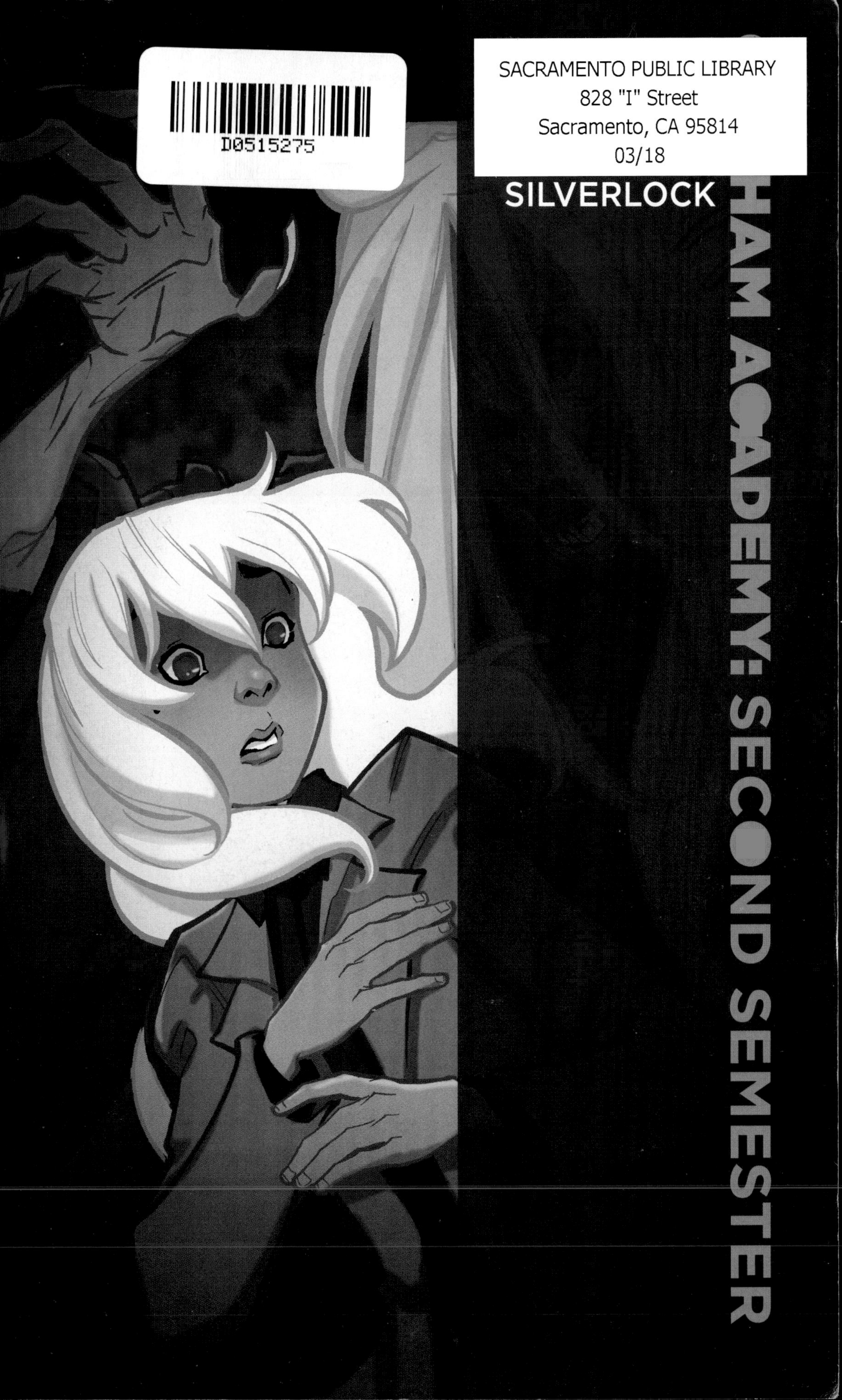
SILVERLOCK
HAM ACADEMY: SECOND SEMESTER

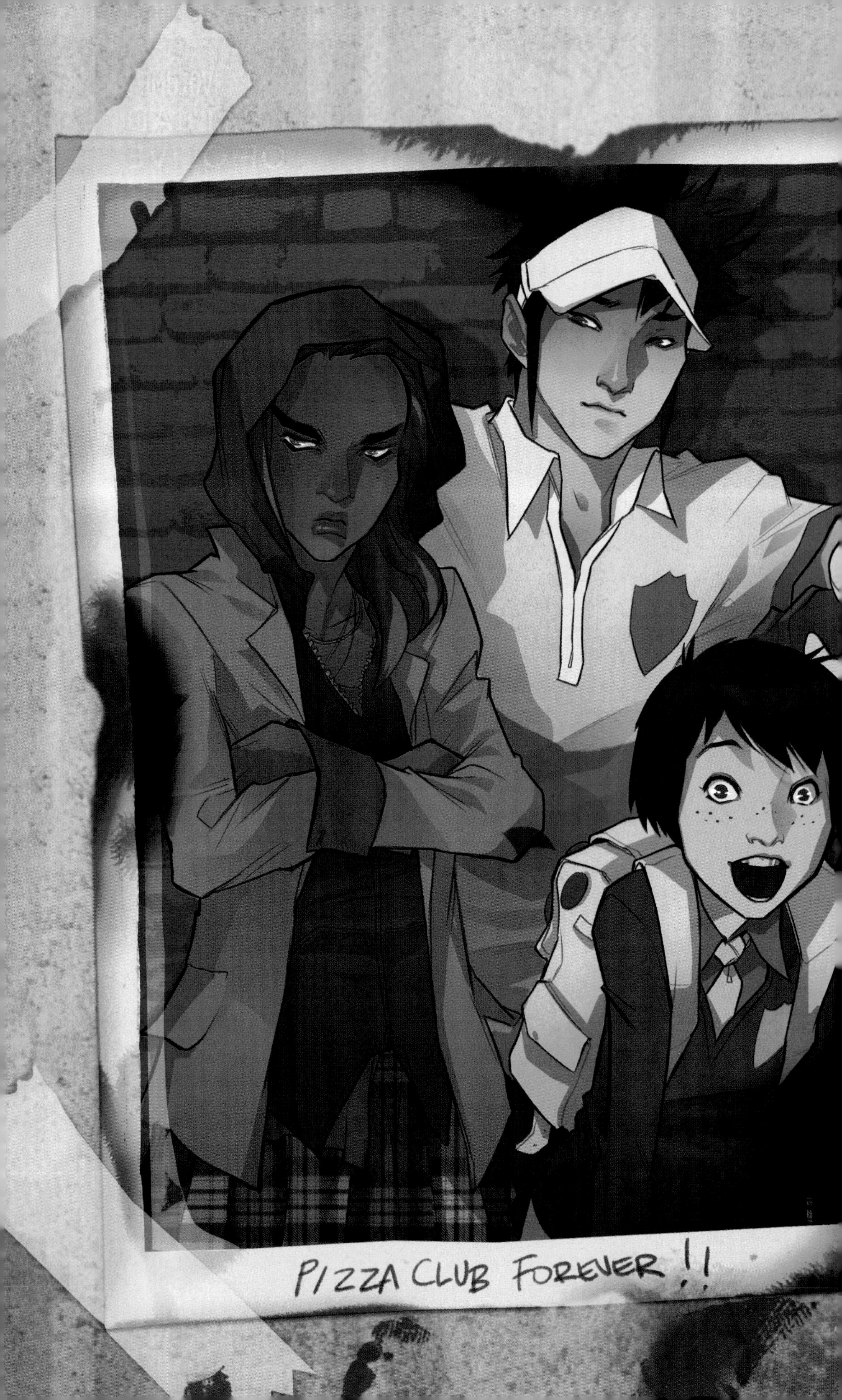
PIZZA CLUB FOREVER !!

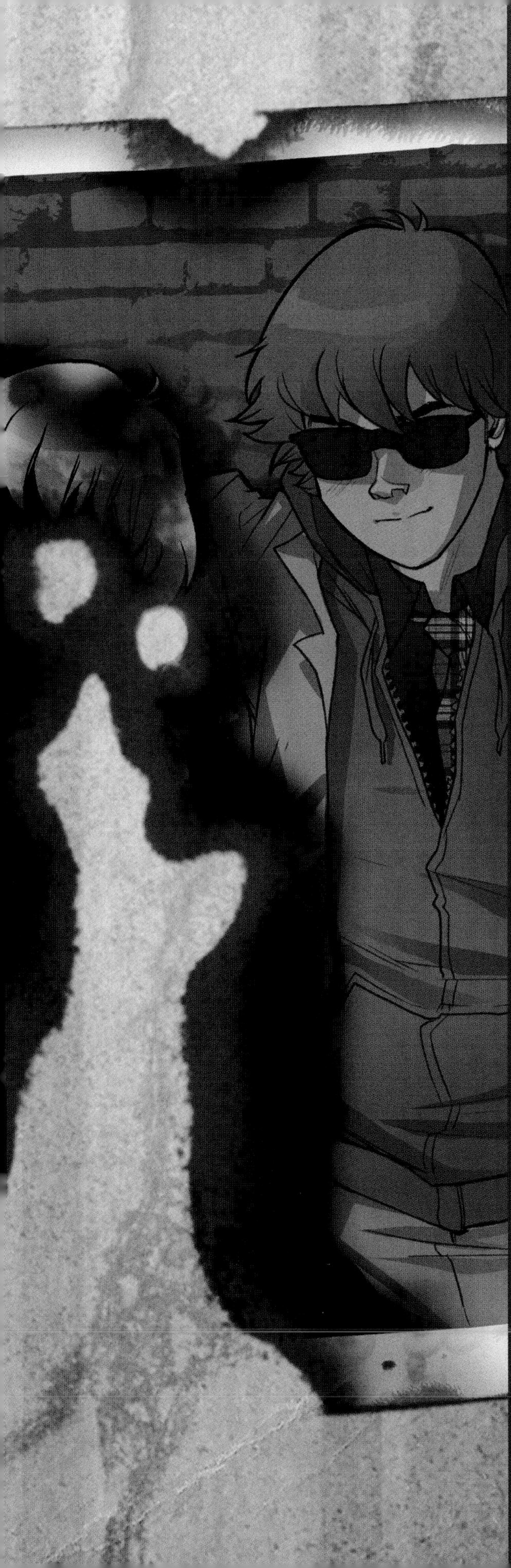

GOTHAM ACADEMY: SECOND SEMESTER

VOLUME 2
THE BALLAD OF OLIVE SILVERLOCK

WRITTEN BY
BRENDEN FLETCHER
BECKY CLOONAN
KARL KERSCHL

PENCILS BY
ADAM ARCHER

INKS BY
SANDRA HOPE

BACKGROUND PAINTING AND COLOR BY
MSASSYK

BREAKDOWNS BY
ROB HAYNES

"THE CARNIVAL MIDNIGHT" ART BY
JON LAM

LETTERS BY
STEVE WANDS

COLLECTION COVER ART BY
KARL KERSCHL

REBECCA TAYLOR Editor - Original Series
JEB WOODARD Group Editor - Collected Editions
ROBIN WILDMAN Editor - Collected Edition
STEVE COOK Design Director - Books
CURTIS KING JR. Publication Design

BOB HARRAS Senior VP - Editor-in-Chief, DC Comics
PAT McCALLUM Executive Editor, DC Comics

DIANE NELSON President
DAN DiDIO Publisher
JIM LEE Publisher
GEOFF JOHNS President & Chief Creative Officer
AMIT DESAI Executive VP - Business & Marketing Strategy, Direct to Consumer & Global Franchise Management
SAM ADES Senior VP & General Manager, Digital Services
BOBBIE CHASE VP & Executive Editor, Young Reader & Talent Development
MARK CHIARELLO Senior VP - Art, Design & Collected Editions
JOHN CUNNINGHAM Senior VP - Sales & Trade Marketing
ANNE DePIES Senior VP - Business Strategy, Finance & Administration
DON FALLETTI VP - Manufacturing Operations
LAWRENCE GANEM VP - Editorial Administration & Talent Relations
ALISON GILL Senior VP - Manufacturing & Operations
HANK KANALZ Senior VP - Editorial Strategy & Administration
JAY KOGAN VP - Legal Affairs
JACK MAHAN VP - Business Affairs
NICK J. NAPOLITANO VP - Manufacturing Administration
EDDIE SCANNELL VP - Consumer Marketing
COURTNEY SIMMONS Senior VP - Publicity & Communications
JIM (SKI) SOKOLOWSKI VP - Comic Book Specialty Sales & Trade Marketing
NANCY SPEARS VP - Mass, Book, Digital Sales & Trade Marketing
MICHELE R. WELLS VP - Content Strategy

GOTHAM ACADEMY: SECOND SEMESTER VOLUME 2—THE BALLAD OF OLIVE SILVERLOCK

DC Comics, 2900 West Alameda Avenue, Burbank, CA 91505
Printed by Vanguard Graphics, LLC, Ithaca, NY, USA. 10/27/17. First Printing.
ISBN: 978-1-4012-7474-0

Library of Congress Cataloging-in-Publication Data is available.

FSC www.fsc.org
MIX
Paper from responsible sources
FSC® C016956

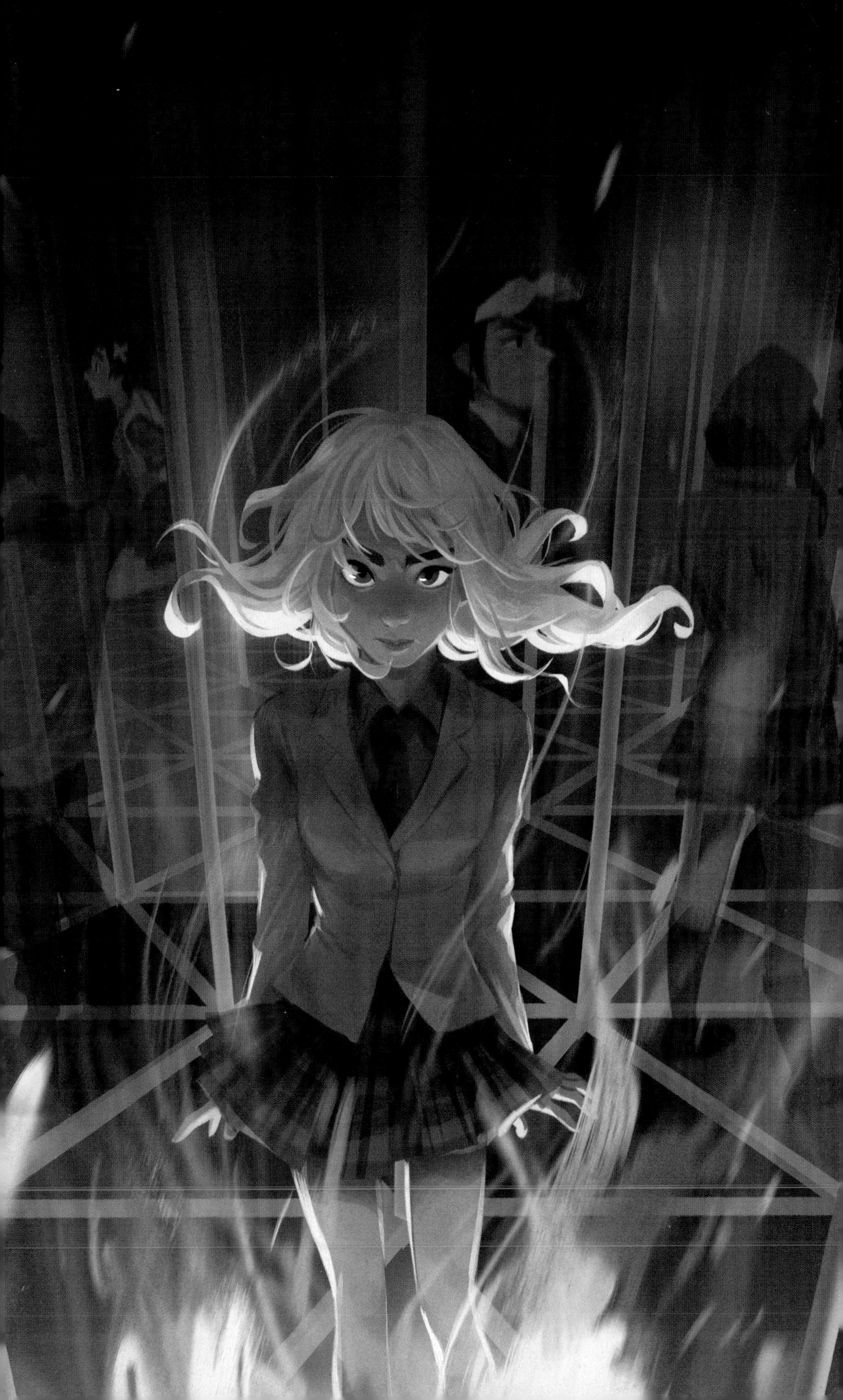

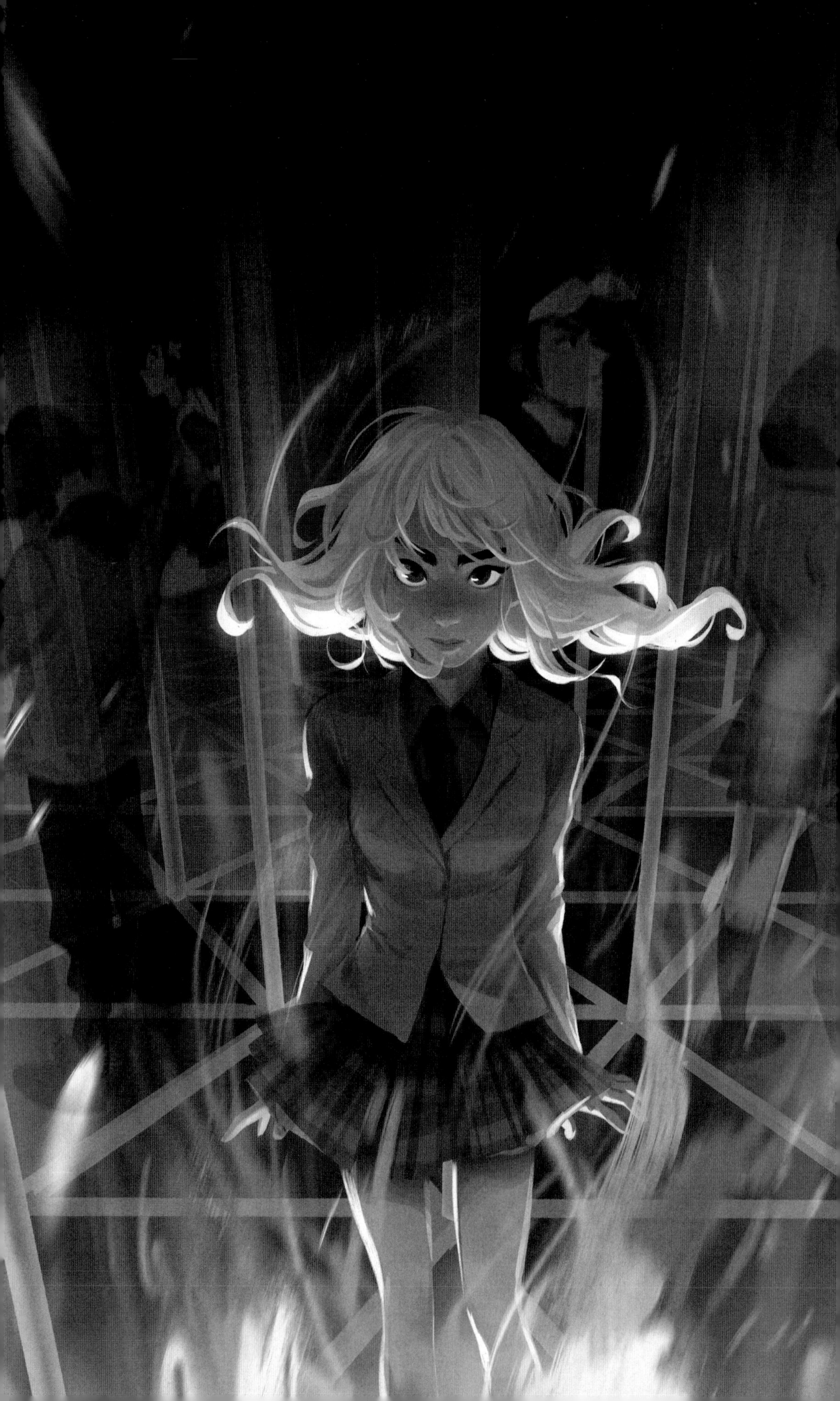

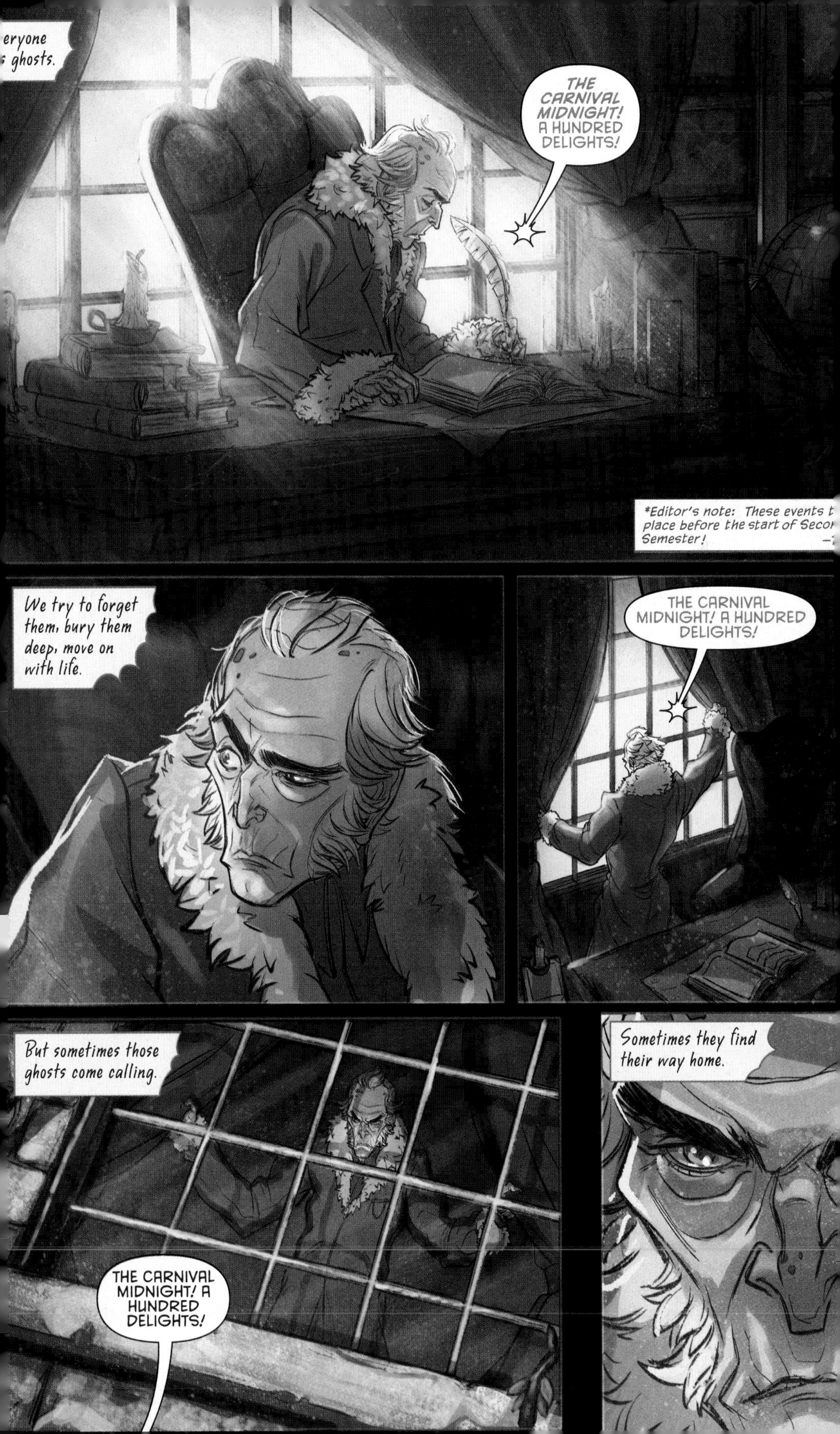
eryone
ghosts.
THE CARNIVAL MIDNIGHT! A HUNDRED DELIGHTS!
*Editor's note: These events t place before the start of Secor Semester! —
We try to forget them, bury them deep, move on with life.
THE CARNIVAL MIDNIGHT! A HUNDRED DELIGHTS!
But sometimes those ghosts come calling.
THE CARNIVAL MIDNIGHT! A HUNDRED DELIGHTS!
Sometimes they find their way home.

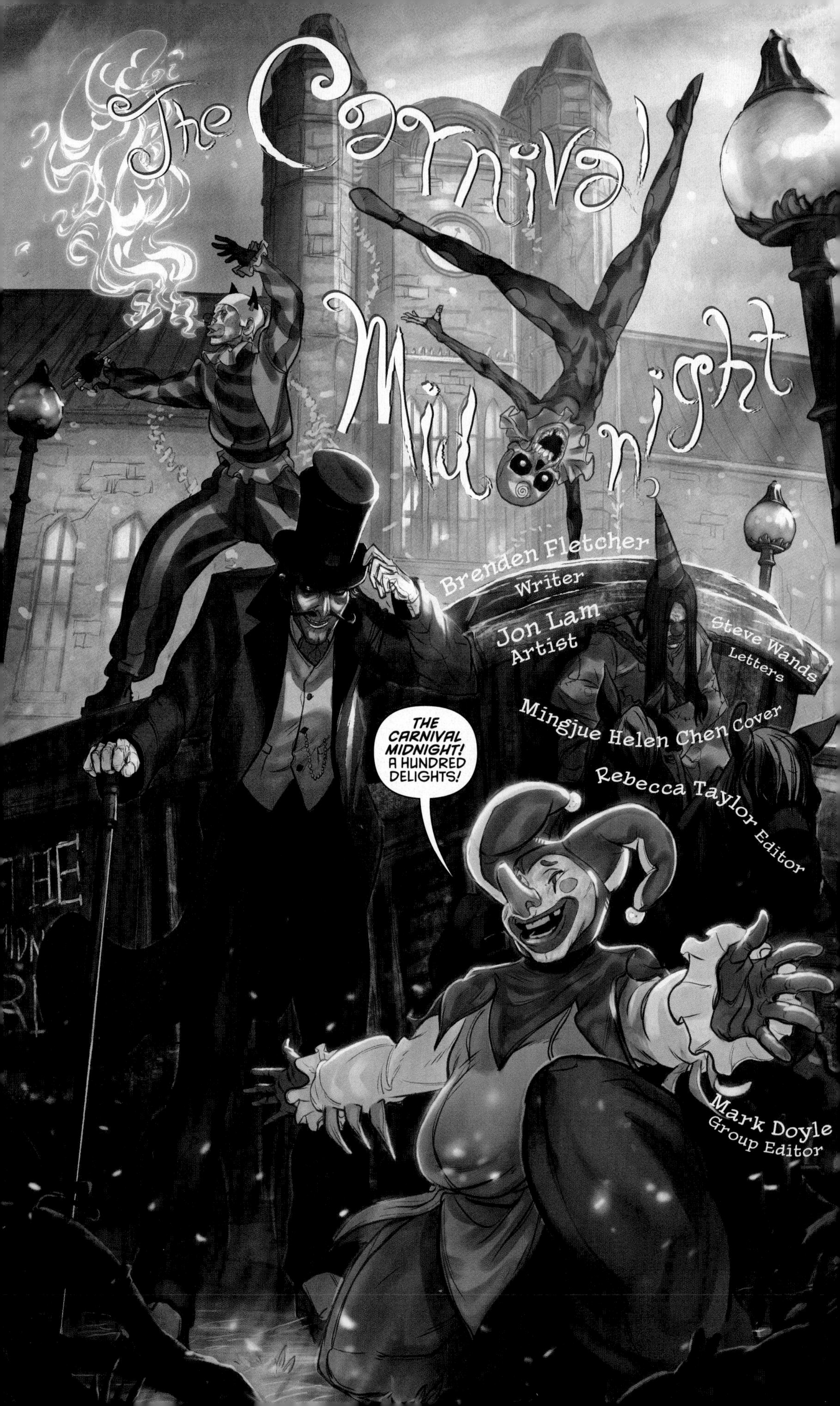
The Carnival Midnight
Brenden Fletcher
Writer
Jon Lam
Artist
Steve Wands
Letters
Mingjue Helen Chen Cover
Rebecca Taylor Editor
Mark Doyle
Group Editor
THE CARNIVAL MIDNIGHT! A HUNDRED DELIGHTS!
THE

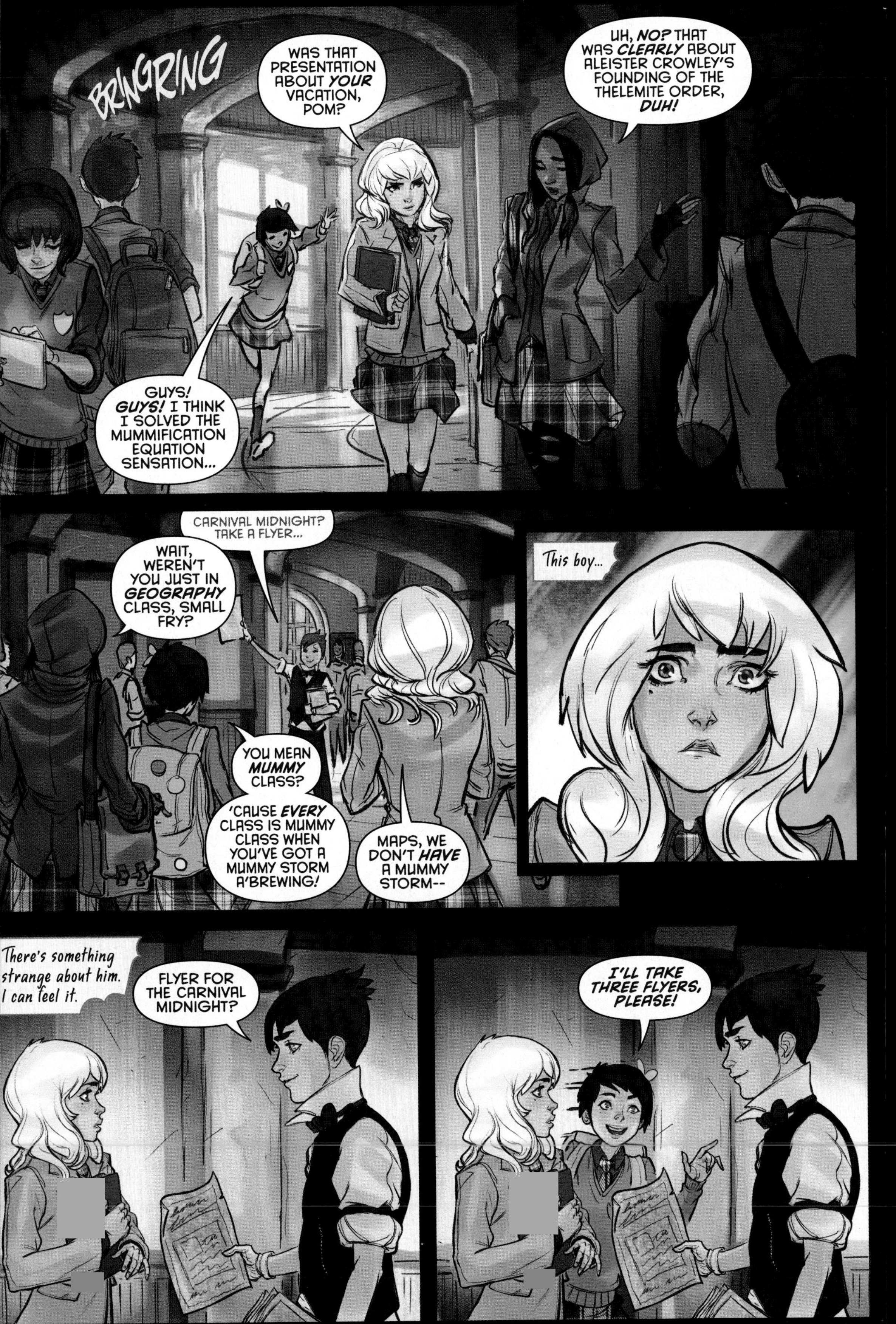
BRINGRING
WAS THAT PRESENTATION ABOUT YOUR VACATION, POM?
UH, NO? THAT WAS CLEARLY ABOUT ALEISTER CROWLEY'S FOUNDING OF THE THELEMITE ORDER, DUH!
GUYS! GUYS! I THINK I SOLVED THE MUMMIFICATION EQUATION SENSATION...
CARNIVAL MIDNIGHT? TAKE A FLYER...
WAIT, WEREN'T YOU JUST IN GEOGRAPHY CLASS, SMALL FRY?
YOU MEAN MUMMY CLASS?
'CAUSE EVERY CLASS IS MUMMY CLASS WHEN YOU'VE GOT A MUMMY STORM A'BREWING!
MAPS, WE DON'T HAVE A MUMMY STORM--
This boy...
There's something strange about him. I can feel it.
FLYER FOR THE CARNIVAL MIDNIGHT?
I'LL TAKE THREE FLYERS, PLEASE!

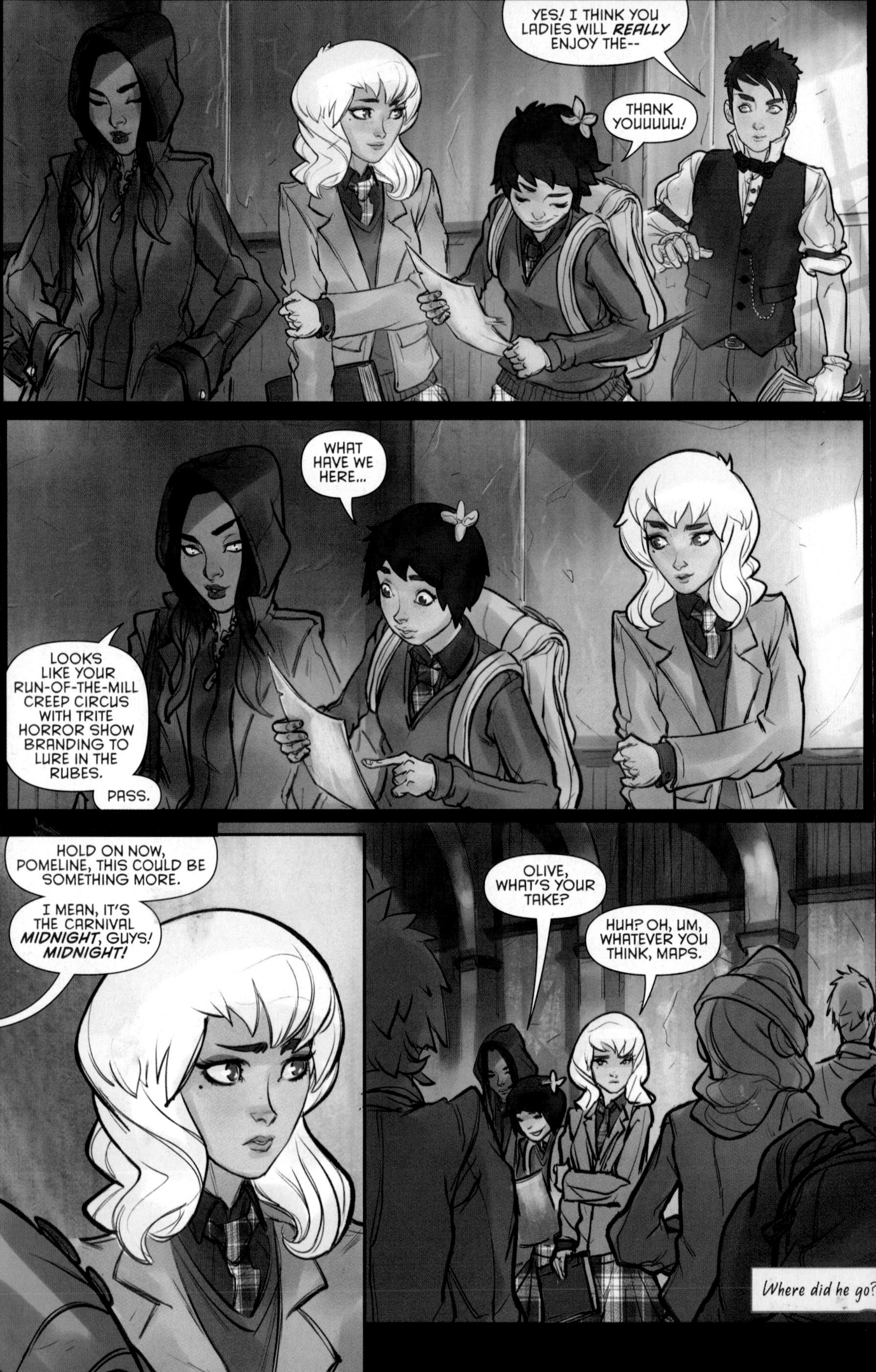
YES! I THINK YOU LADIES WILL REALLY ENJOY THE--
THANK YOUUUUU!
WHAT HAVE WE HERE...
LOOKS LIKE YOUR RUN-OF-THE-MILL CREEP CIRCUS WITH TRITE HORROR SHOW BRANDING TO LURE IN THE RUBES.
PASS.
HOLD ON NOW, POMELINE, THIS COULD BE SOMETHING MORE.
I MEAN, IT'S THE CARNIVAL MIDNIGHT, GUYS! MIDNIGHT!
OLIVE, WHAT'S YOUR TAKE?
HUH? OH, UM, WHATEVER YOU THINK, MAPS.
Where did he go?

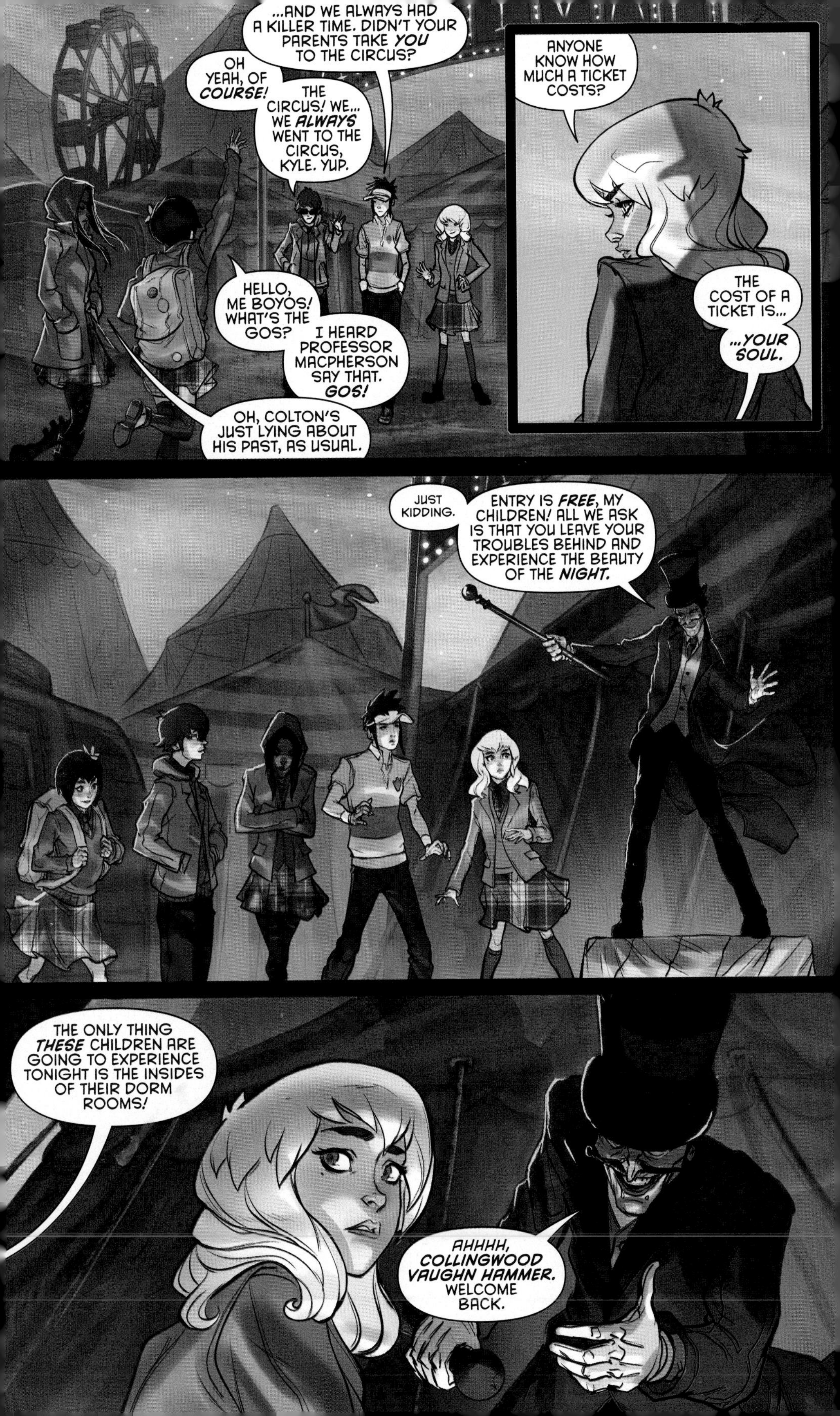
...AND WE ALWAYS HAD A KILLER TIME. DIDN'T YOUR PARENTS TAKE *YOU* TO THE CIRCUS?
OH YEAH, OF *COURSE!*
THE CIRCUS! WE... WE *ALWAYS* WENT TO THE CIRCUS, KYLE. YUP.
HELLO, ME BOYOS! WHAT'S THE GOS?
I HEARD PROFESSOR MACPHERSON SAY THAT. *GOS!*
OH, COLTON'S JUST LYING ABOUT HIS PAST, AS USUAL.
ANYONE KNOW HOW MUCH A TICKET COSTS?
THE COST OF A TICKET IS...
...YOUR SOUL.
JUST KIDDING.
ENTRY IS *FREE*, MY CHILDREN! ALL WE ASK IS THAT YOU LEAVE YOUR TROUBLES BEHIND AND EXPERIENCE THE BEAUTY OF THE *NIGHT.*
THE ONLY THING *THESE* CHILDREN ARE GOING TO EXPERIENCE TONIGHT IS THE INSIDES OF THEIR DORM ROOMS!
AHHHH, *COLLINGWOOD VAUGHN HAMMER.* WELCOME BACK.

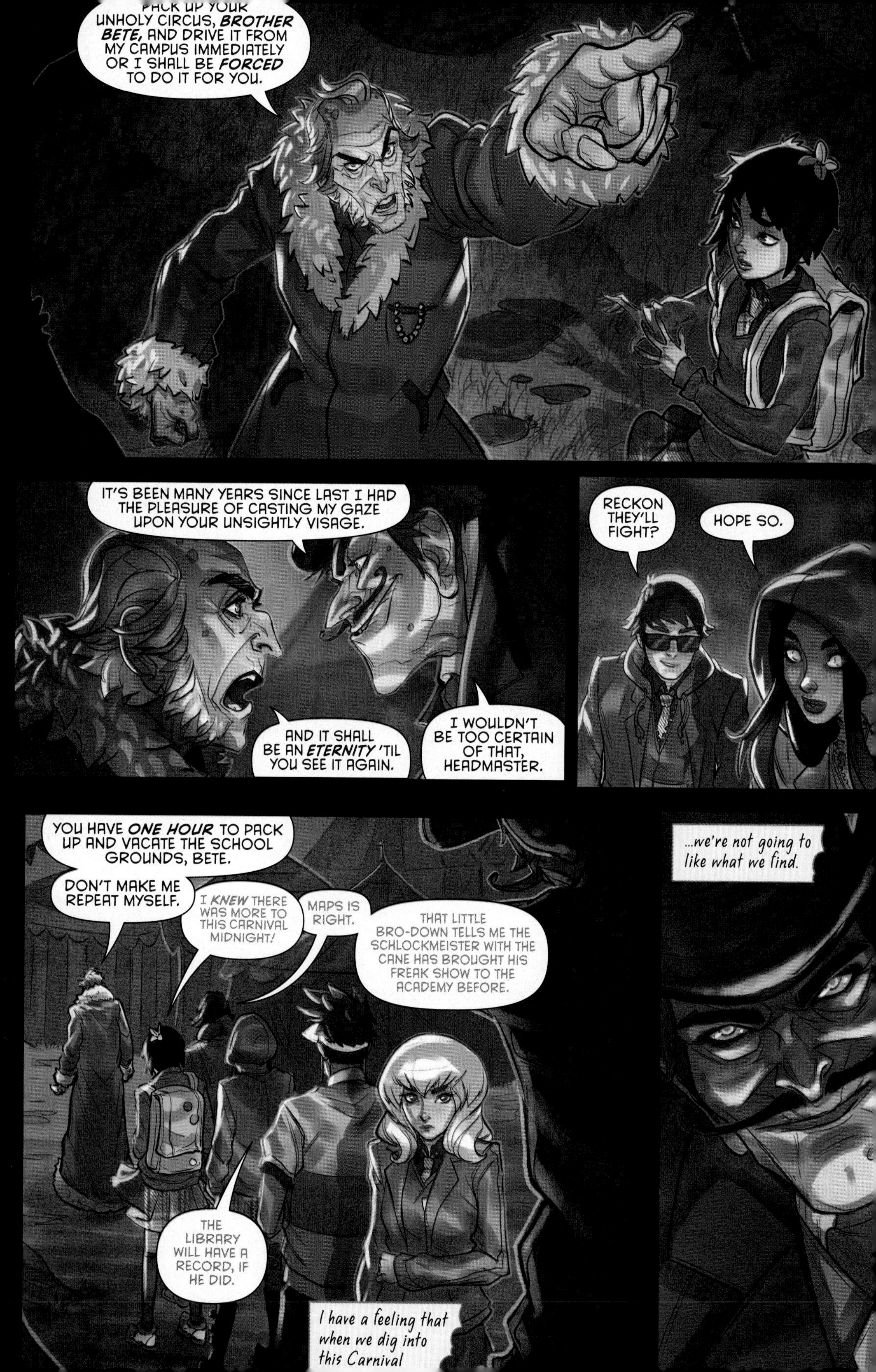
PACK UP YOUR UNHOLY CIRCUS, BROTHER BETE, AND DRIVE IT FROM MY CAMPUS IMMEDIATELY OR I SHALL BE FORCED TO DO IT FOR YOU.
IT'S BEEN MANY YEARS SINCE LAST I HAD THE PLEASURE OF CASTING MY GAZE UPON YOUR UNSIGHTLY VISAGE.
AND IT SHALL BE AN ETERNITY 'TIL YOU SEE IT AGAIN.
I WOULDN'T BE TOO CERTAIN OF THAT, HEADMASTER.
RECKON THEY'LL FIGHT?
HOPE SO.
YOU HAVE ONE HOUR TO PACK UP AND VACATE THE SCHOOL GROUNDS, BETE.
DON'T MAKE ME REPEAT MYSELF.
I KNEW THERE WAS MORE TO THIS CARNIVAL MIDNIGHT!
MAPS IS RIGHT.
THAT LITTLE BRO-DOWN TELLS ME THE SCHLOCKMEISTER WITH THE CANE HAS BROUGHT HIS FREAK SHOW TO THE ACADEMY BEFORE.
THE LIBRARY WILL HAVE A RECORD, IF HE DID.
I have a feeling that when we dig into this Carnival
...we're not going to like what we find.

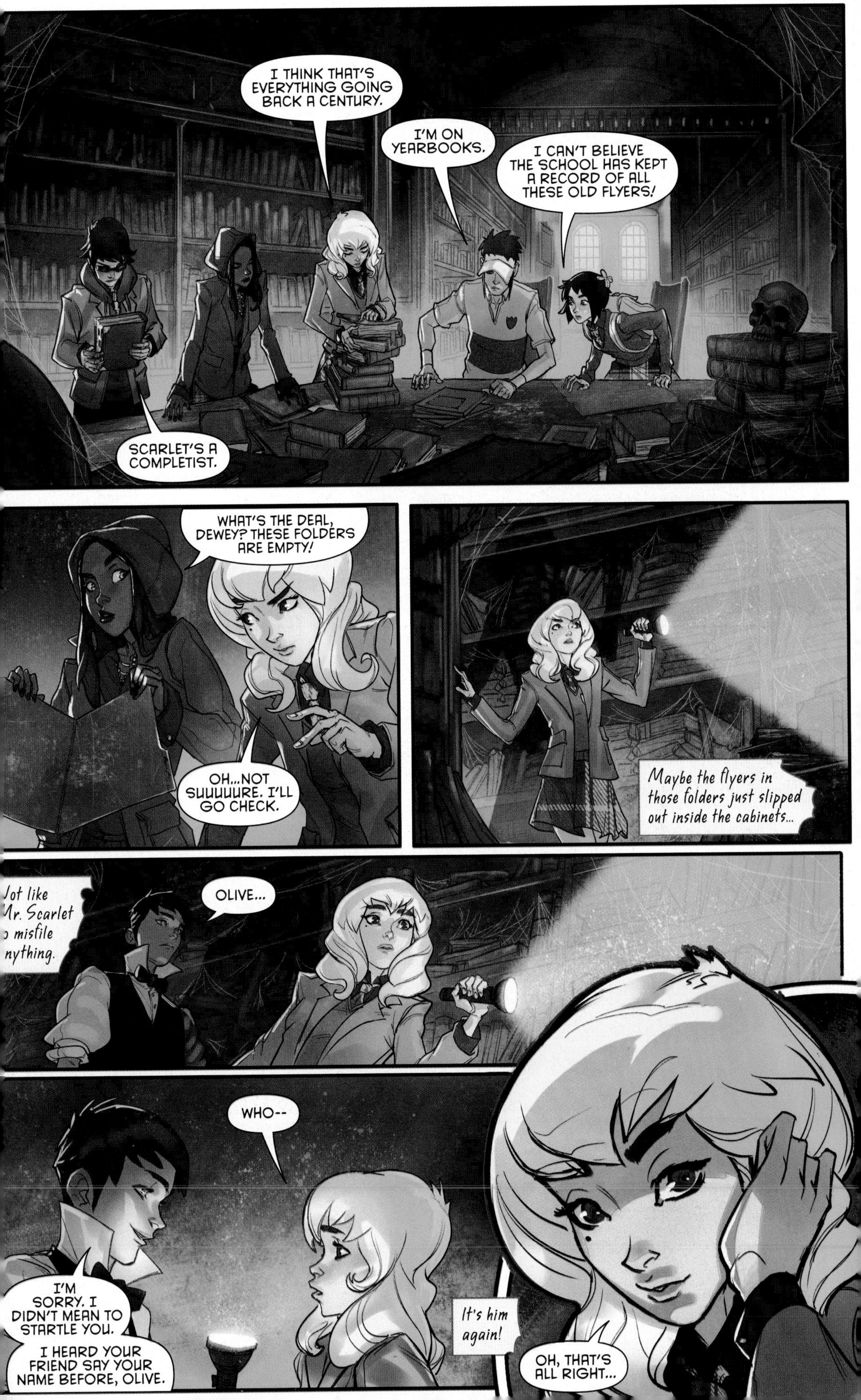
I THINK THAT'S EVERYTHING GOING BACK A CENTURY.
I'M ON YEARBOOKS.
I CAN'T BELIEVE THE SCHOOL HAS KEPT A RECORD OF ALL THESE OLD FLYERS!
SCARLET'S A COMPLETIST.
WHAT'S THE DEAL, DEWEY? THESE FOLDERS ARE EMPTY!
OH...NOT SUUUUURE. I'LL GO CHECK.
Maybe the flyers in those folders just slipped out inside the cabinets...
ot like Mr. Scarlet misfile nything.
OLIVE...
WHO--
I'M SORRY. I DIDN'T MEAN TO STARTLE YOU.
I HEARD YOUR FRIEND SAY YOUR NAME BEFORE, OLIVE.
It's him again!
OH, THAT'S ALL RIGHT...

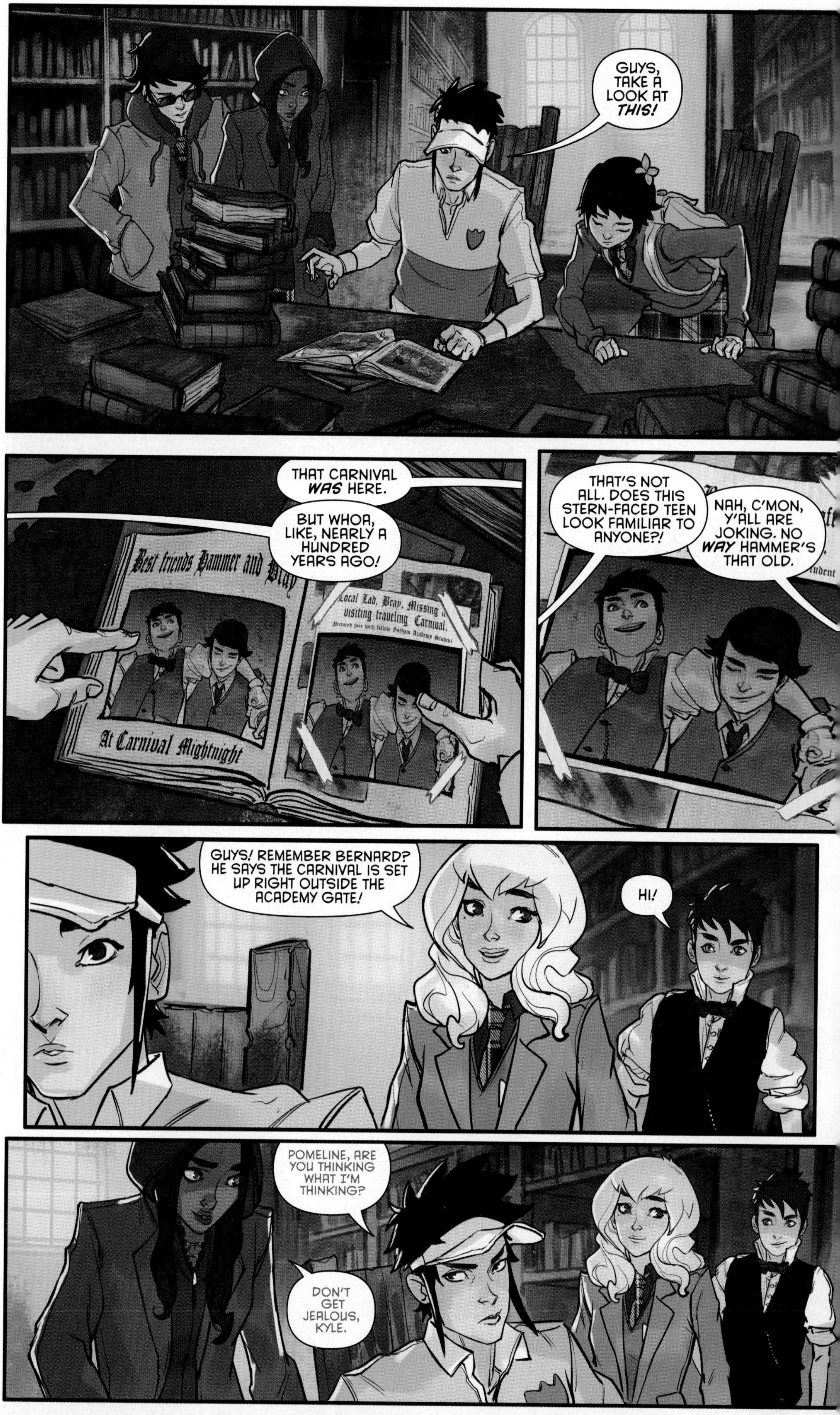
GUYS, TAKE A LOOK AT THIS!
THAT CARNIVAL WAS HERE.
BUT WHOA, LIKE, NEARLY A HUNDRED YEARS AGO!
Best friends Hammer and Bray
At Carnival Mightnight
Local Lad, Bray, Missing after visiting traveling Carnival.
Pictured here with fellow Gotham Academy Student
THAT'S NOT ALL. DOES THIS STERN-FACED TEEN LOOK FAMILIAR TO ANYONE?!
NAH, C'MON, Y'ALL ARE JOKING. NO WAY HAMMER'S THAT OLD.
GUYS! REMEMBER BERNARD? HE SAYS THE CARNIVAL IS SET UP RIGHT OUTSIDE THE ACADEMY GATE!
HI!
POMELINE, ARE YOU THINKING WHAT I'M THINKING?
DON'T GET JEALOUS, KYLE.

WE SHOULDN'T BE HERE, POM. HEADMASTER HAMMER SPECIFICALLY FORBID--

WHATEVER, LAWFUL GOOD. YOU SAID IT YOURSELF--THAT BERNARD KID LOOKS LIKE THE BOY IN THE OLD PIC WITH HAMMER. THE ONE WHO WENT MISSING. DON'T YOU WANNA GET SOME ANSWERS?

THIS IS IT!

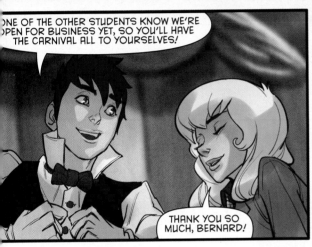

ONE OF THE OTHER STUDENTS KNOW WE'RE OPEN FOR BUSINESS YET, SO YOU'LL HAVE THE CARNIVAL ALL TO YOURSELVES!

THANK YOU SO MUCH, BERNARD!

YES! COME INSIDE AND BE THE FIRST IN YOUR CLASS TO ENJOY THE SPECTACLE!

WELCOME...

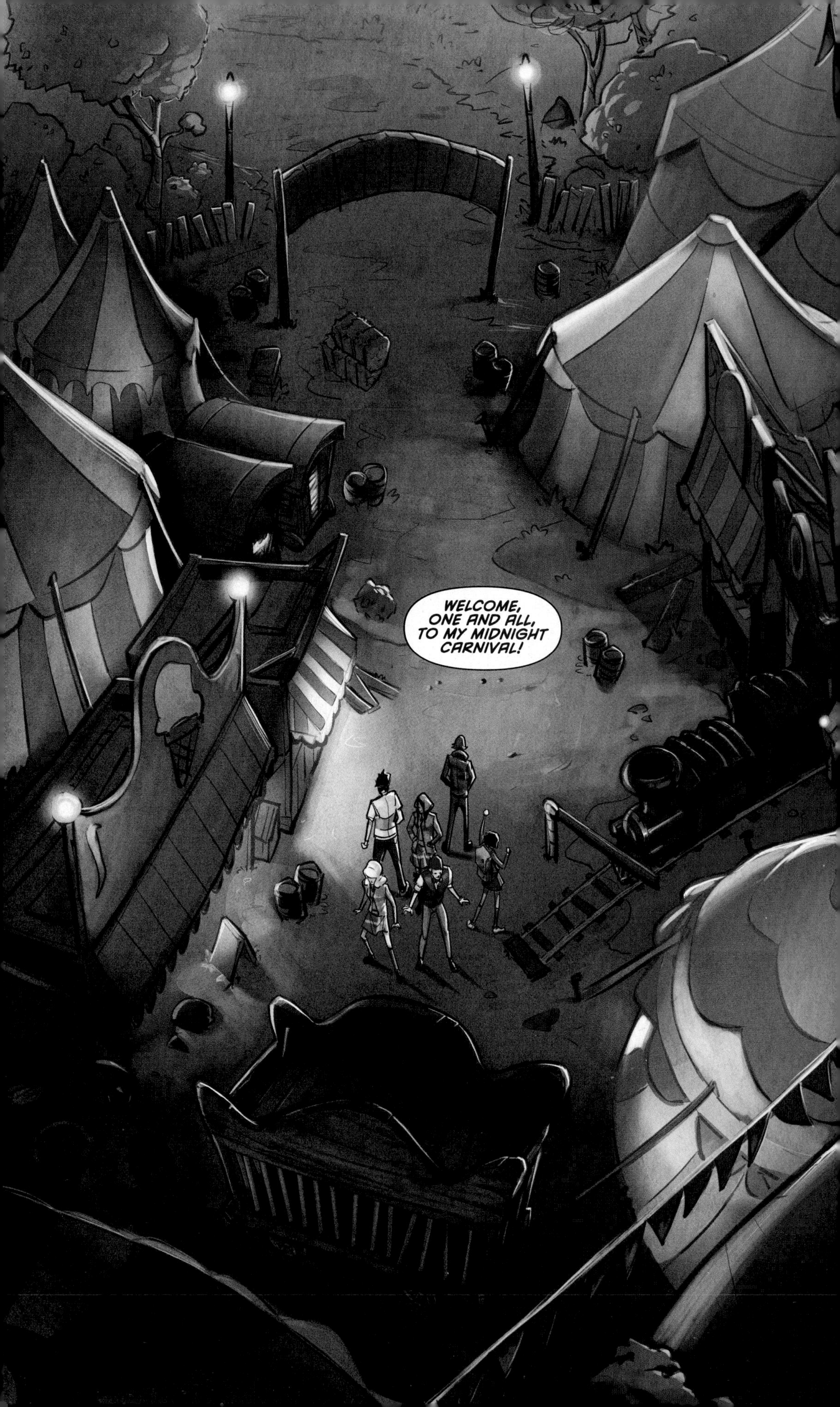
WELCOME, ONE AND ALL, TO MY MIDNIGHT CARNIVAL!

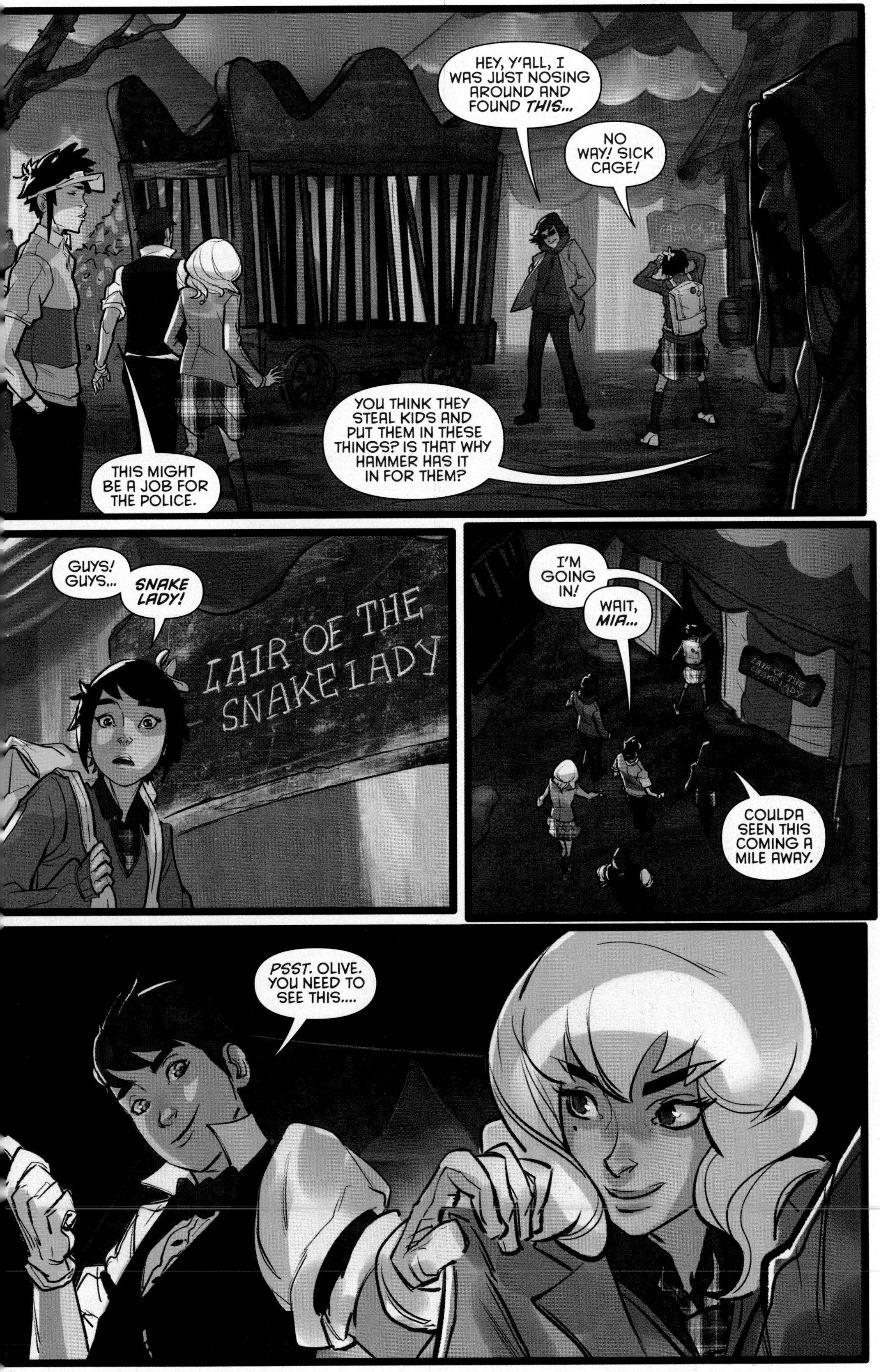

HEY, Y'ALL, I WAS JUST NOSING AROUND AND FOUND *THIS*...
NO WAY! SICK CAGE!
YOU THINK THEY STEAL KIDS AND PUT THEM IN THESE THINGS? IS THAT WHY HAMMER HAS IT IN FOR THEM?
THIS MIGHT BE A JOB FOR THE POLICE.
LAIR OF THE SNAKE LADY
GUYS! GUYS...
SNAKE LADY!
LAIR OF THE SNAKE LADY
I'M GOING IN!
WAIT, *MIA*...
COULDA SEEN THIS COMING A MILE AWAY.
PSST. OLIVE. YOU NEED TO SEE THIS....

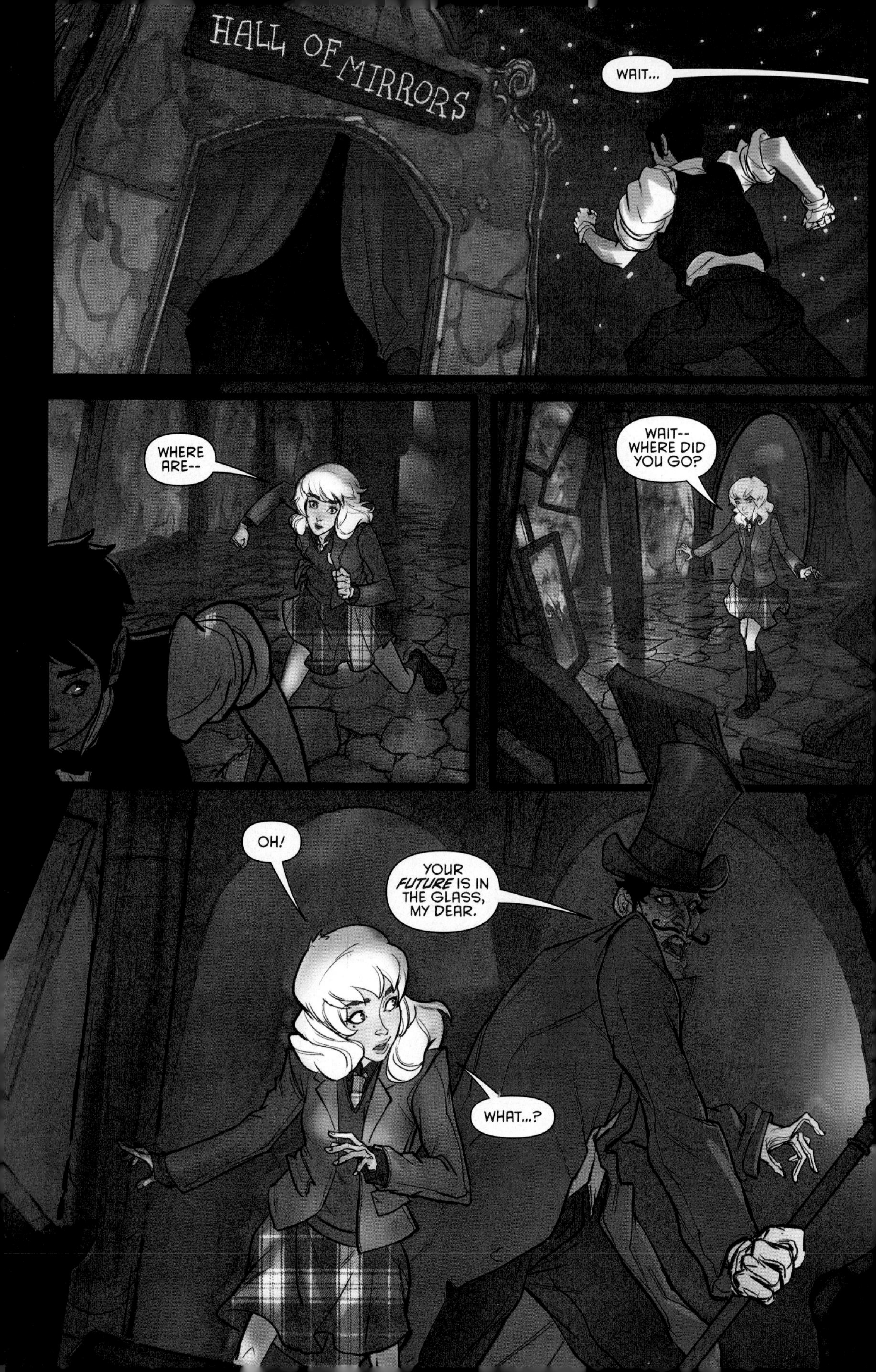
HALL OF MIRRORS
WAIT...
WHERE ARE--
WAIT-- WHERE DID YOU GO?
OH!
YOUR *FUTURE* IS IN THE GLASS, MY DEAR.
WHAT...?

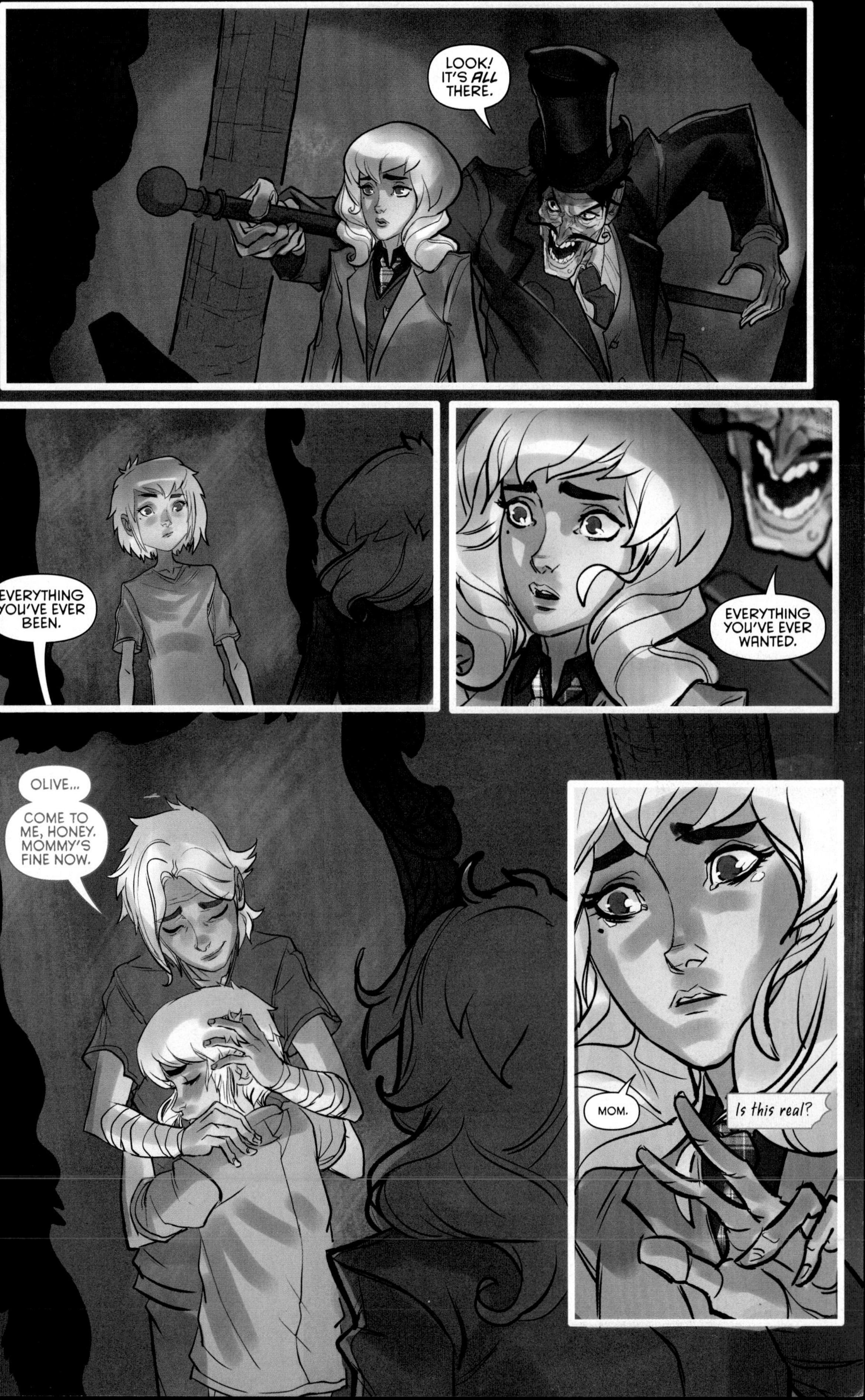
LOOK! IT'S ALL THERE.
EVERYTHING YOU'VE EVER BEEN.
EVERYTHING YOU'VE EVER WANTED.
OLIVE...
COME TO ME, HONEY. MOMMY'S FINE NOW.
MOM.
Is this real?

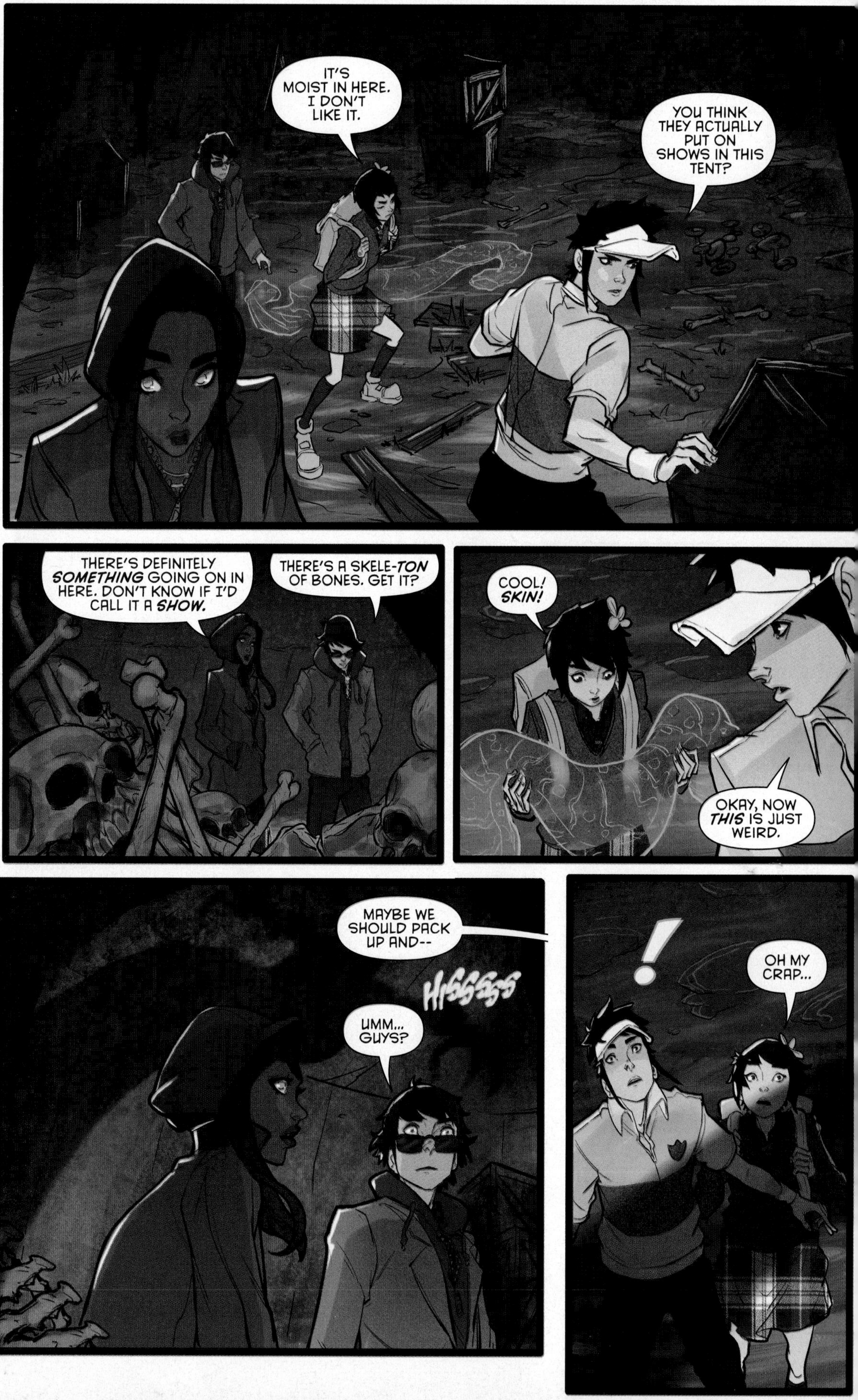
IT'S MOIST IN HERE. I DON'T LIKE IT.
YOU THINK THEY ACTUALLY PUT ON SHOWS IN THIS TENT?
THERE'S DEFINITELY SOMETHING GOING ON IN HERE. DON'T KNOW IF I'D CALL IT A SHOW.
THERE'S A SKELE-TON OF BONES. GET IT?
COOL! SKIN!
OKAY, NOW THIS IS JUST WEIRD.
MAYBE WE SHOULD PACK UP AND--
HISSSSS
UMM... GUYS?
!
OH MY CRAP...

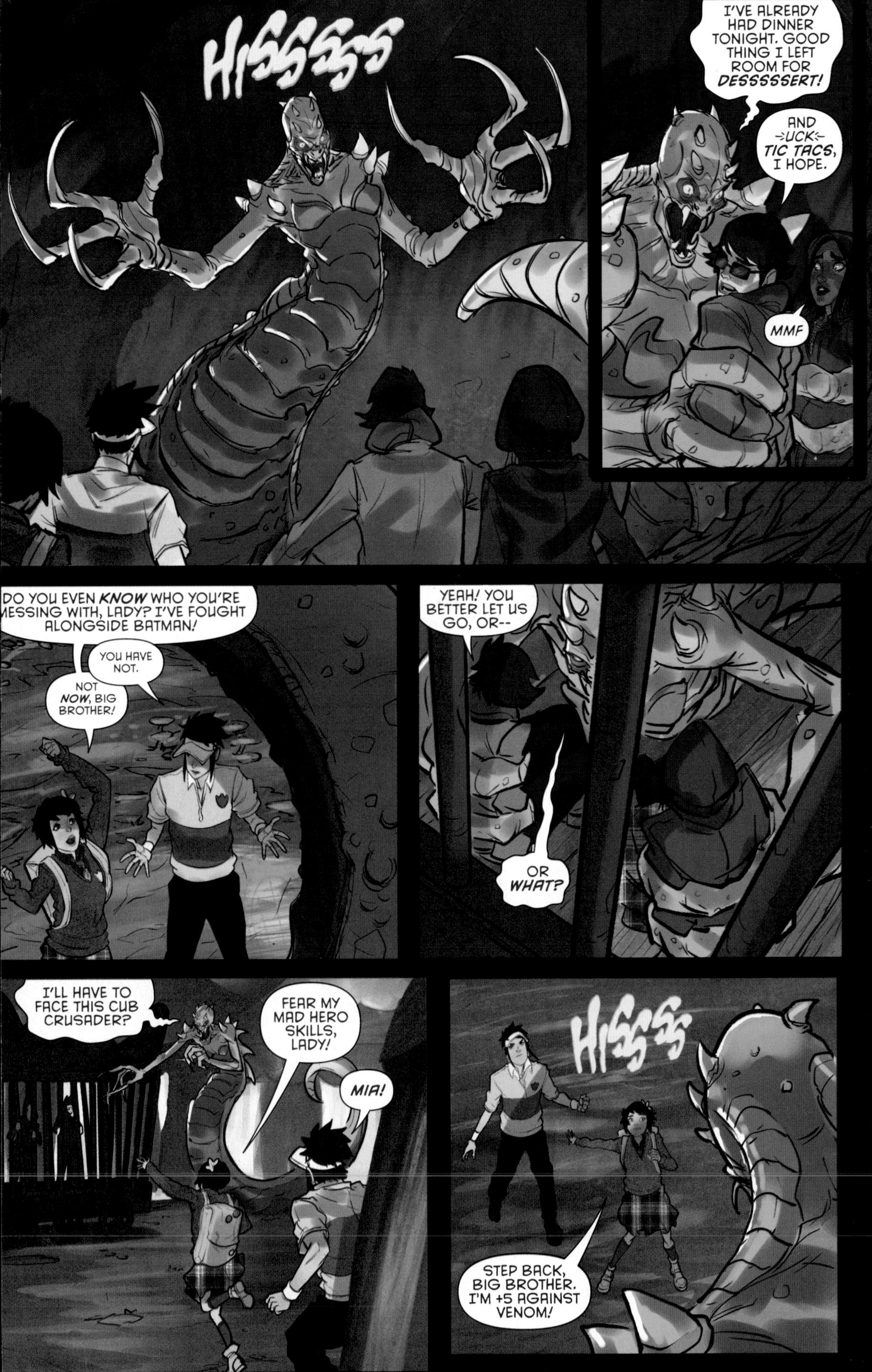
HISSSSS
I'VE ALREADY HAD DINNER TONIGHT. GOOD THING I LEFT ROOM FOR DESSSSSERT!
AND UCK TIC TACS, I HOPE.
MMF
DO YOU EVEN KNOW WHO YOU'RE MESSING WITH, LADY? I'VE FOUGHT ALONGSIDE BATMAN!
YOU HAVE NOT.
NOT NOW, BIG BROTHER!
YEAH! YOU BETTER LET US GO, OR--
OR WHAT?
I'LL HAVE TO FACE THIS CUB CRUSADER?
FEAR MY MAD HERO SKILLS, LADY!
MIA!
HISSSS
STEP BACK, BIG BROTHER. I'M +5 AGAINST VENOM!

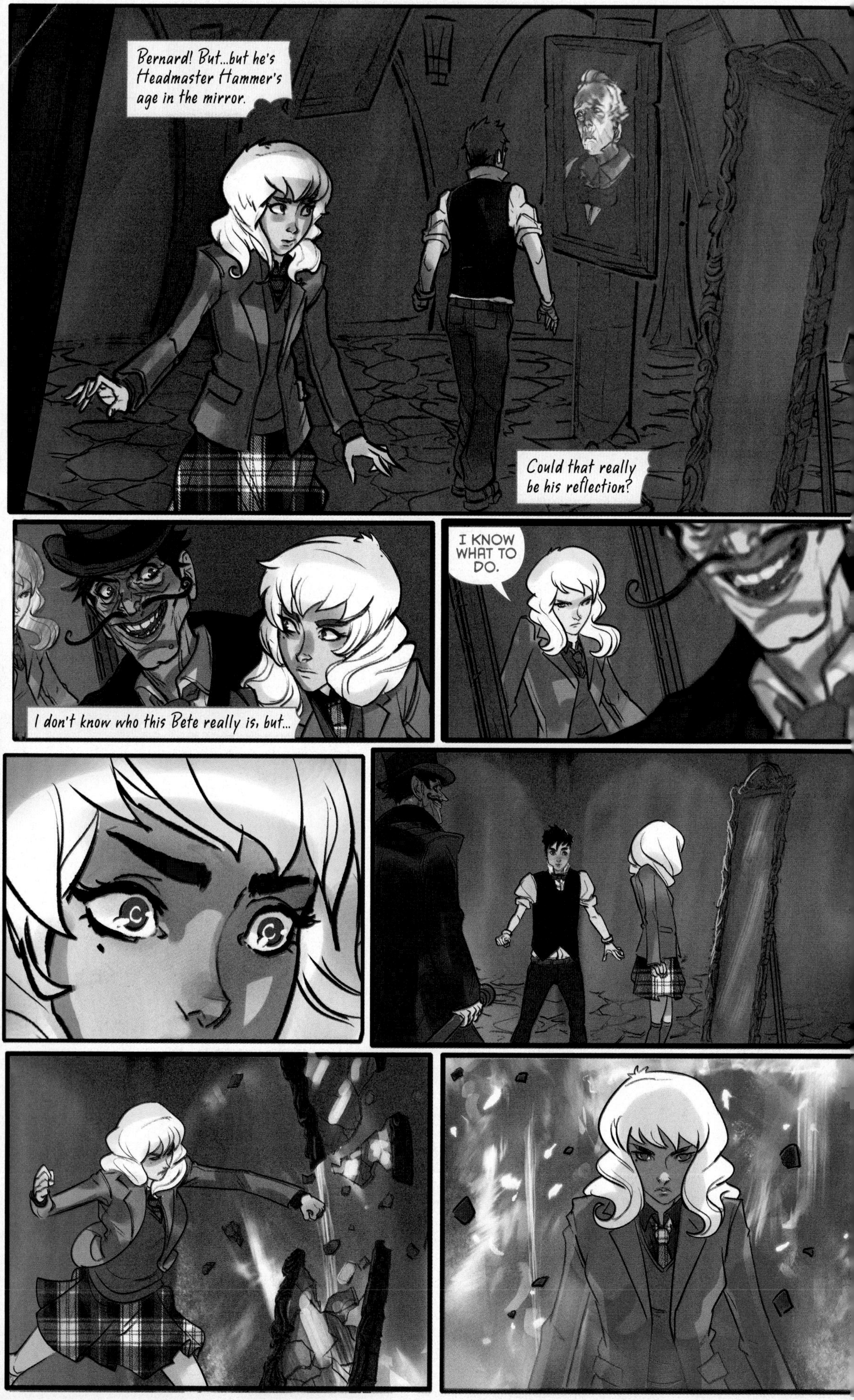
Bernard! But...but he's Headmaster Hammer's age in the mirror.
Could that really be his reflection?
I don't know who this Bete really is, but...
I KNOW WHAT TO DO.

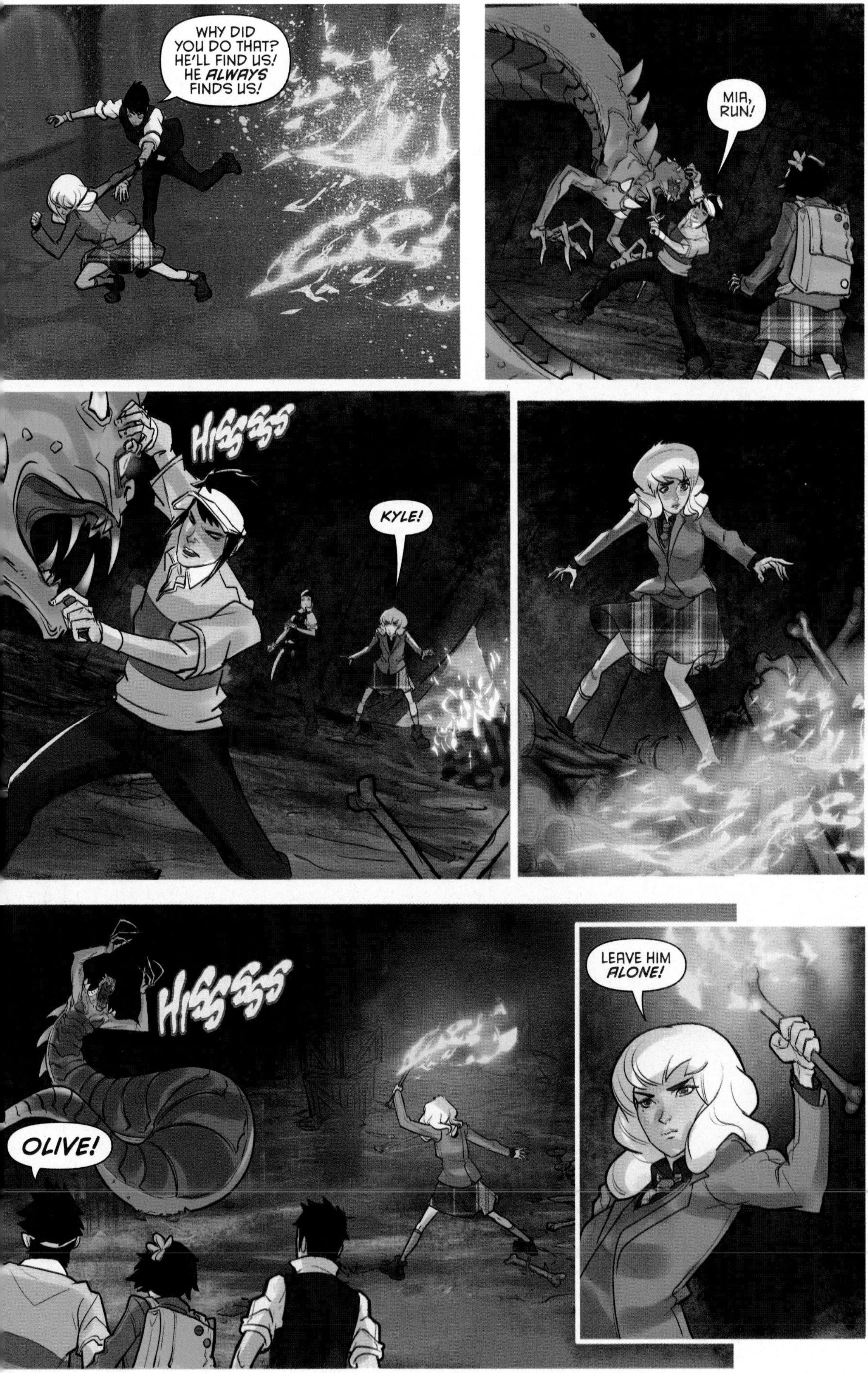
WHY DID YOU DO THAT? HE'LL FIND US! HE ALWAYS FINDS US!
MIA, RUN!
HISSSSS
KYLE!
HISSSSS
OLIVE!
LEAVE HIM ALONE!

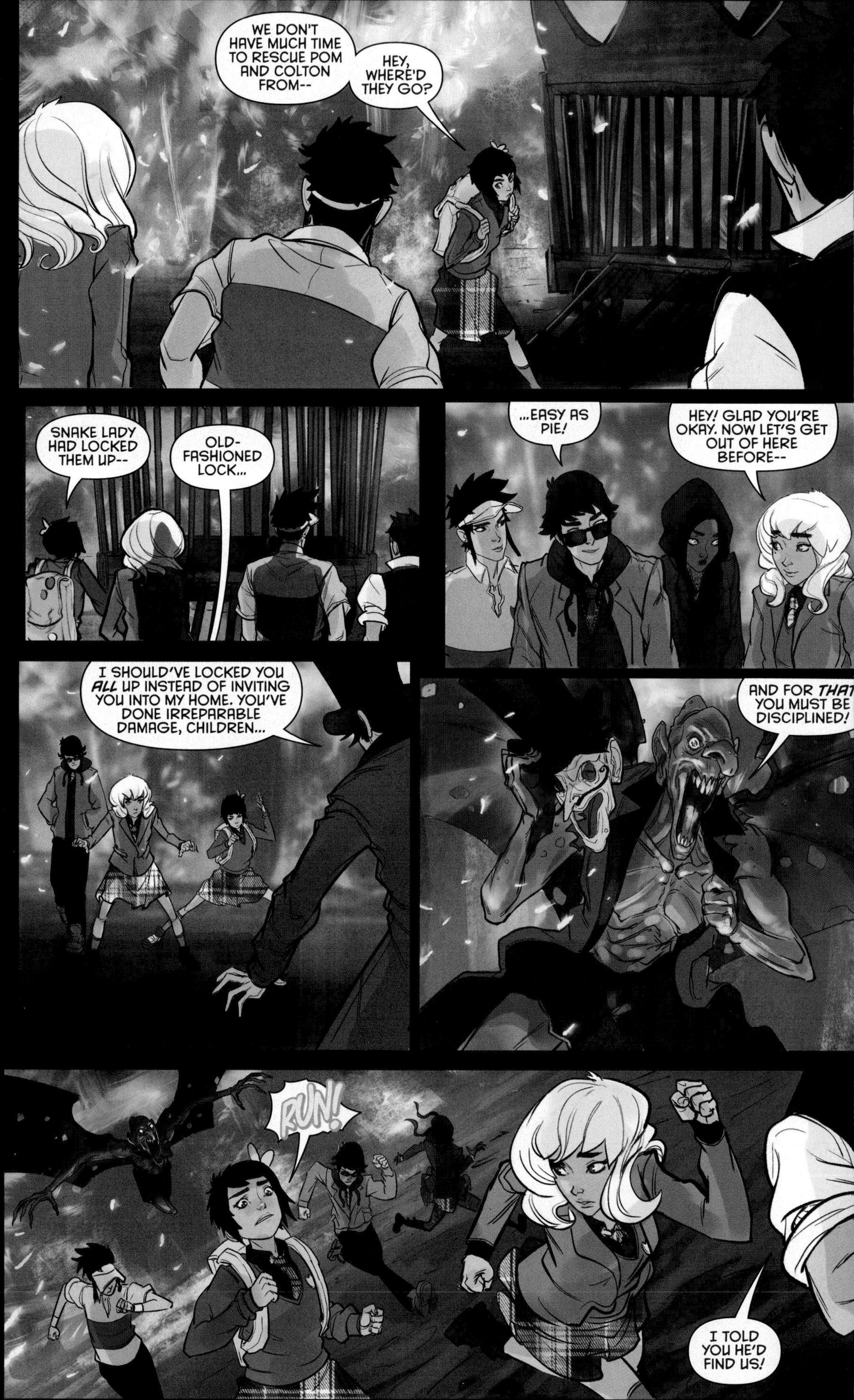

WE DON'T HAVE MUCH TIME TO RESCUE POM AND COLTON FROM--
HEY, WHERE'D THEY GO?
SNAKE LADY HAD LOCKED THEM UP--
OLD-FASHIONED LOCK...
...EASY AS PIE!
HEY! GLAD YOU'RE OKAY. NOW LET'S GET OUT OF HERE BEFORE--
I SHOULD'VE LOCKED YOU ALL UP INSTEAD OF INVITING YOU INTO MY HOME. YOU'VE DONE IRREPARABLE DAMAGE, CHILDREN...
AND FOR THAT YOU MUST BE DISCIPLINED!
RUN!
I TOLD YOU HE'D FIND US!

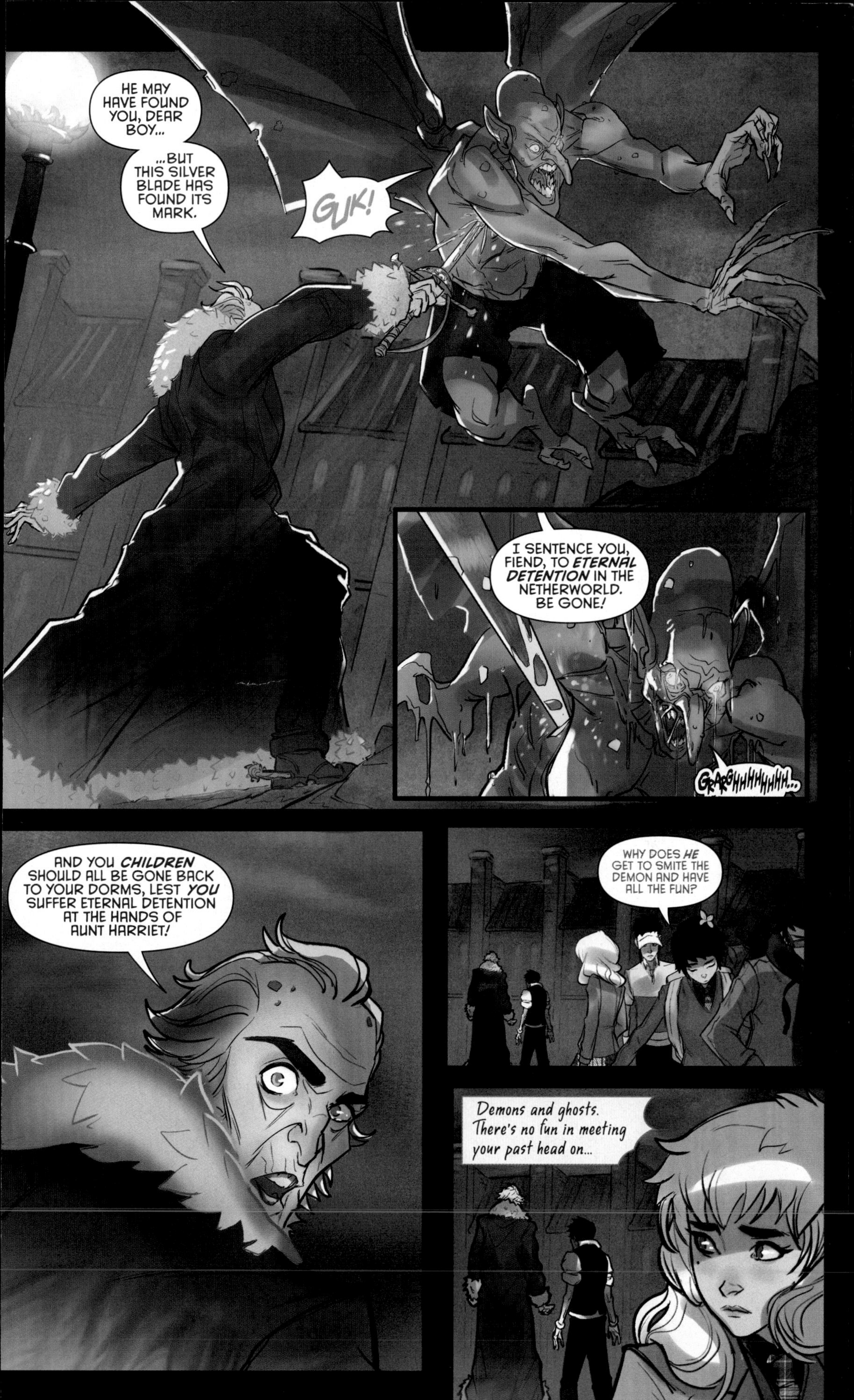
HE MAY HAVE FOUND YOU, DEAR BOY...
...BUT THIS SILVER BLADE HAS FOUND ITS MARK.
GUK!
I SENTENCE YOU, FIEND, TO ETERNAL DETENTION IN THE NETHERWORLD. BE GONE!
GRARGHHHHHHHH...
AND YOU CHILDREN SHOULD ALL BE GONE BACK TO YOUR DORMS, LEST YOU SUFFER ETERNAL DETENTION AT THE HANDS OF AUNT HARRIET!
WHY DOES HE GET TO SMITE THE DEMON AND HAVE ALL THE FUN?
Demons and ghosts. There's no fun in meeting your past head on...

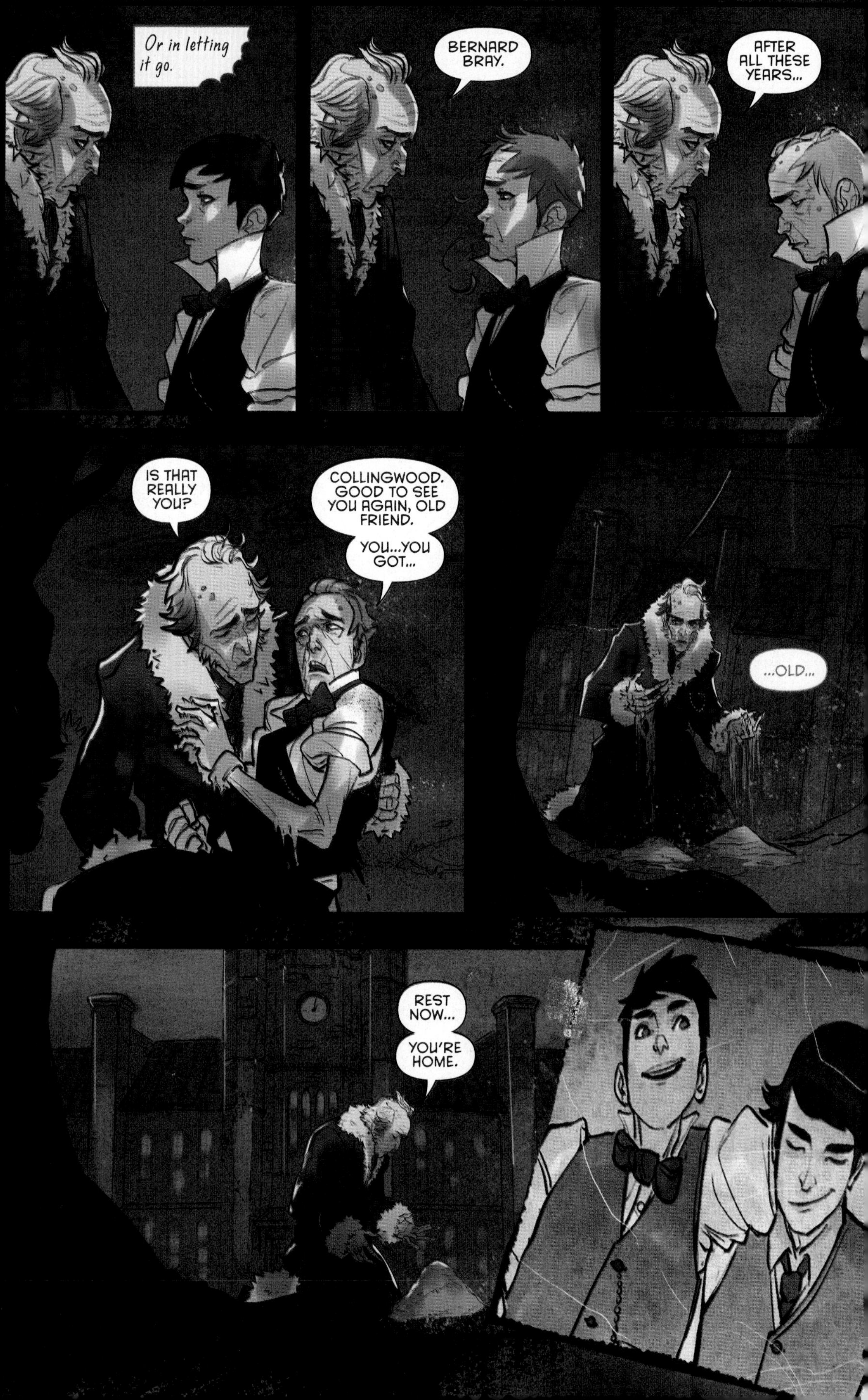
Or in letting it go.
BERNARD BRAY.
AFTER ALL THESE YEARS...
IS THAT REALLY YOU?
COLLINGWOOD. GOOD TO SEE YOU AGAIN, OLD FRIEND.
YOU...YOU GOT...
...OLD...
REST NOW...
YOU'RE HOME.

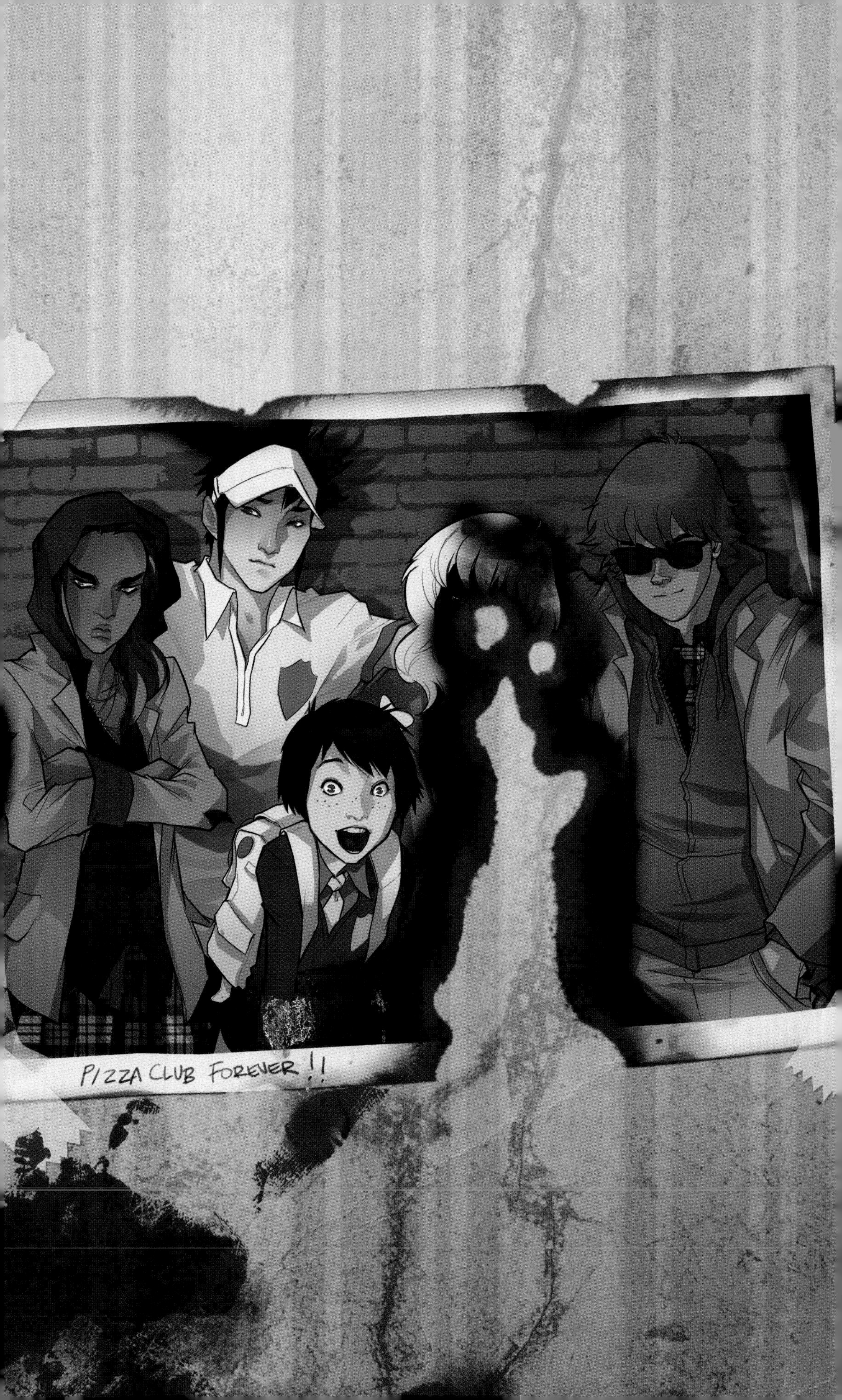
PIZZA CLUB FOREVER!!

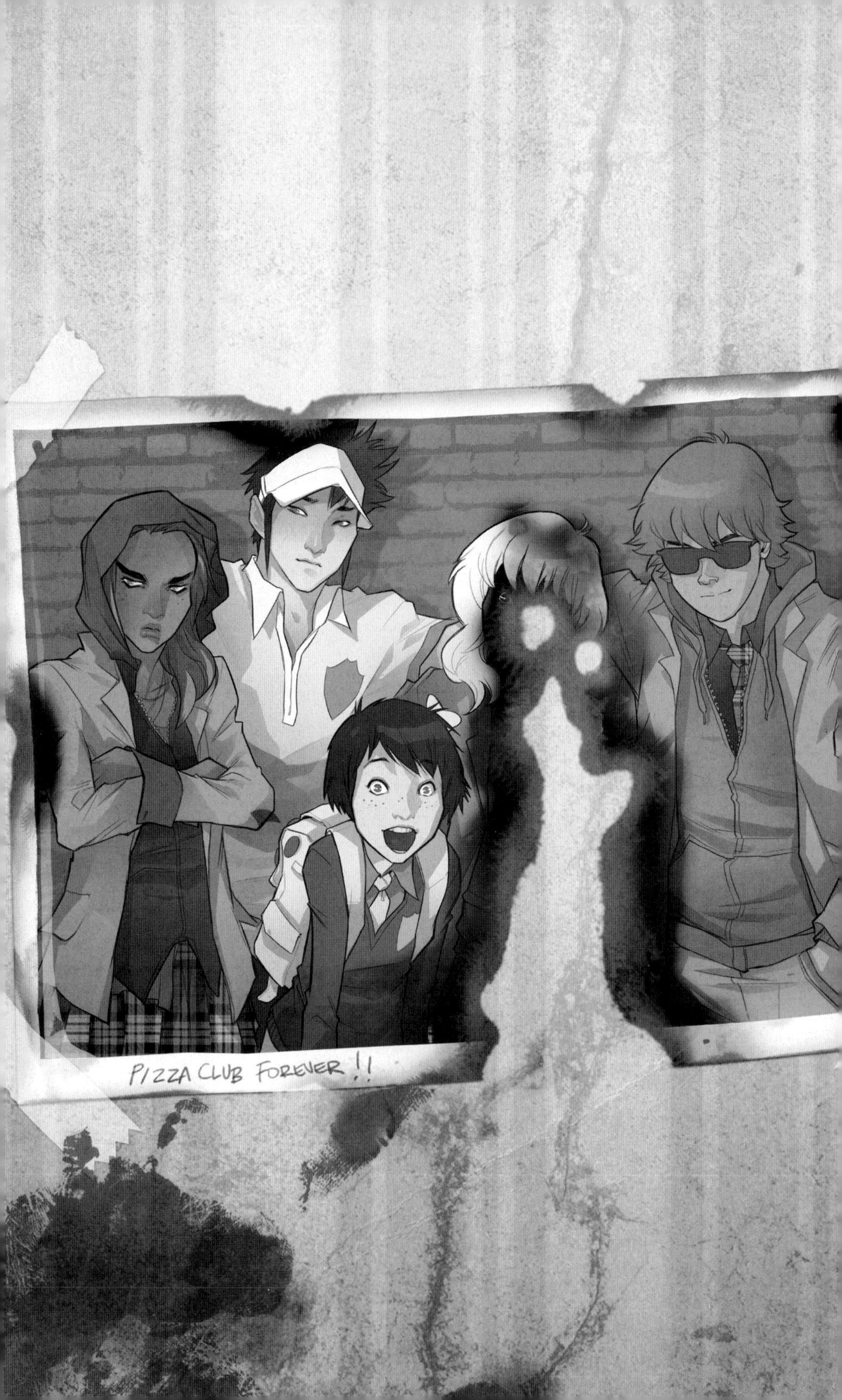
PIZZA CLUB FOREVER!!

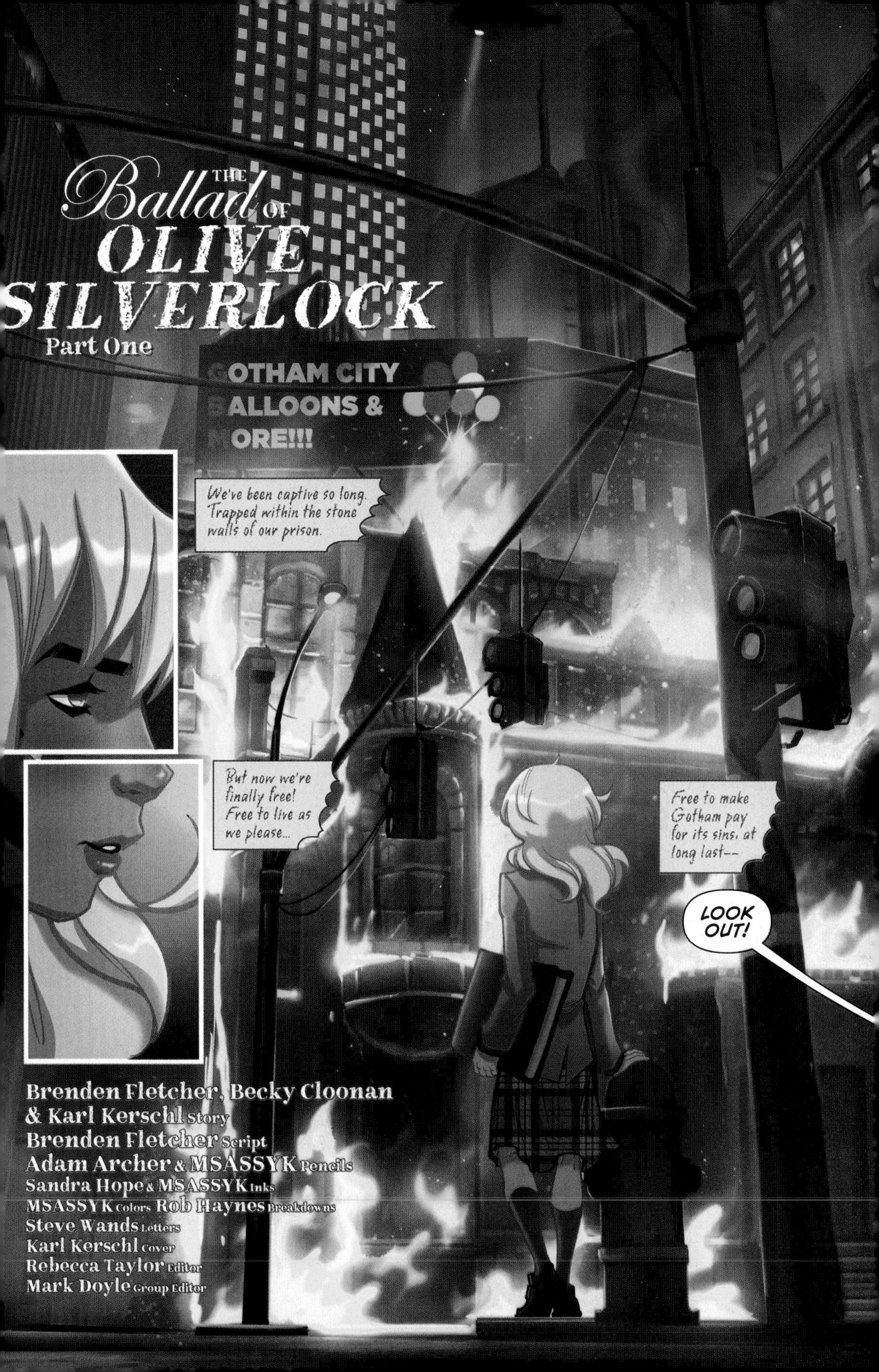
THE Ballad OF OLIVE SILVERLOCK
Part One
GOTHAM CITY BALLOONS & MORE!!!
We've been captive so long. Trapped within the stone walls of our prison.
But now we're finally free! Free to live as we please...
Free to make Gotham pay for its sins, at long last--
LOOK OUT!
Brenden Fletcher, Becky Cloonan & Karl Kerschl Story
Brenden Fletcher Script
Adam Archer & MSASSYK Pencils
Sandra Hope & MSASSYK Inks
MSASSYK Colors Rob Haynes Breakdowns
Steve Wands Letters
Karl Kerschl Cover
Rebecca Taylor Editor
Mark Doyle Group Editor

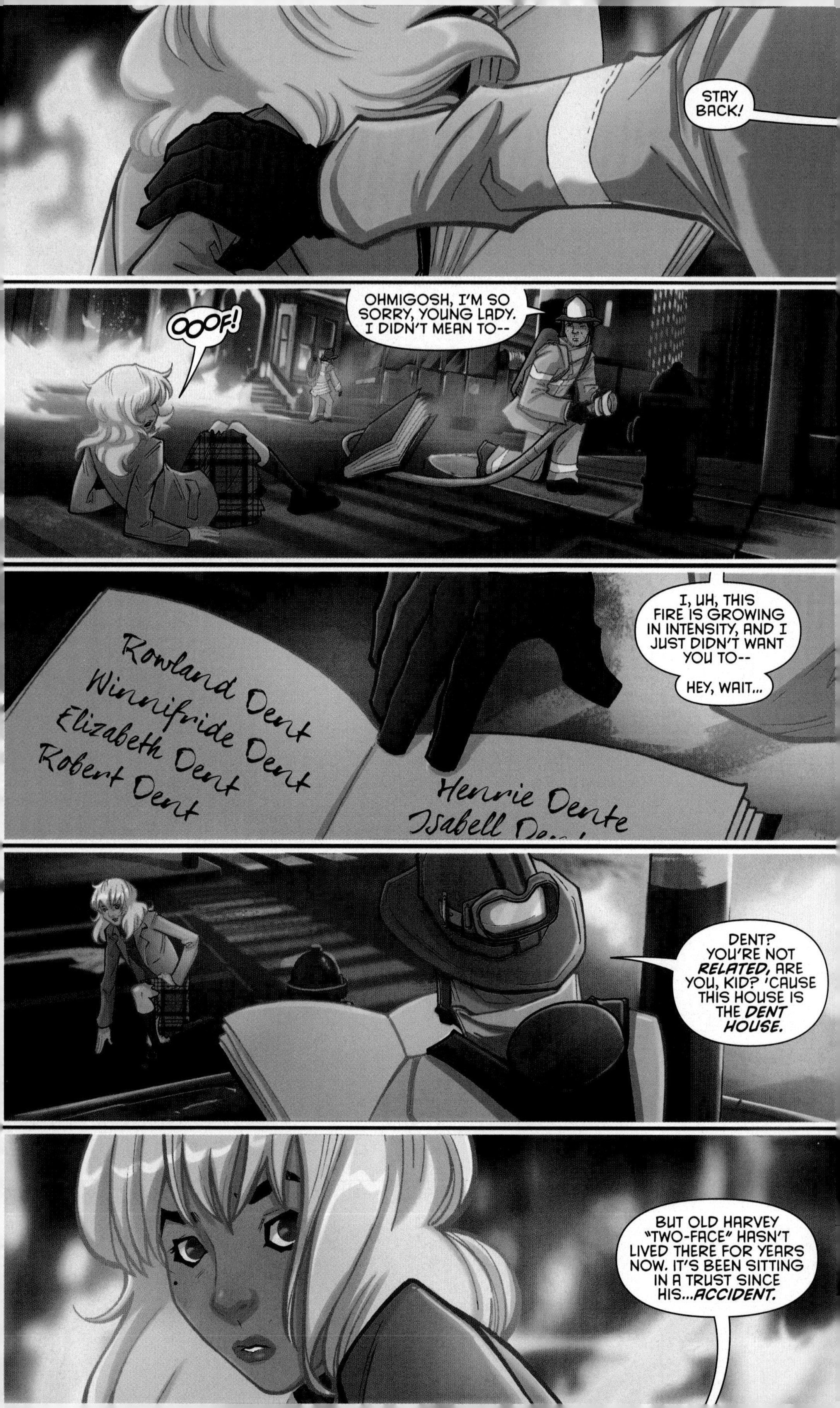
STAY BACK!
OOOF!
OHMIGOSH, I'M SO SORRY, YOUNG LADY. I DIDN'T MEAN TO--
Rowland Dent
Winnifride Dent
Elizabeth Dent
Robert Dent
Henrie Dente
I, UH, THIS FIRE IS GROWING IN INTENSITY, AND I JUST DIDN'T WANT YOU TO--
HEY, WAIT...
DENT? YOU'RE NOT RELATED, ARE YOU, KID? 'CAUSE THIS HOUSE IS THE DENT HOUSE.
BUT OLD HARVEY "TWO-FACE" HASN'T LIVED THERE FOR YEARS NOW. IT'S BEEN SITTING IN A TRUST SINCE HIS...ACCIDENT.

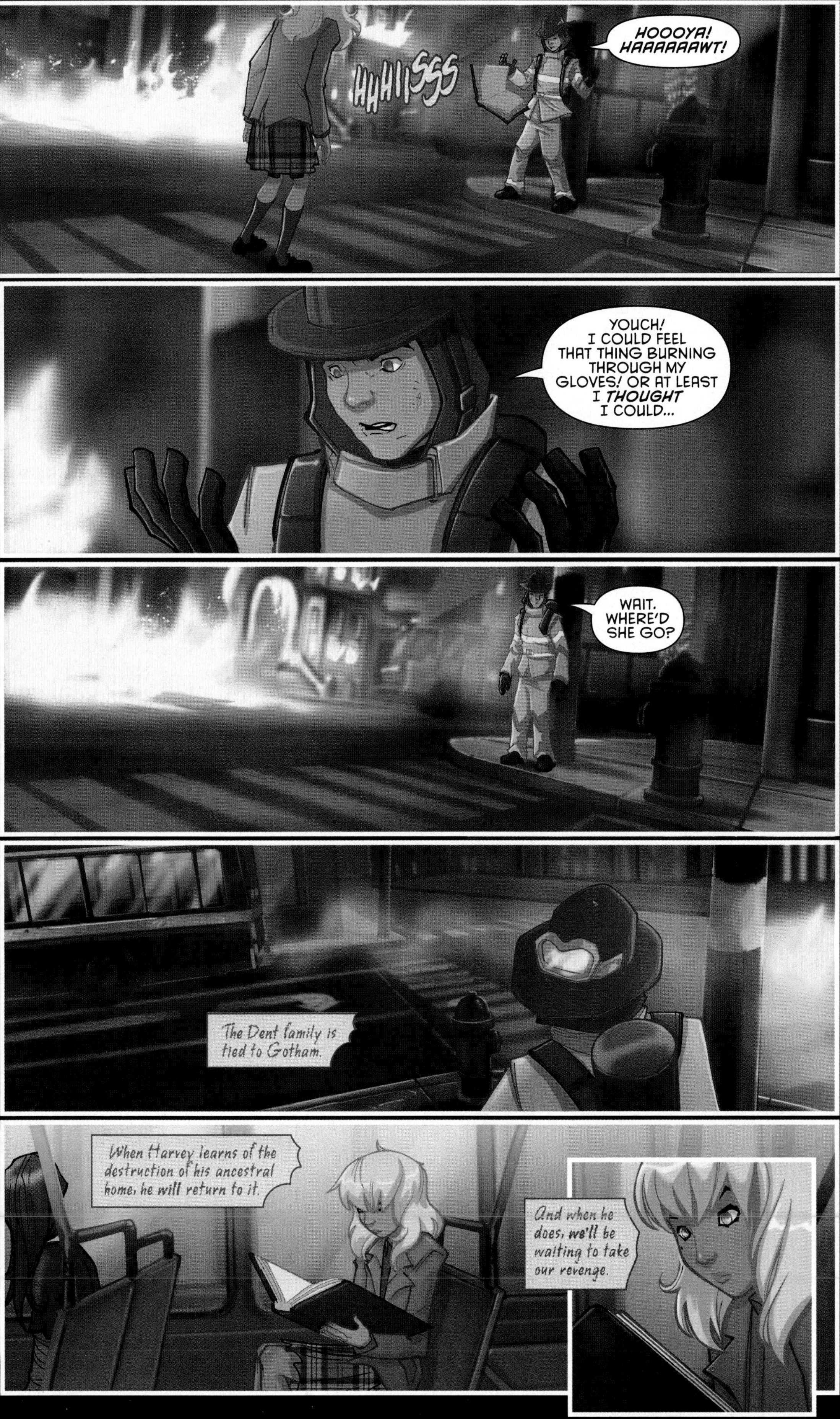
HOOOYA! HAAAAAAWT!
HHHIISSS
YOUCH! I COULD FEEL THAT THING BURNING THROUGH MY GLOVES! OR AT LEAST I THOUGHT I COULD...
WAIT. WHERE'D SHE GO?
The Dent family is tied to Gotham.
When Harvey learns of the destruction of his ancestral home, he will return to it.
And when he does, we'll be waiting to take our revenge.

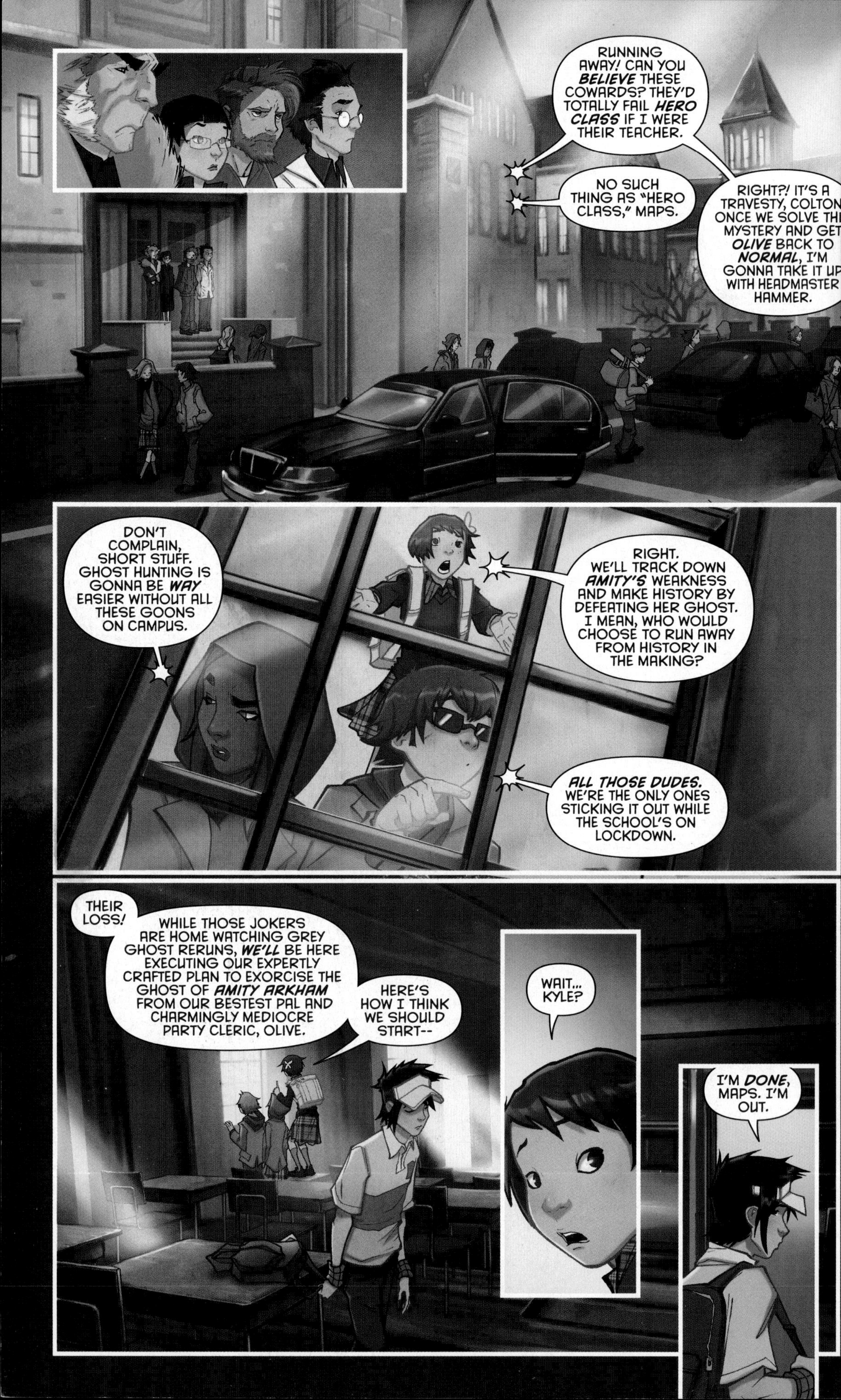
RUNNING AWAY! CAN YOU BELIEVE THESE COWARDS? THEY'D TOTALLY FAIL HERO CLASS IF I WERE THEIR TEACHER.
NO SUCH THING AS "HERO CLASS," MAPS.
RIGHT?! IT'S A TRAVESTY, COLTON. ONCE WE SOLVE THE MYSTERY AND GET OLIVE BACK TO NORMAL, I'M GONNA TAKE IT UP WITH HEADMASTER HAMMER.
DON'T COMPLAIN, SHORT STUFF. GHOST HUNTING IS GONNA BE WAY EASIER WITHOUT ALL THESE GOONS ON CAMPUS.
RIGHT. WE'LL TRACK DOWN AMITY'S WEAKNESS AND MAKE HISTORY BY DEFEATING HER GHOST. I MEAN, WHO WOULD CHOOSE TO RUN AWAY FROM HISTORY IN THE MAKING?
ALL THOSE DUDES. WE'RE THE ONLY ONES STICKING IT OUT WHILE THE SCHOOL'S ON LOCKDOWN.
THEIR LOSS!
WHILE THOSE JOKERS ARE HOME WATCHING GREY GHOST RERUNS, WE'LL BE HERE EXECUTING OUR EXPERTLY CRAFTED PLAN TO EXORCISE THE GHOST OF AMITY ARKHAM FROM OUR BESTEST PAL AND CHARMINGLY MEDIOCRE PARTY CLERIC, OLIVE.
HERE'S HOW I THINK WE SHOULD START--
WAIT... KYLE?
I'M DONE, MAPS. I'M OUT.

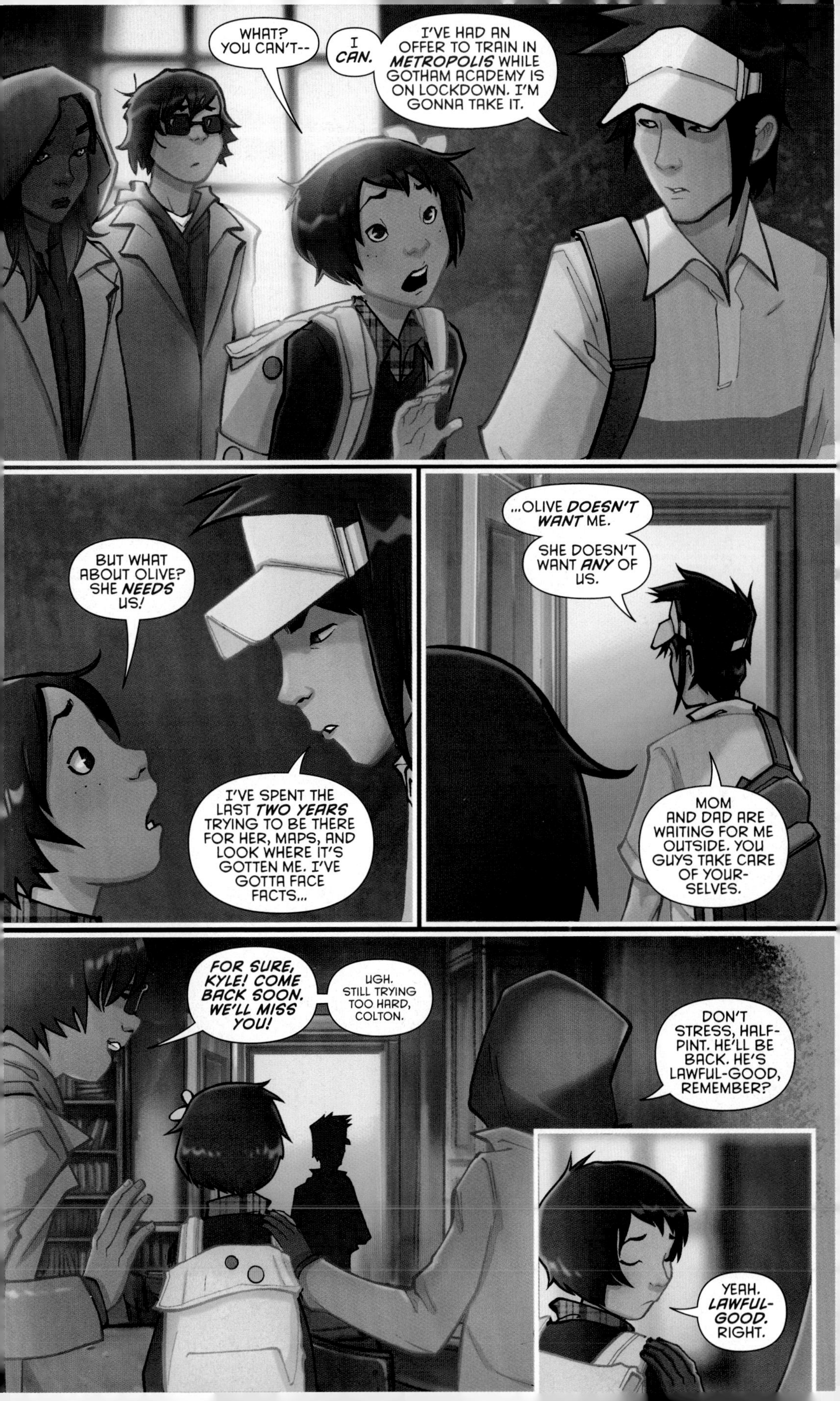
WHAT? YOU CAN'T--
I CAN.
I'VE HAD AN OFFER TO TRAIN IN METROPOLIS WHILE GOTHAM ACADEMY IS ON LOCKDOWN. I'M GONNA TAKE IT.
BUT WHAT ABOUT OLIVE? SHE NEEDS US!
I'VE SPENT THE LAST TWO YEARS TRYING TO BE THERE FOR HER, MAPS, AND LOOK WHERE IT'S GOTTEN ME. I'VE GOTTA FACE FACTS...
...OLIVE DOESN'T WANT ME.
SHE DOESN'T WANT ANY OF US.
MOM AND DAD ARE WAITING FOR ME OUTSIDE. YOU GUYS TAKE CARE OF YOUR-SELVES.
FOR SURE, KYLE! COME BACK SOON. WE'LL MISS YOU!
UGH. STILL TRYING TOO HARD, COLTON.
DON'T STRESS, HALF-PINT. HE'LL BE BACK. HE'S LAWFUL-GOOD, REMEMBER?
YEAH. LAWFUL-GOOD. RIGHT.

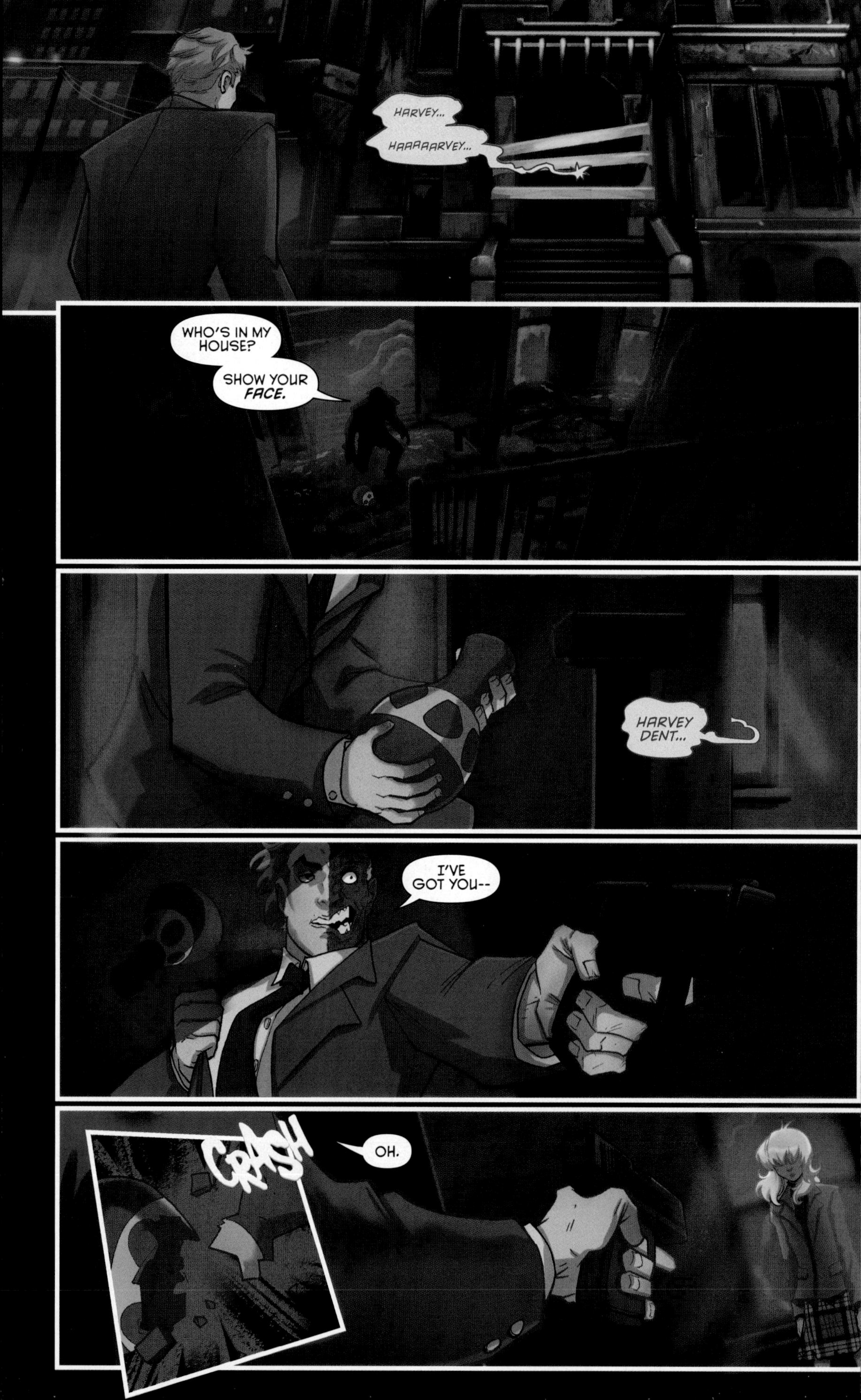
HARVEY...
HAAAAARVEY...
WHO'S IN MY HOUSE?
SHOW YOUR FACE.
HARVEY DENT...
I'VE GOT YOU--
CRASH
OH.

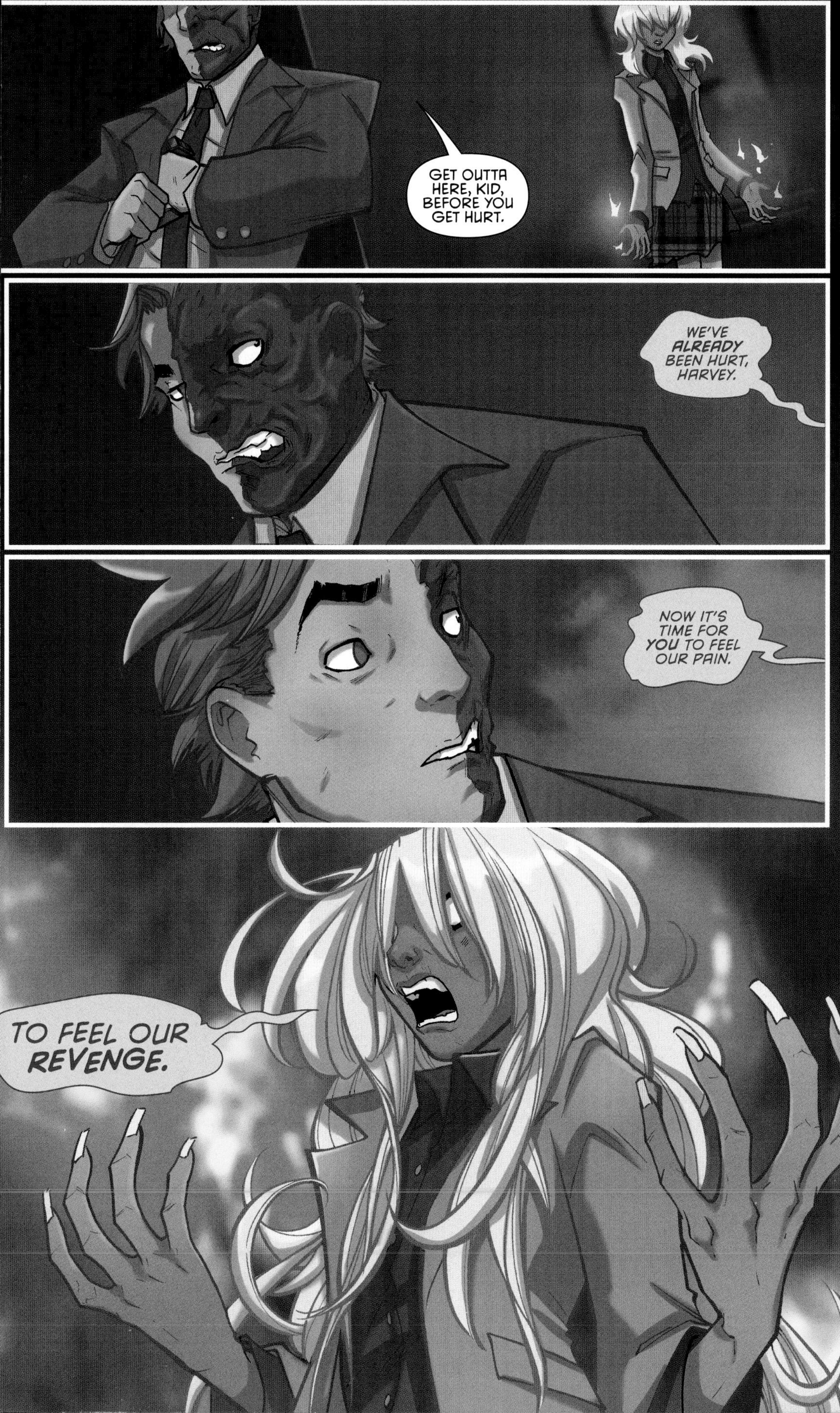
GET OUTTA HERE, KID, BEFORE YOU GET HURT.
WE'VE ALREADY BEEN HURT, HARVEY.
NOW IT'S TIME FOR YOU TO FEEL OUR PAIN.
TO FEEL OUR REVENGE.

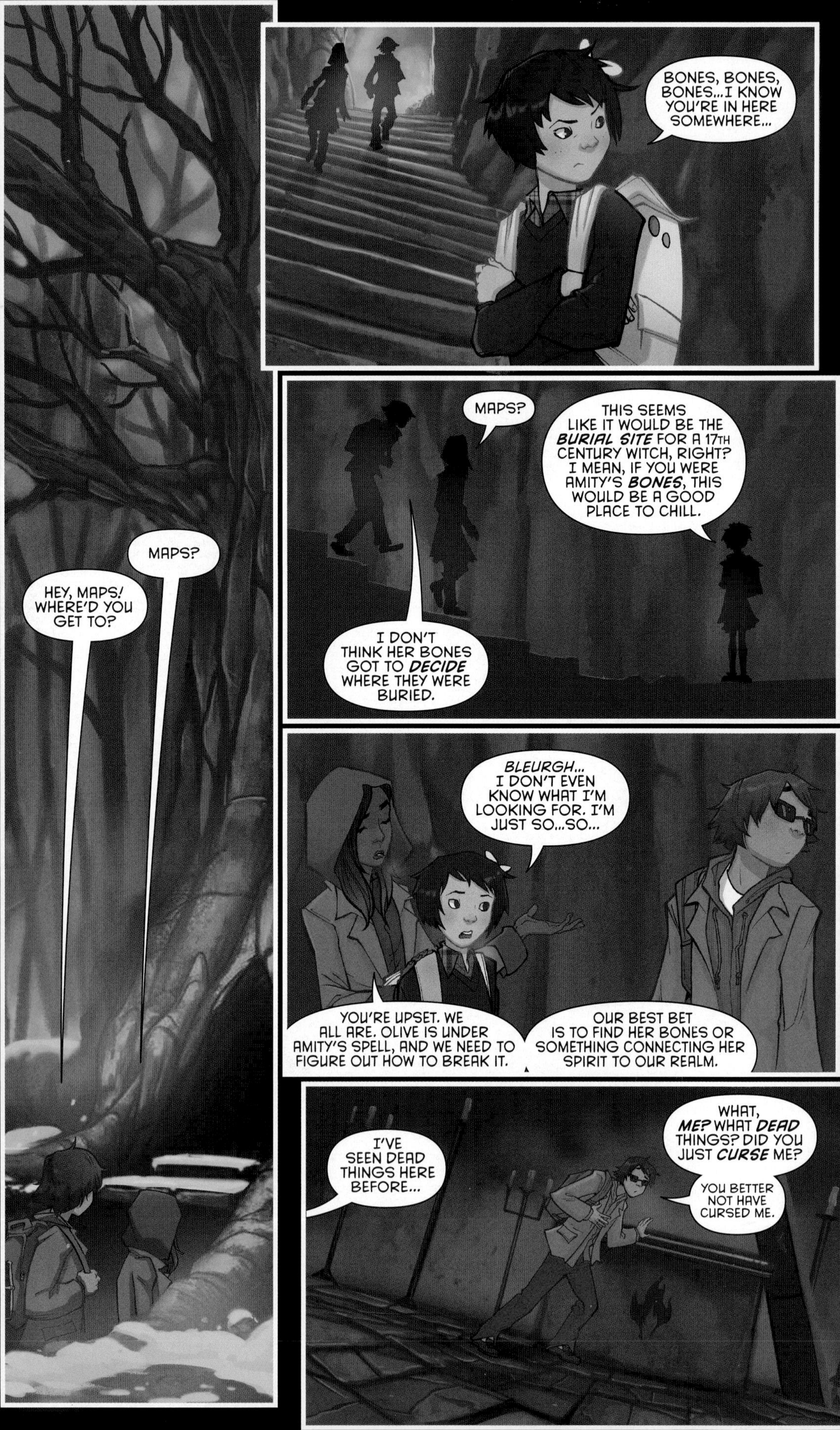
MAPS?
HEY, MAPS! WHERE'D YOU GET TO?
BONES, BONES, BONES...I KNOW YOU'RE IN HERE SOMEWHERE...
MAPS?
THIS SEEMS LIKE IT WOULD BE THE BURIAL SITE FOR A 17TH CENTURY WITCH, RIGHT? I MEAN, IF YOU WERE AMITY'S BONES, THIS WOULD BE A GOOD PLACE TO CHILL.
I DON'T THINK HER BONES GOT TO DECIDE WHERE THEY WERE BURIED.
BLEURGH... I DON'T EVEN KNOW WHAT I'M LOOKING FOR. I'M JUST SO...SO...
YOU'RE UPSET. WE ALL ARE. OLIVE IS UNDER AMITY'S SPELL, AND WE NEED TO FIGURE OUT HOW TO BREAK IT.
OUR BEST BET IS TO FIND HER BONES OR SOMETHING CONNECTING HER SPIRIT TO OUR REALM.
I'VE SEEN DEAD THINGS HERE BEFORE...
WHAT, ME? WHAT DEAD THINGS? DID YOU JUST CURSE ME?
YOU BETTER NOT HAVE CURSED ME.

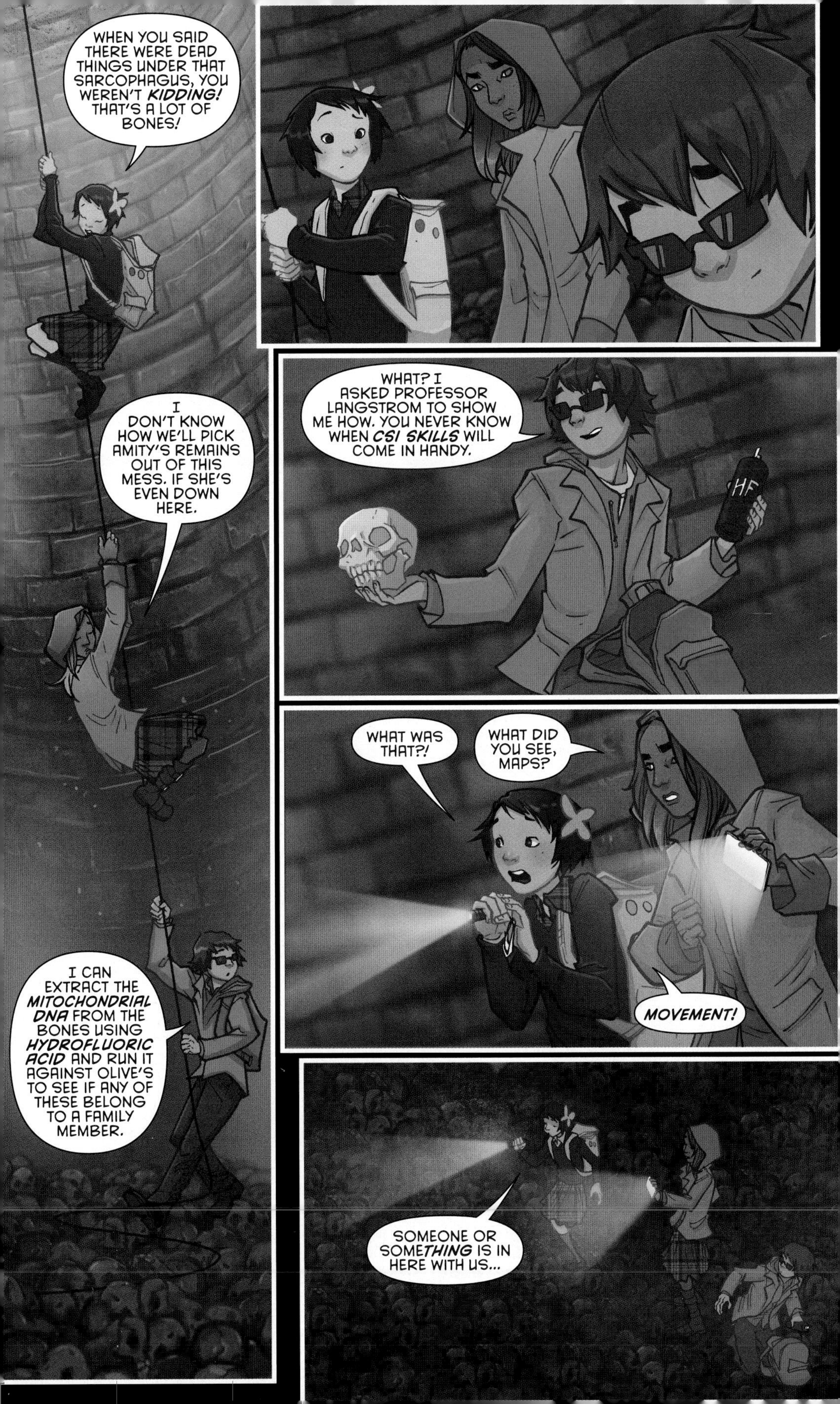
WHEN YOU SAID THERE WERE DEAD THINGS UNDER THAT SARCOPHAGUS, YOU WEREN'T KIDDING! THAT'S A LOT OF BONES!
I DON'T KNOW HOW WE'LL PICK AMITY'S REMAINS OUT OF THIS MESS. IF SHE'S EVEN DOWN HERE.
I CAN EXTRACT THE MITOCHONDRIAL DNA FROM THE BONES USING HYDROFLUORIC ACID AND RUN IT AGAINST OLIVE'S TO SEE IF ANY OF THESE BELONG TO A FAMILY MEMBER.
WHAT? I ASKED PROFESSOR LANGSTROM TO SHOW ME HOW. YOU NEVER KNOW WHEN CSI SKILLS WILL COME IN HANDY.
HF
WHAT WAS THAT?!
WHAT DID YOU SEE, MAPS?
MOVEMENT!
SOMEONE OR SOMETHING IS IN HERE WITH US...

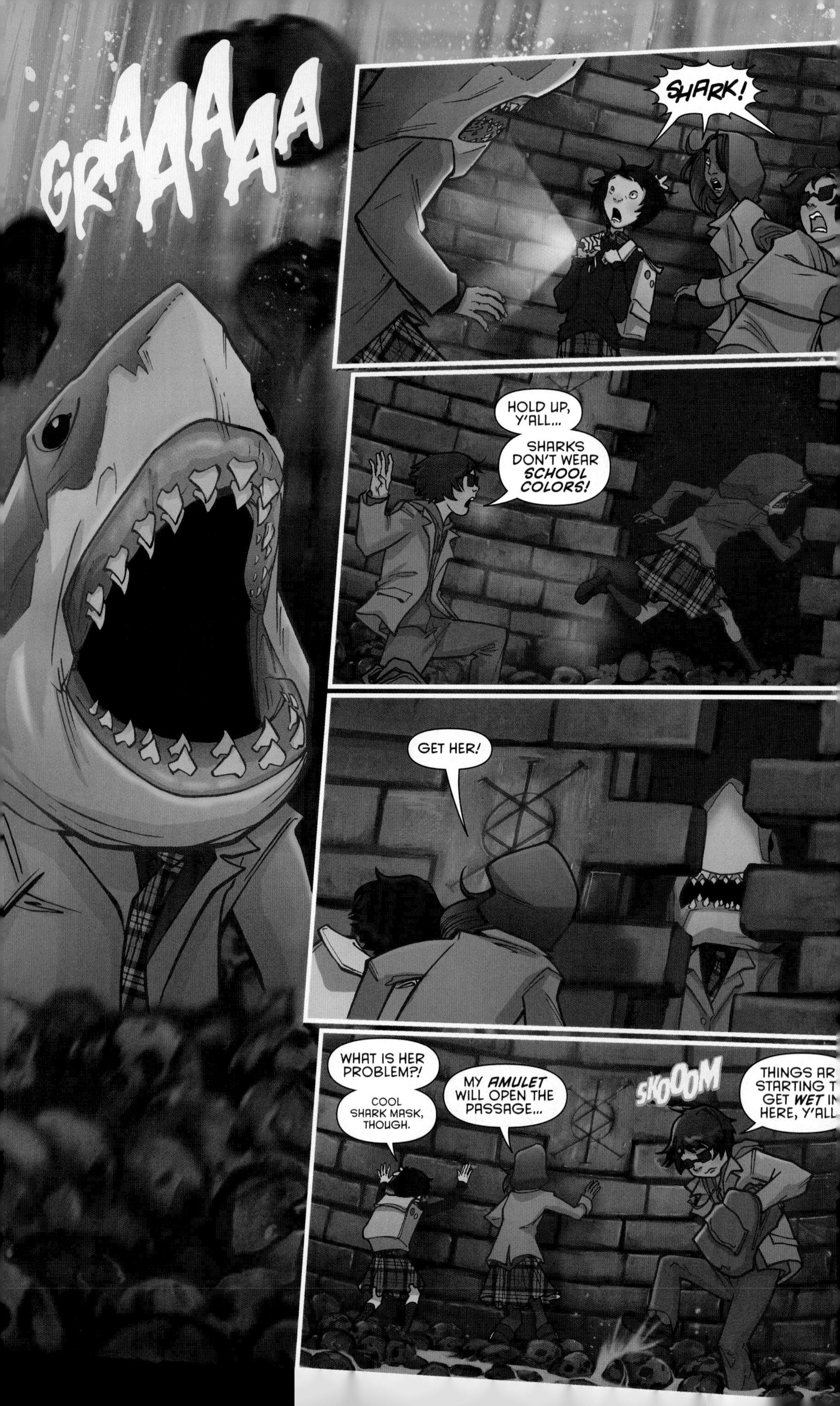
GRAAAAA
SHARK!
HOLD UP, Y'ALL...
SHARKS DON'T WEAR SCHOOL COLORS!
GET HER!
WHAT IS HER PROBLEM?!
COOL SHARK MASK, THOUGH.
MY AMULET WILL OPEN THE PASSAGE...
SKOOOM
THINGS AR STARTING T GET WET IN HERE, Y'ALL

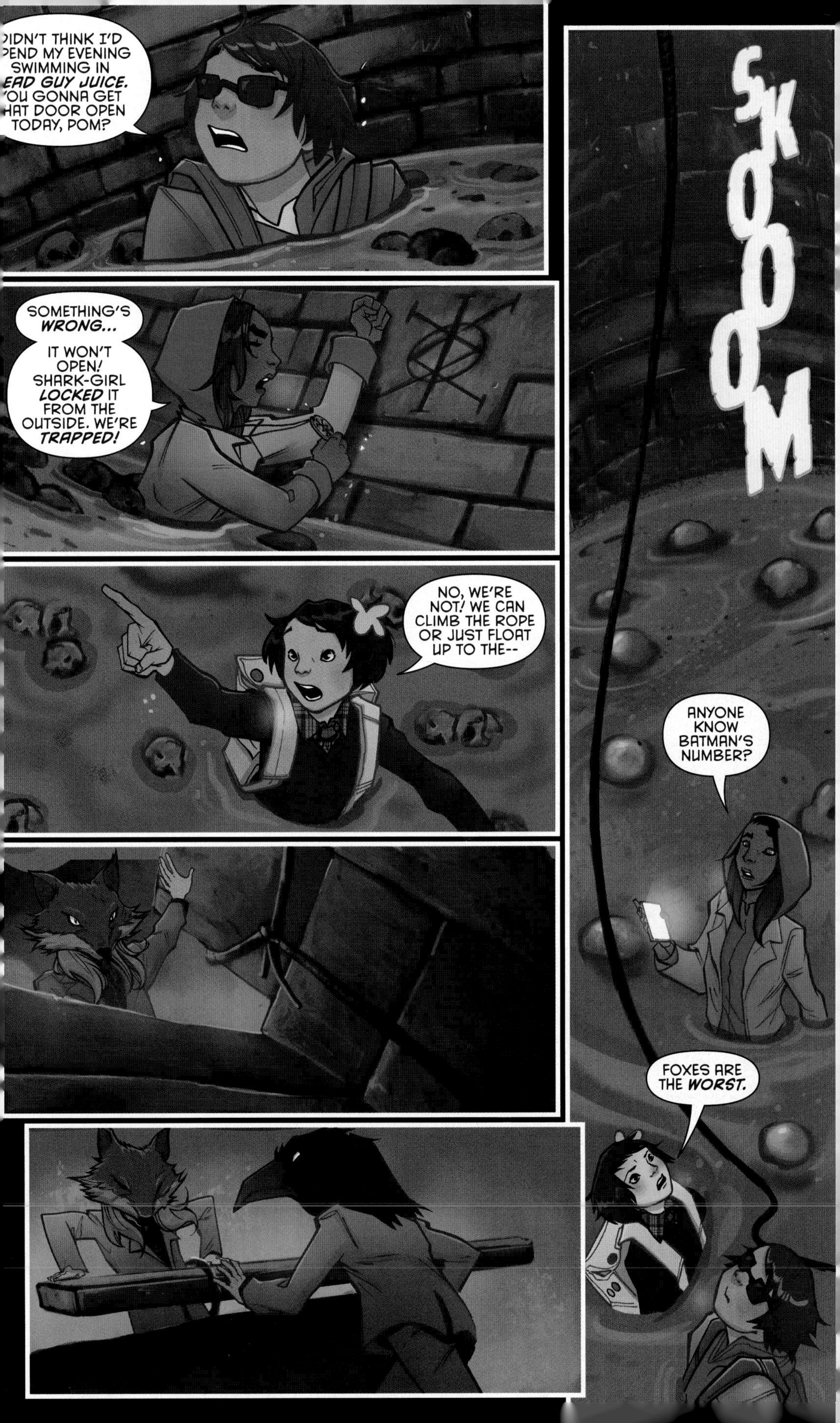

DIDN'T THINK I'D SPEND MY EVENING SWIMMING IN DEAD GUY JUICE. YOU GONNA GET THAT DOOR OPEN TODAY, POM?
SOMETHING'S WRONG...
IT WON'T OPEN! SHARK-GIRL LOCKED IT FROM THE OUTSIDE. WE'RE TRAPPED!
NO, WE'RE NOT! WE CAN CLIMB THE ROPE OR JUST FLOAT UP TO THE--
SKOOOOM
ANYONE KNOW BATMAN'S NUMBER?
FOXES ARE THE WORST.

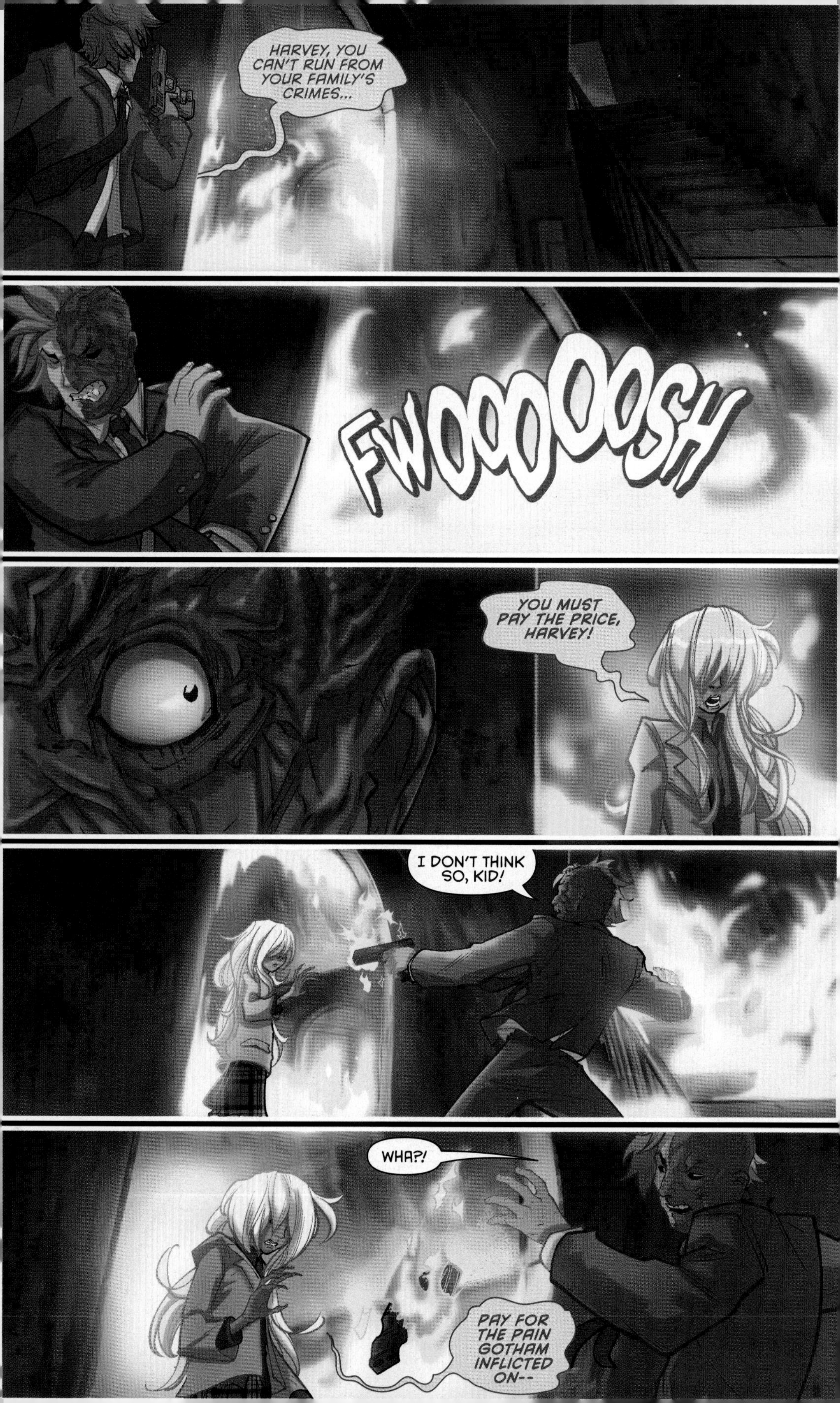
HARVEY, YOU CAN'T RUN FROM YOUR FAMILY'S CRIMES...
FWOOOOOOSH
YOU MUST PAY THE PRICE, HARVEY!
I DON'T THINK SO, KID!
WHA?!
PAY FOR THE PAIN GOTHAM INFLICTED ON--

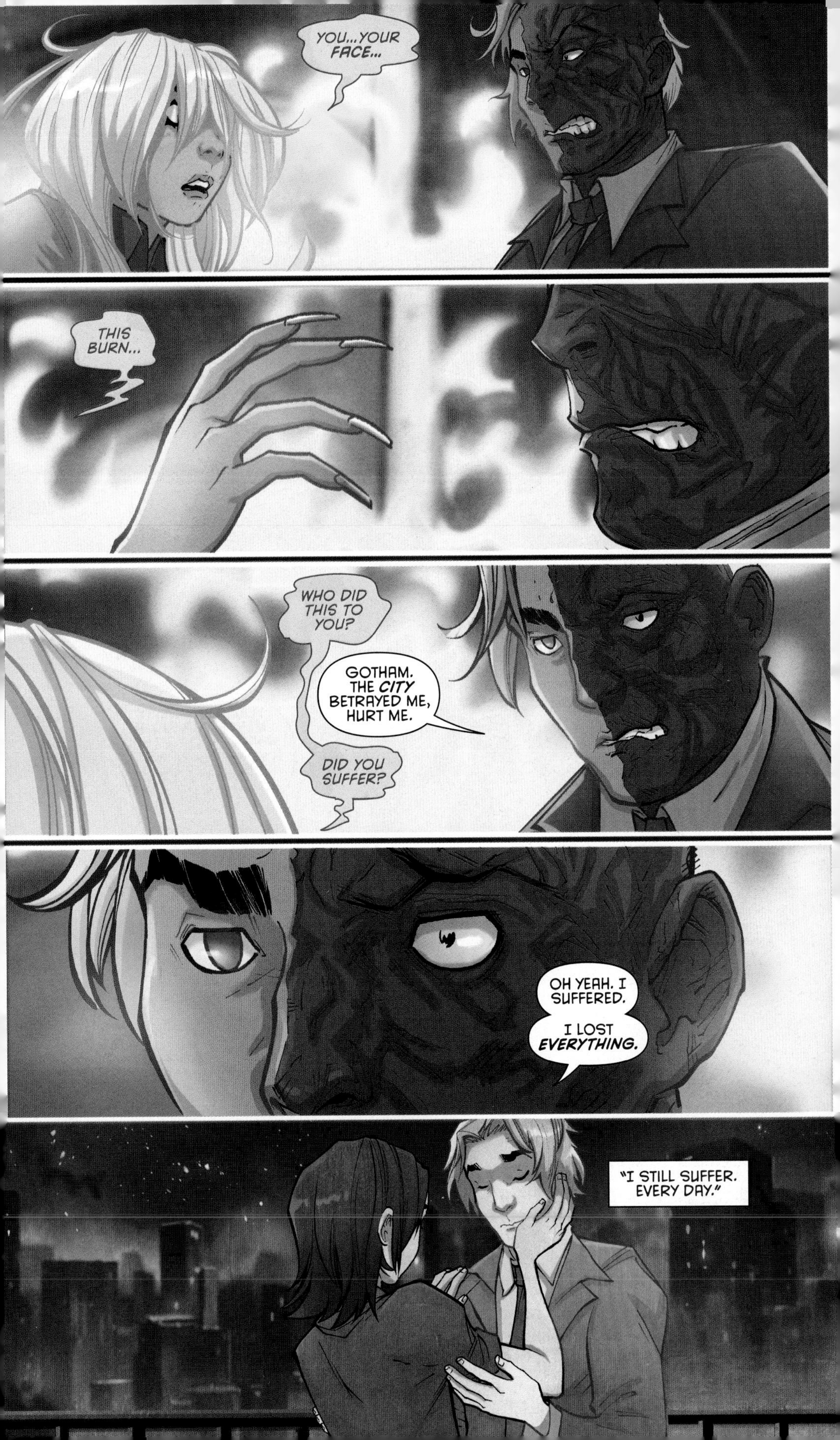
YOU...YOUR FACE...
THIS BURN...
WHO DID THIS TO YOU?
GOTHAM. THE CITY BETRAYED ME, HURT ME.
DID YOU SUFFER?
OH YEAH. I SUFFERED.
I LOST EVERYTHING.
"I STILL SUFFER. EVERY DAY."

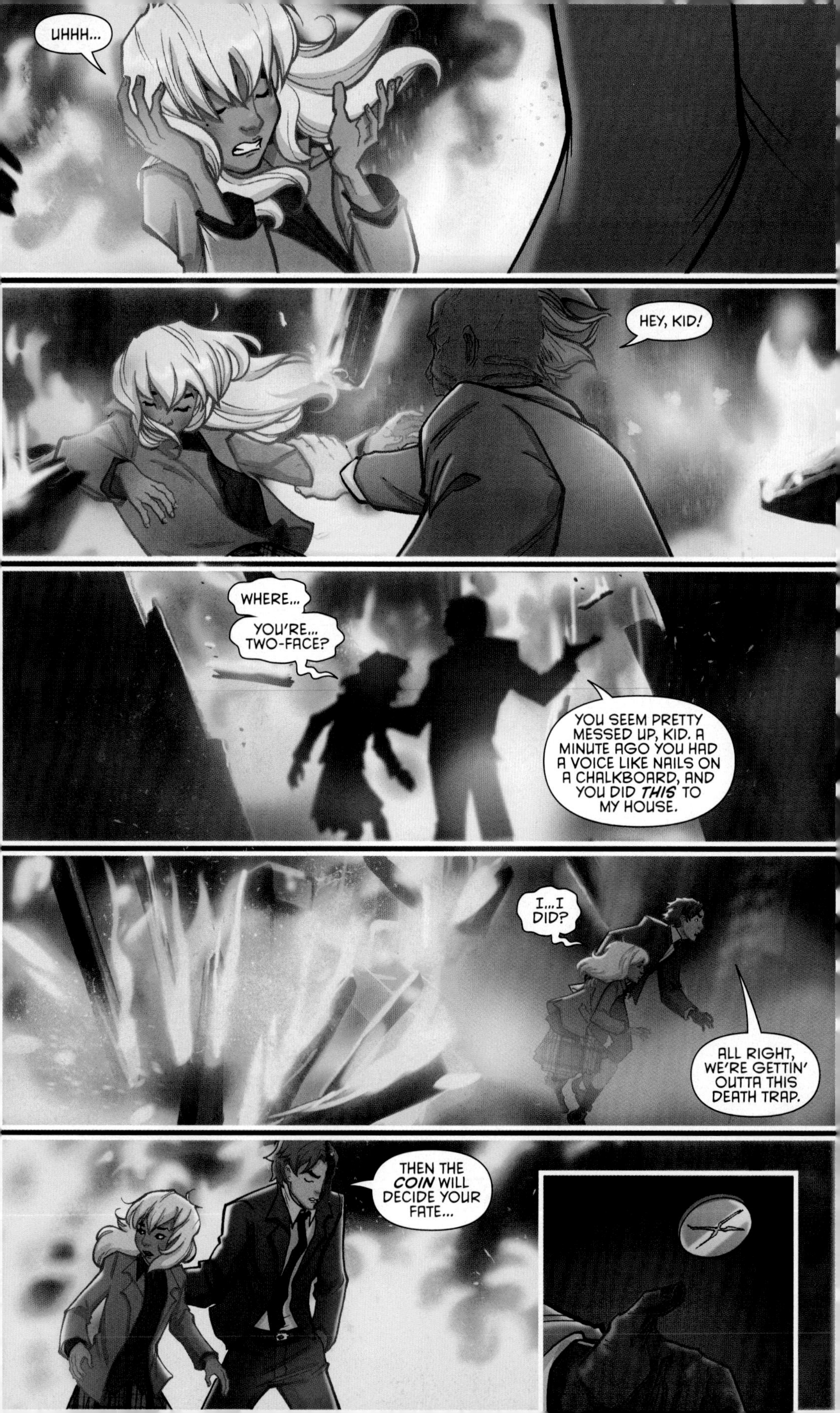
UHHH...
HEY, KID!
WHERE...
YOU'RE... TWO-FACE?
YOU SEEM PRETTY MESSED UP, KID. A MINUTE AGO YOU HAD A VOICE LIKE NAILS ON A CHALKBOARD, AND YOU DID *THIS* TO MY HOUSE.
I...I DID?
ALL RIGHT, WE'RE GETTIN' OUTTA THIS DEATH TRAP.
THEN THE *COIN* WILL DECIDE YOUR FATE...

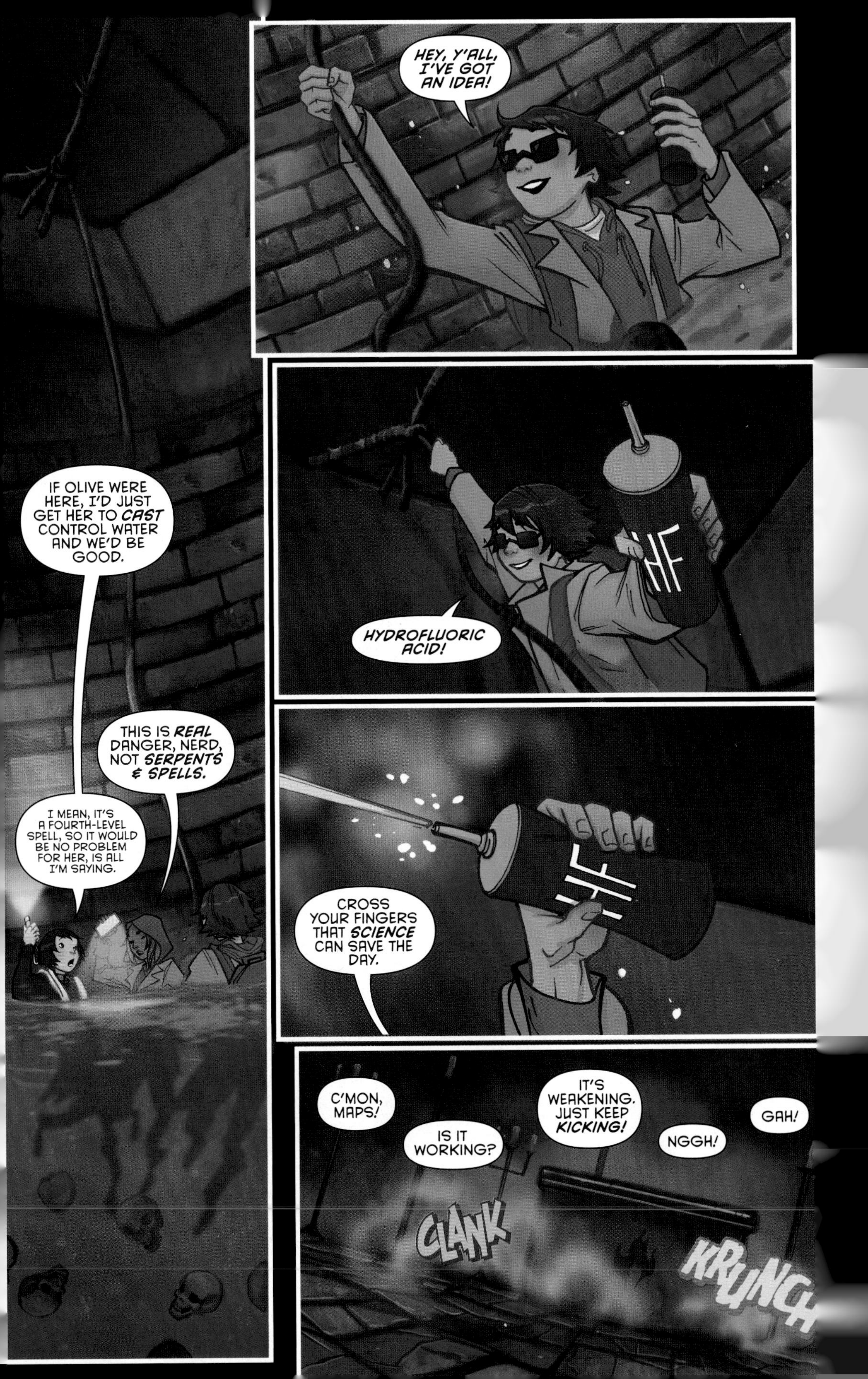
HEY, Y'ALL, I'VE GOT AN IDEA!
IF OLIVE WERE HERE, I'D JUST GET HER TO CAST CONTROL WATER AND WE'D BE GOOD.
I MEAN, IT'S A FOURTH-LEVEL SPELL, SO IT WOULD BE NO PROBLEM FOR HER, IS ALL I'M SAYING.
THIS IS REAL DANGER, NERD, NOT SERPENTS & SPELLS.
HYDROFLUORIC ACID!
HF
CROSS YOUR FINGERS THAT SCIENCE CAN SAVE THE DAY.
C'MON, MAPS!
IS IT WORKING?
IT'S WEAKENING. JUST KEEP KICKING!
NGGH!
GAH!
CLANK
KRUNCH

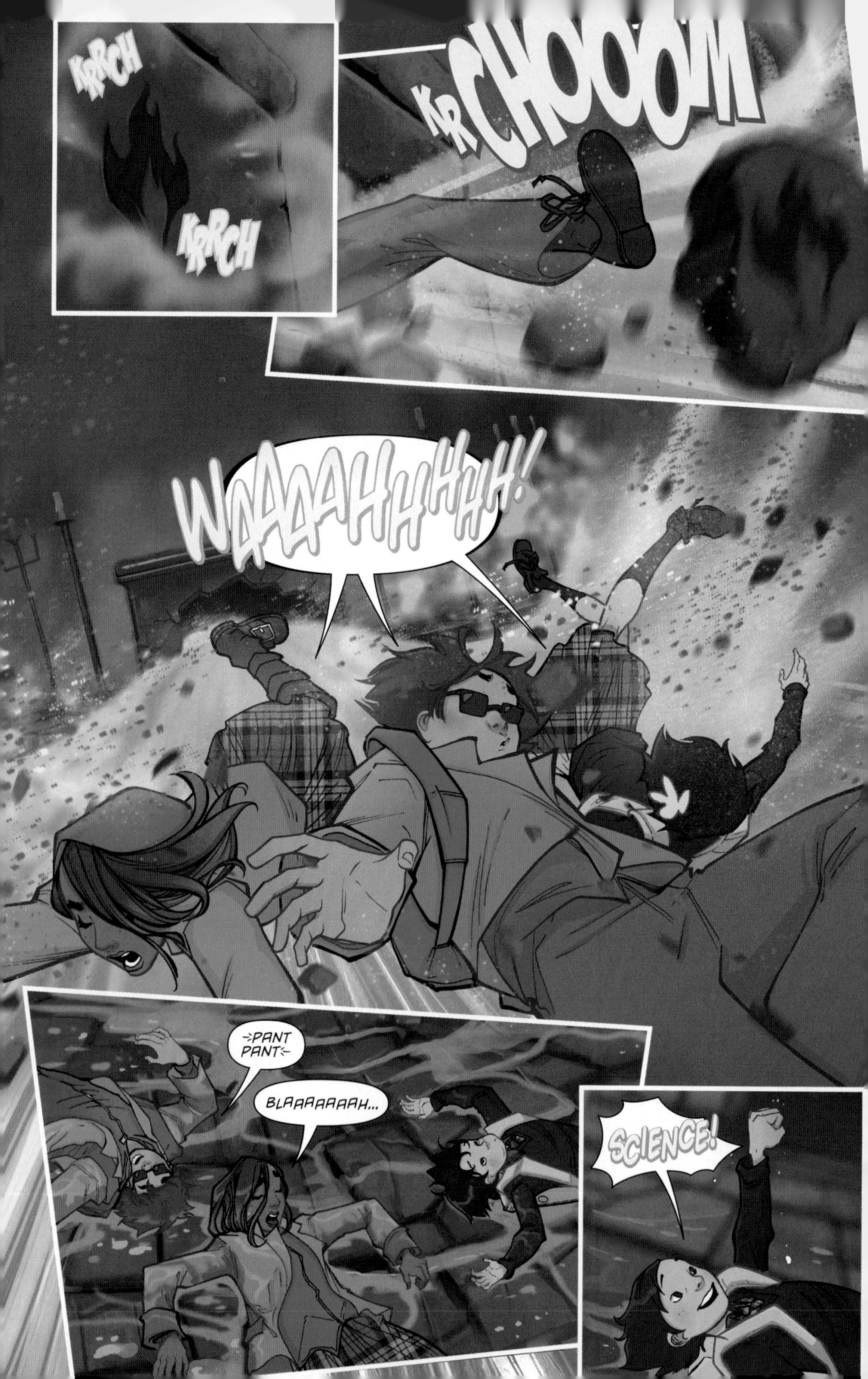

KRRCH
KRRCH
KRCHOOOOM
WAAAAHHHHH!
PANT PANT
BLAAAAAAAH...
SCIENCE!

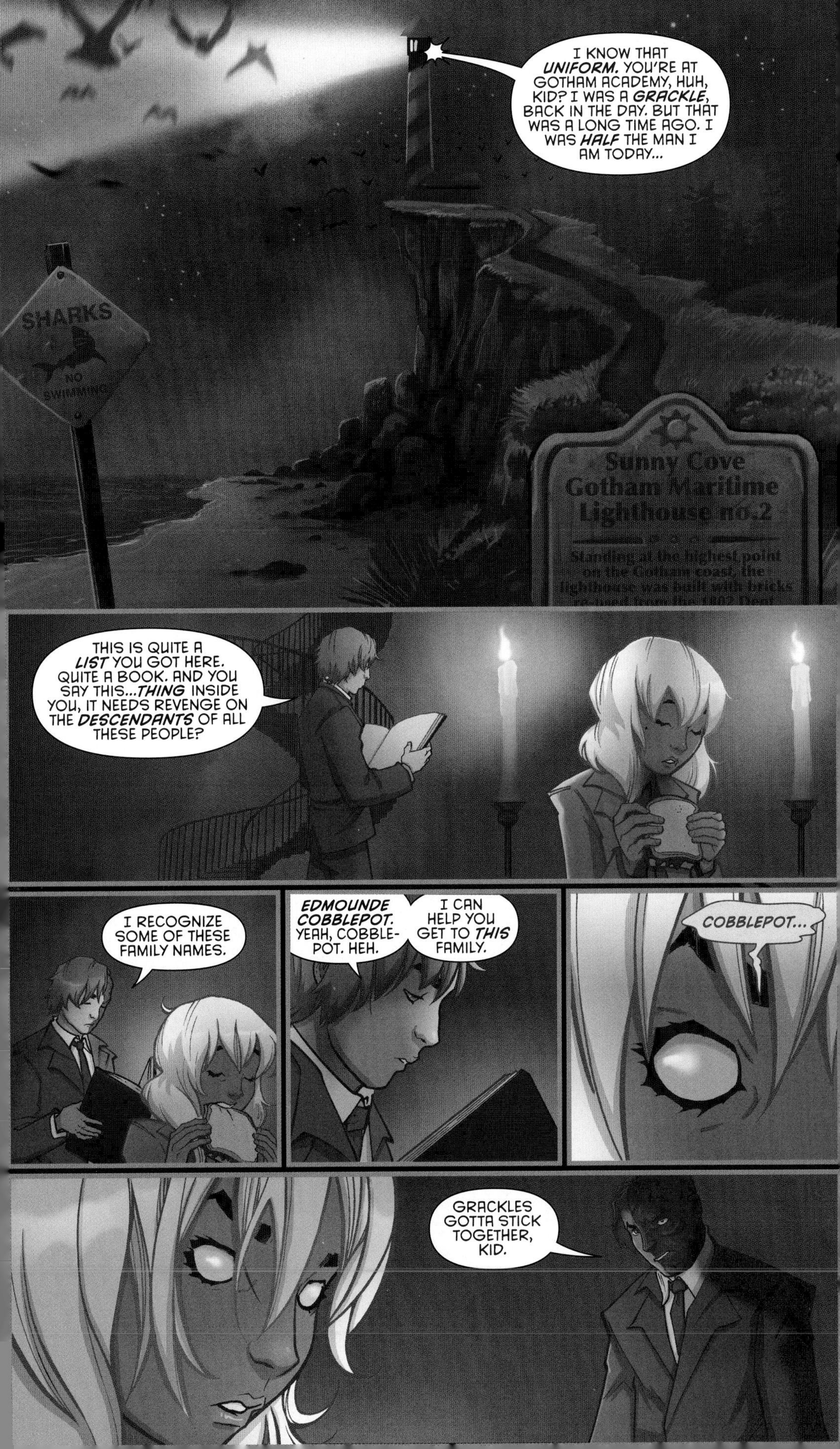

I KNOW THAT UNIFORM. YOU'RE AT GOTHAM ACADEMY, HUH, KID? I WAS A GRACKLE, BACK IN THE DAY. BUT THAT WAS A LONG TIME AGO. I WAS HALF THE MAN I AM TODAY...
SHARKS
NO SWIMMING
Sunny Cove
Gotham Maritime
Lighthouse no.2
Standing at the highest point on the Gotham coast, the lighthouse was built with bricks
THIS IS QUITE A LIST YOU GOT HERE. QUITE A BOOK. AND YOU SAY THIS...THING INSIDE YOU, IT NEEDS REVENGE ON THE DESCENDANTS OF ALL THESE PEOPLE?
I RECOGNIZE SOME OF THESE FAMILY NAMES.
EDMOUNDE COBBLEPOT. YEAH, COBBLE-POT. HEH.
I CAN HELP YOU GET TO THIS FAMILY.
COBBLEPOT...
GRACKLES GOTTA STICK TOGETHER, KID.

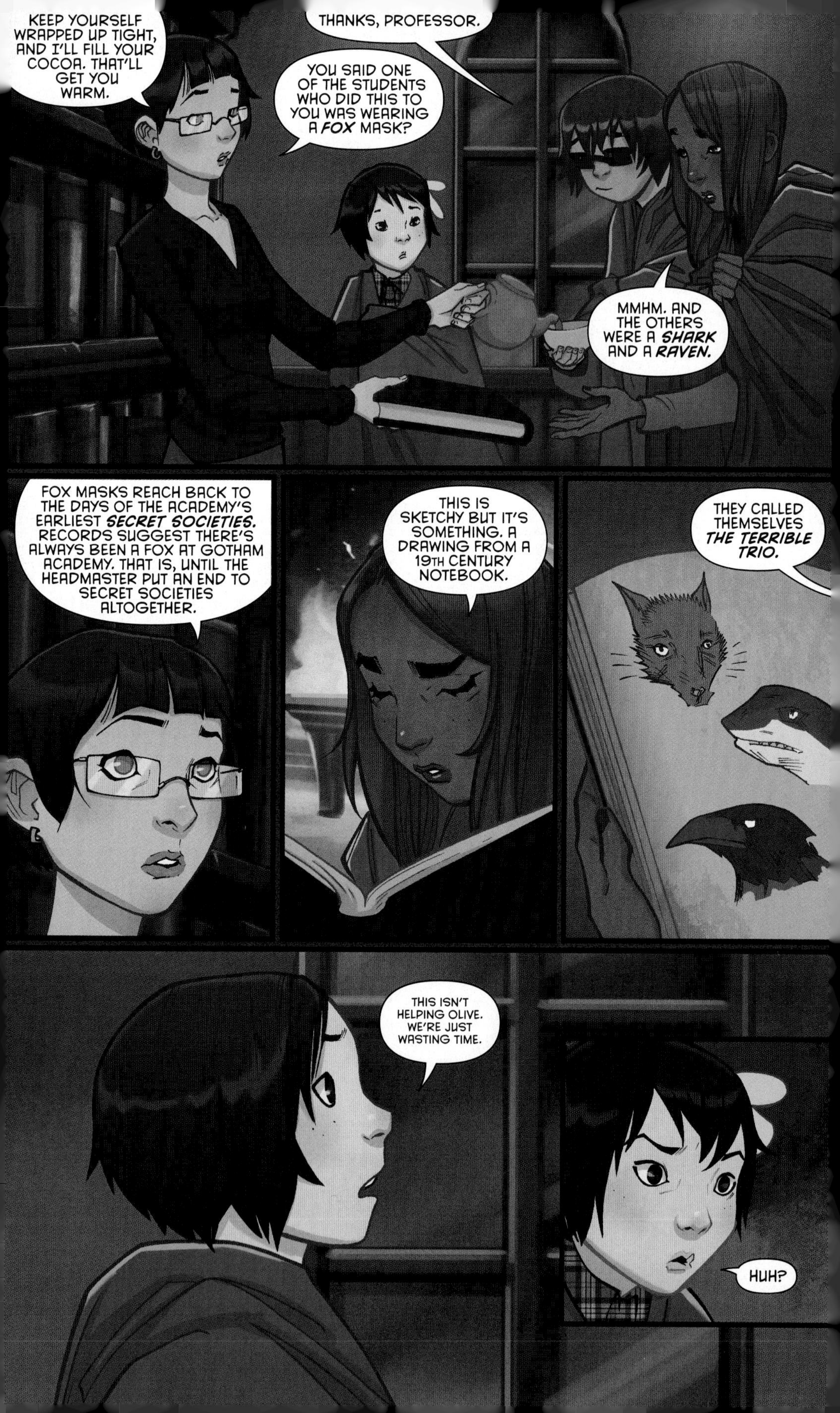
KEEP YOURSELF WRAPPED UP TIGHT, AND I'LL FILL YOUR COCOA. THAT'LL GET YOU WARM.
THANKS, PROFESSOR.
YOU SAID ONE OF THE STUDENTS WHO DID THIS TO YOU WAS WEARING A FOX MASK?
MMHM. AND THE OTHERS WERE A SHARK AND A RAVEN.
FOX MASKS REACH BACK TO THE DAYS OF THE ACADEMY'S EARLIEST SECRET SOCIETIES. RECORDS SUGGEST THERE'S ALWAYS BEEN A FOX AT GOTHAM ACADEMY. THAT IS, UNTIL THE HEADMASTER PUT AN END TO SECRET SOCIETIES ALTOGETHER.
THIS IS SKETCHY BUT IT'S SOMETHING. A DRAWING FROM A 19TH CENTURY NOTEBOOK.
THEY CALLED THEMSELVES THE TERRIBLE TRIO.
THIS ISN'T HELPING OLIVE. WE'RE JUST WASTING TIME.
HUH?

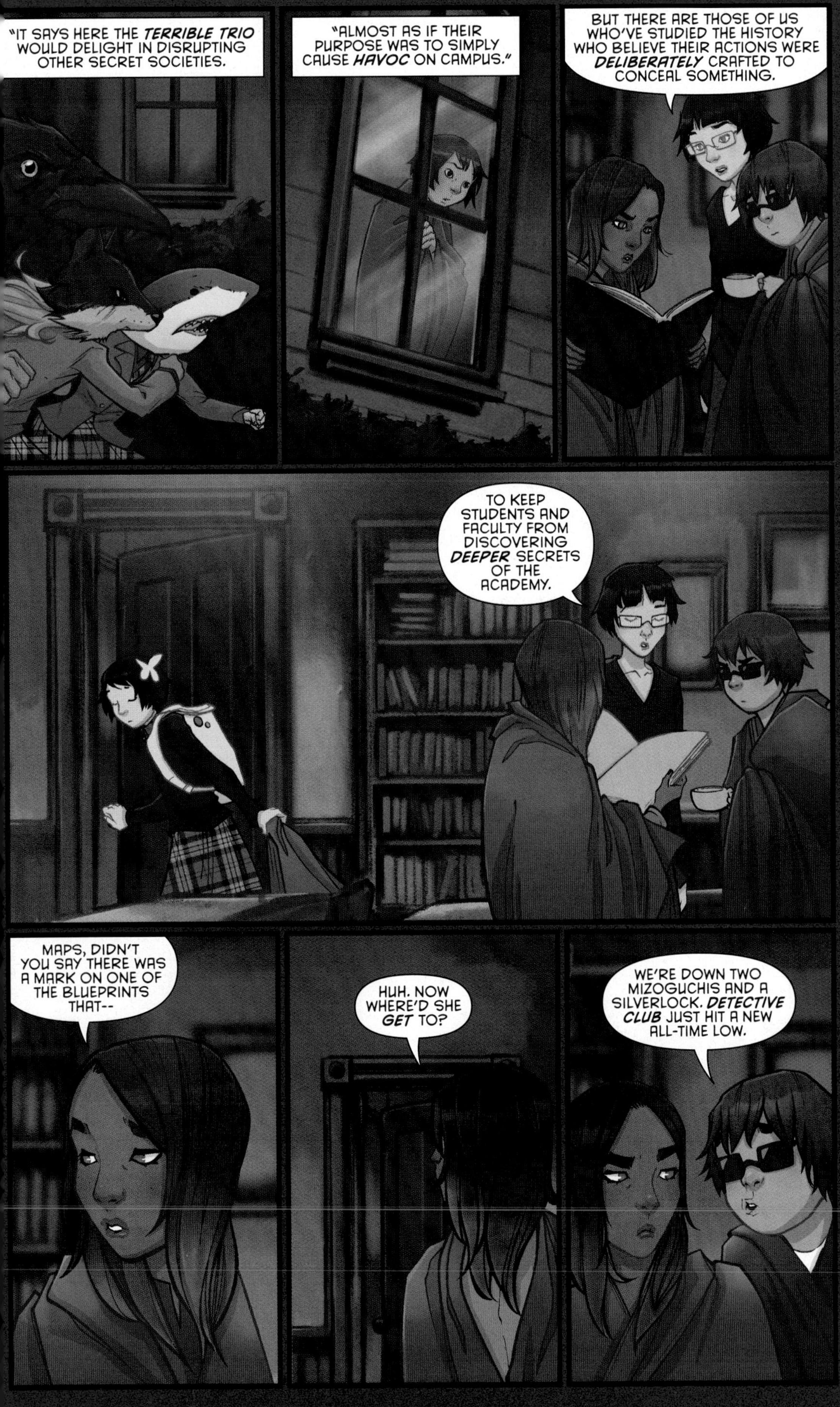

"IT SAYS HERE THE TERRIBLE TRIO WOULD DELIGHT IN DISRUPTING OTHER SECRET SOCIETIES.
"ALMOST AS IF THEIR PURPOSE WAS TO SIMPLY CAUSE HAVOC ON CAMPUS."
BUT THERE ARE THOSE OF US WHO'VE STUDIED THE HISTORY WHO BELIEVE THEIR ACTIONS WERE DELIBERATELY CRAFTED TO CONCEAL SOMETHING.
TO KEEP STUDENTS AND FACULTY FROM DISCOVERING DEEPER SECRETS OF THE ACADEMY.
MAPS, DIDN'T YOU SAY THERE WAS A MARK ON ONE OF THE BLUEPRINTS THAT--
HUH. NOW WHERE'D SHE GET TO?
WE'RE DOWN TWO MIZOGUCHIS AND A SILVERLOCK. DETECTIVE CLUB JUST HIT A NEW ALL-TIME LOW.

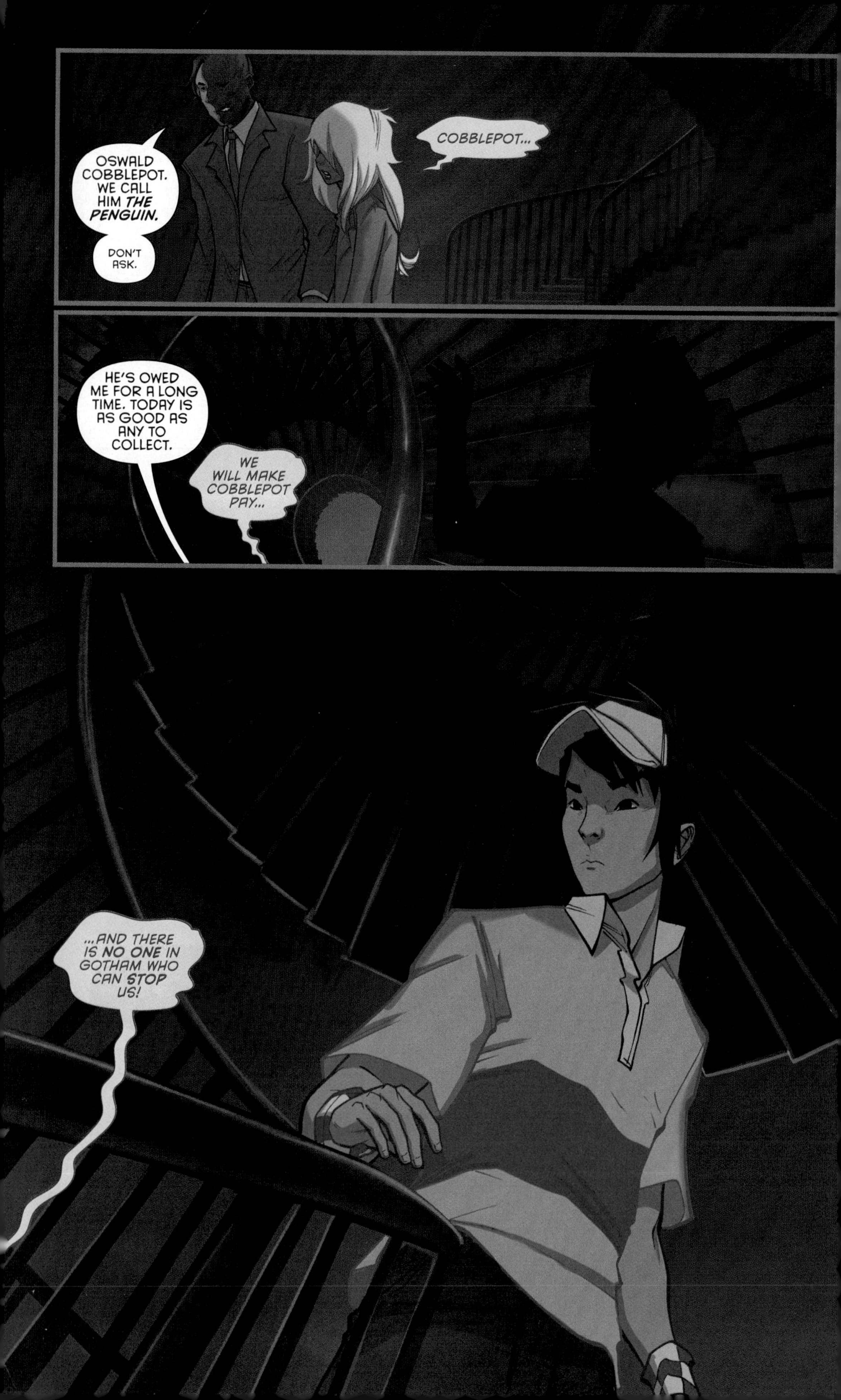
OSWALD COBBLEPOT. WE CALL HIM ***THE PENGUIN.***
DON'T ASK.
COBBLEPOT...
HE'S OWED ME FOR A LONG TIME. TODAY IS AS GOOD AS ANY TO COLLECT.
WE WILL MAKE COBBLEPOT PAY...
...AND THERE IS ***NO ONE*** *IN GOTHAM WHO CAN* ***STOP*** *US!*

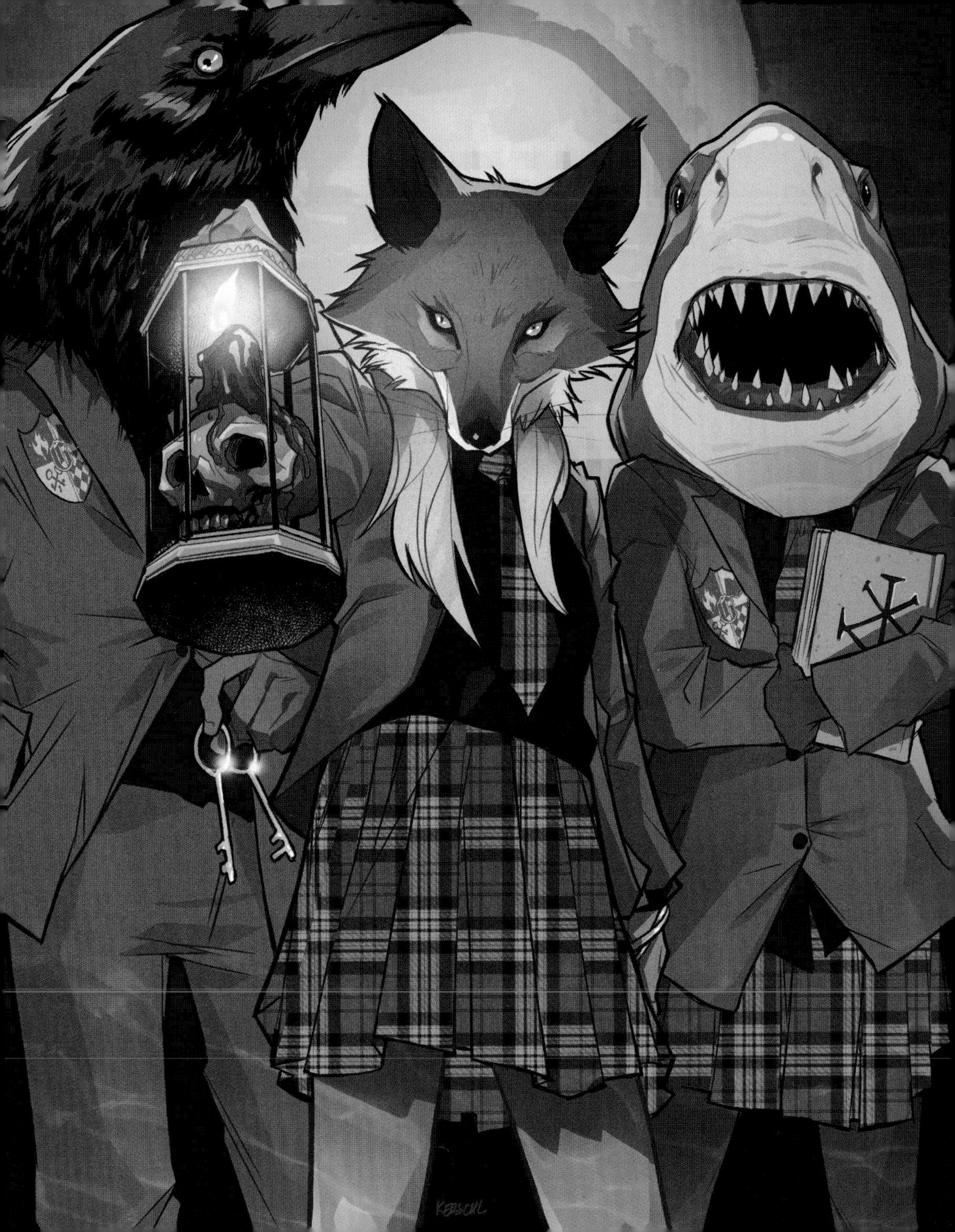
KERSCHL

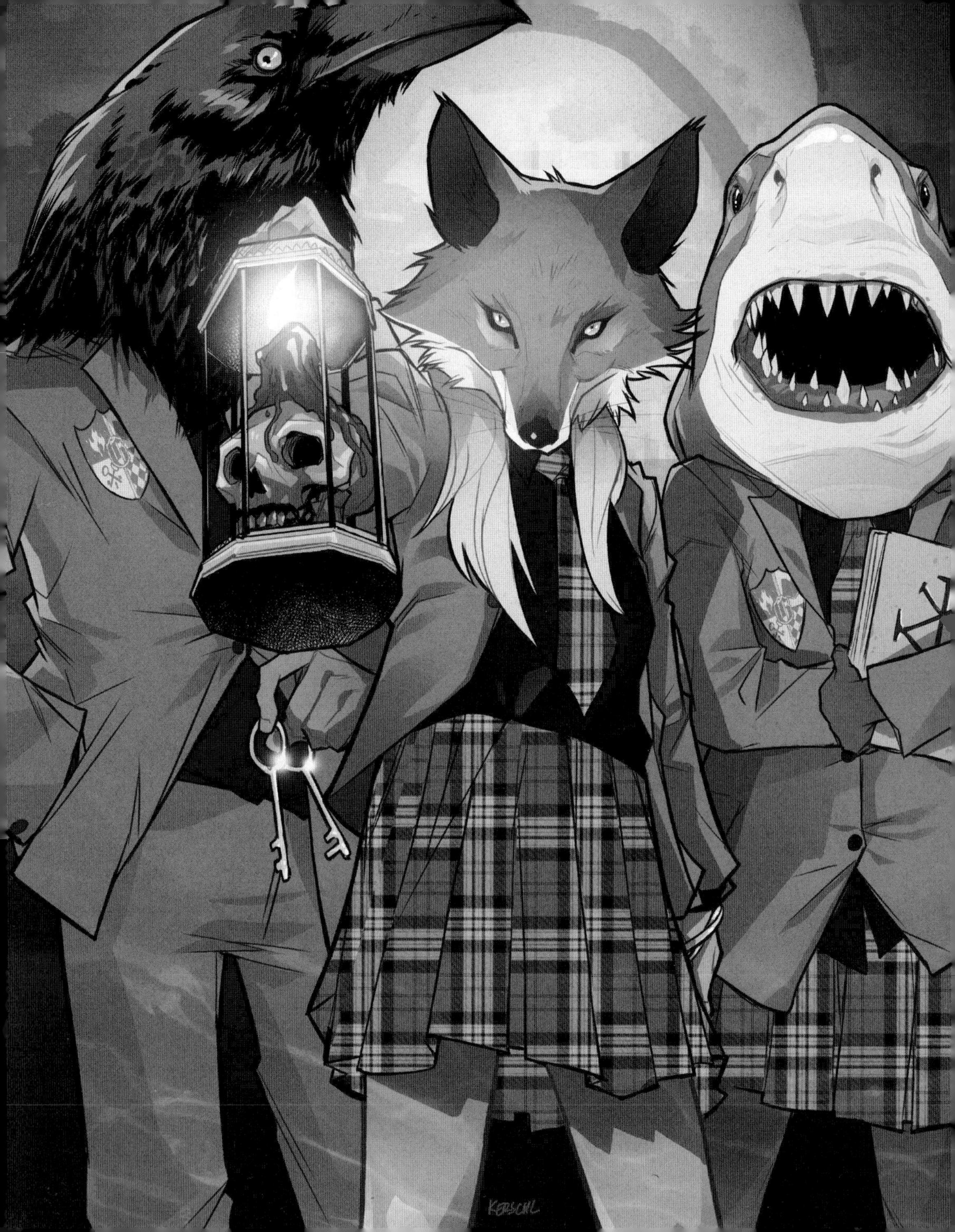
KERSCHL

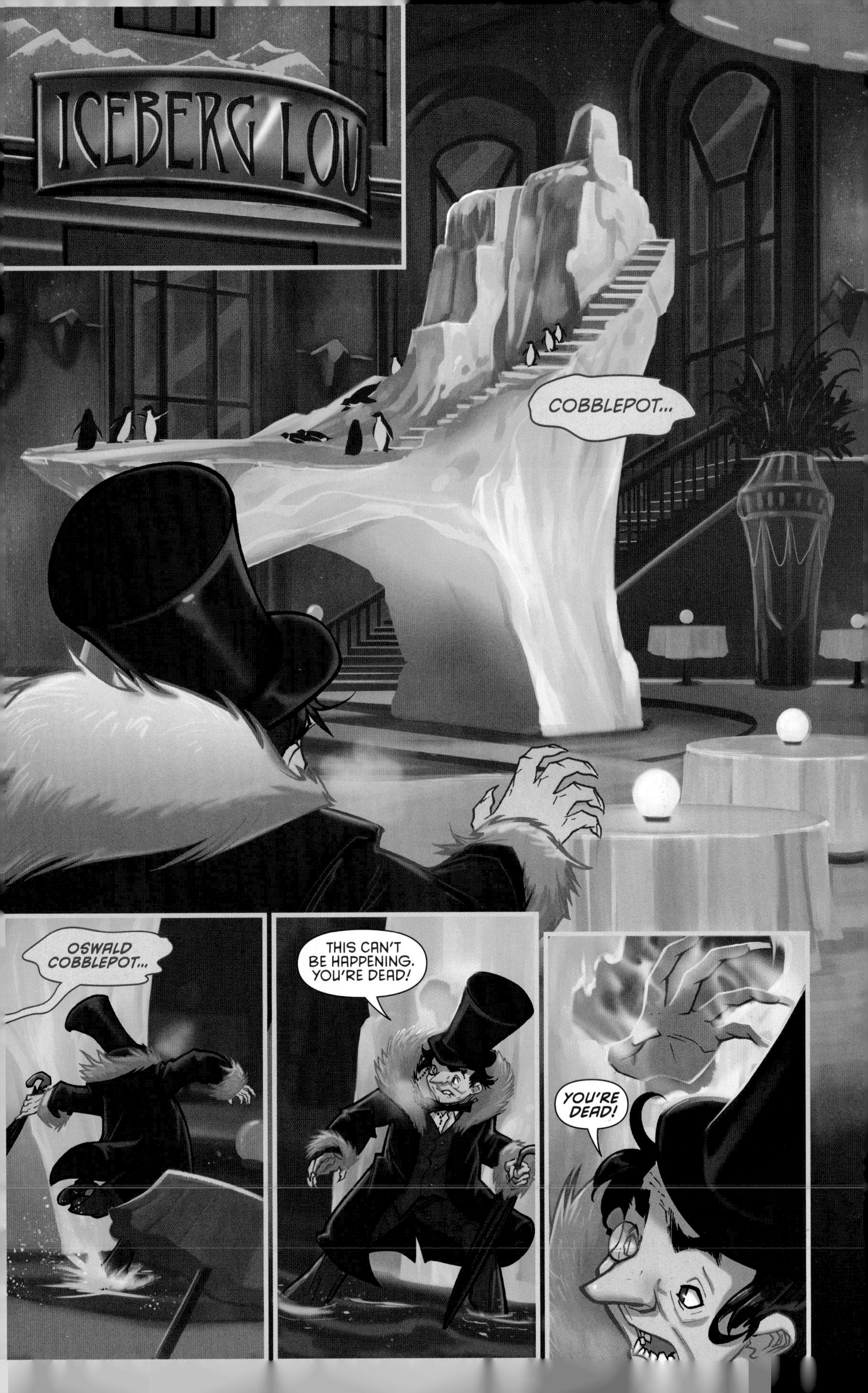
ICEBERG LOU
COBBLEPOT...
OSWALD COBBLEPOT...
THIS CAN'T BE HAPPENING. YOU'RE DEAD!
YOU'RE DEAD!

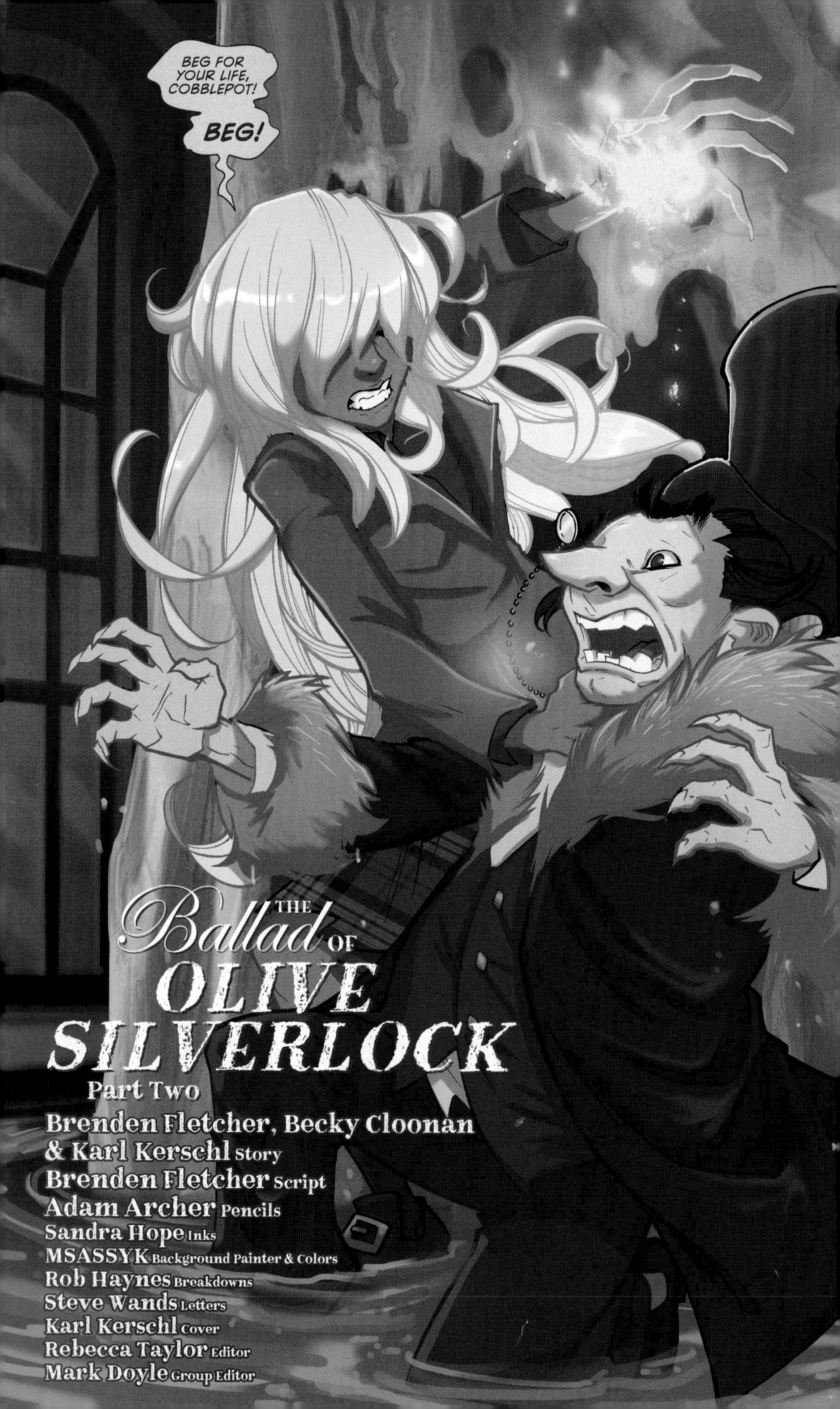
BEG FOR YOUR LIFE, COBBLEPOT!
BEG!
THE Ballad OF OLIVE SILVERLOCK
Part Two
Brenden Fletcher, Becky Cloonan & Karl Kerschl story
Brenden Fletcher script
Adam Archer Pencils
Sandra Hope Inks
MSASSYK Background Painter & Colors
Rob Haynes Breakdowns
Steve Wands Letters
Karl Kerschl cover
Rebecca Taylor Editor
Mark Doyle Group Editor

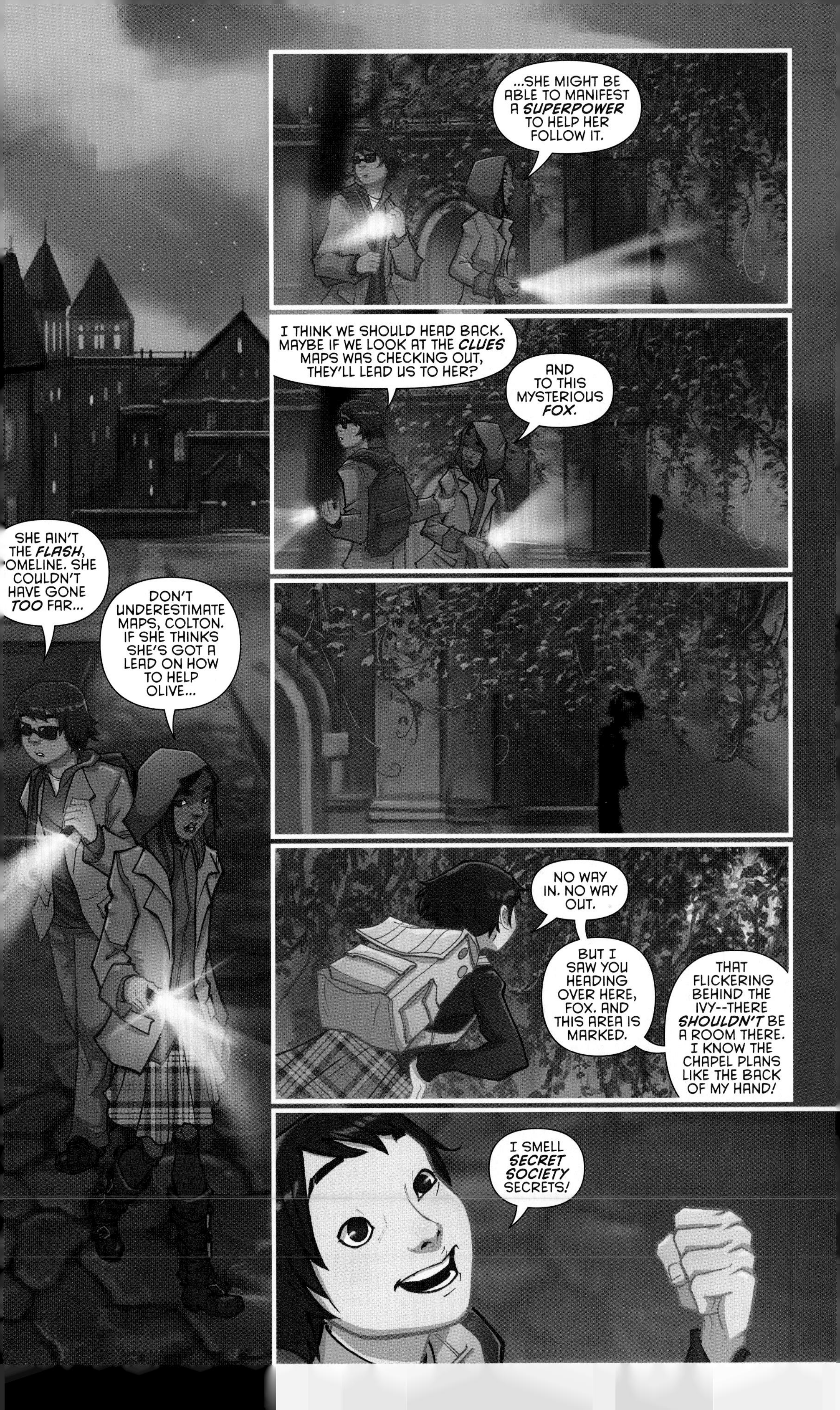

SHE AIN'T THE *FLASH*, OMELINE. SHE COULDN'T HAVE GONE *TOO* FAR...
DON'T UNDERESTIMATE MAPS, COLTON. IF SHE THINKS SHE'S GOT A LEAD ON HOW TO HELP OLIVE...
...SHE MIGHT BE ABLE TO MANIFEST A *SUPERPOWER* TO HELP HER FOLLOW IT.
I THINK WE SHOULD HEAD BACK. MAYBE IF WE LOOK AT THE *CLUES* MAPS WAS CHECKING OUT, THEY'LL LEAD US TO HER?
AND TO THIS MYSTERIOUS *FOX*.
NO WAY IN. NO WAY OUT.
BUT I SAW YOU HEADING OVER HERE, FOX. AND THIS AREA IS MARKED.
THAT FLICKERING BEHIND THE IVY--THERE *SHOULDN'T* BE A ROOM THERE. I KNOW THE CHAPEL PLANS LIKE THE BACK OF MY HAND!
I SMELL *SECRET SOCIETY* SECRETS!

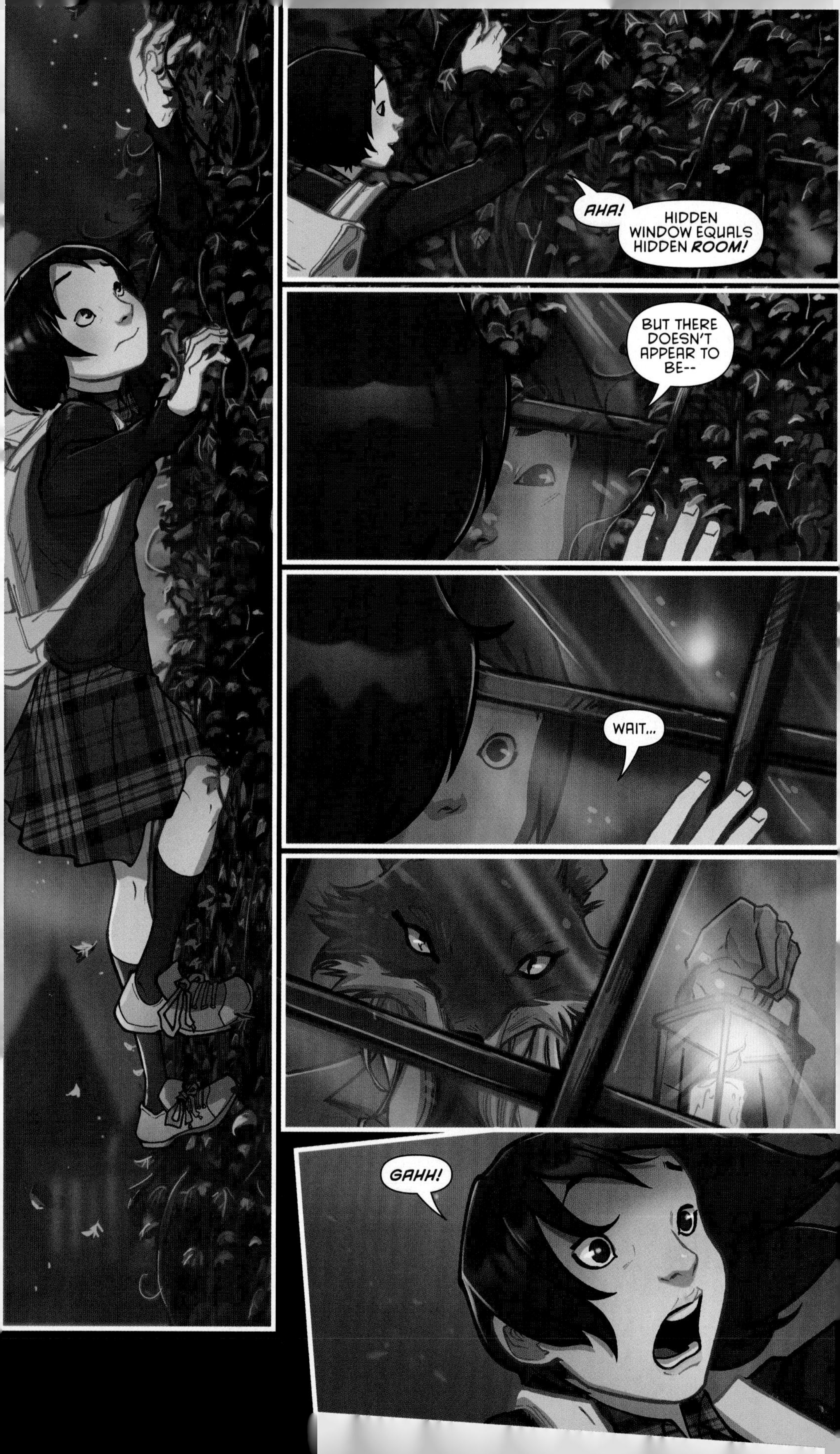
AHA!
HIDDEN WINDOW EQUALS HIDDEN ROOM!
BUT THERE DOESN'T APPEAR TO BE--
WAIT...
GAHH!

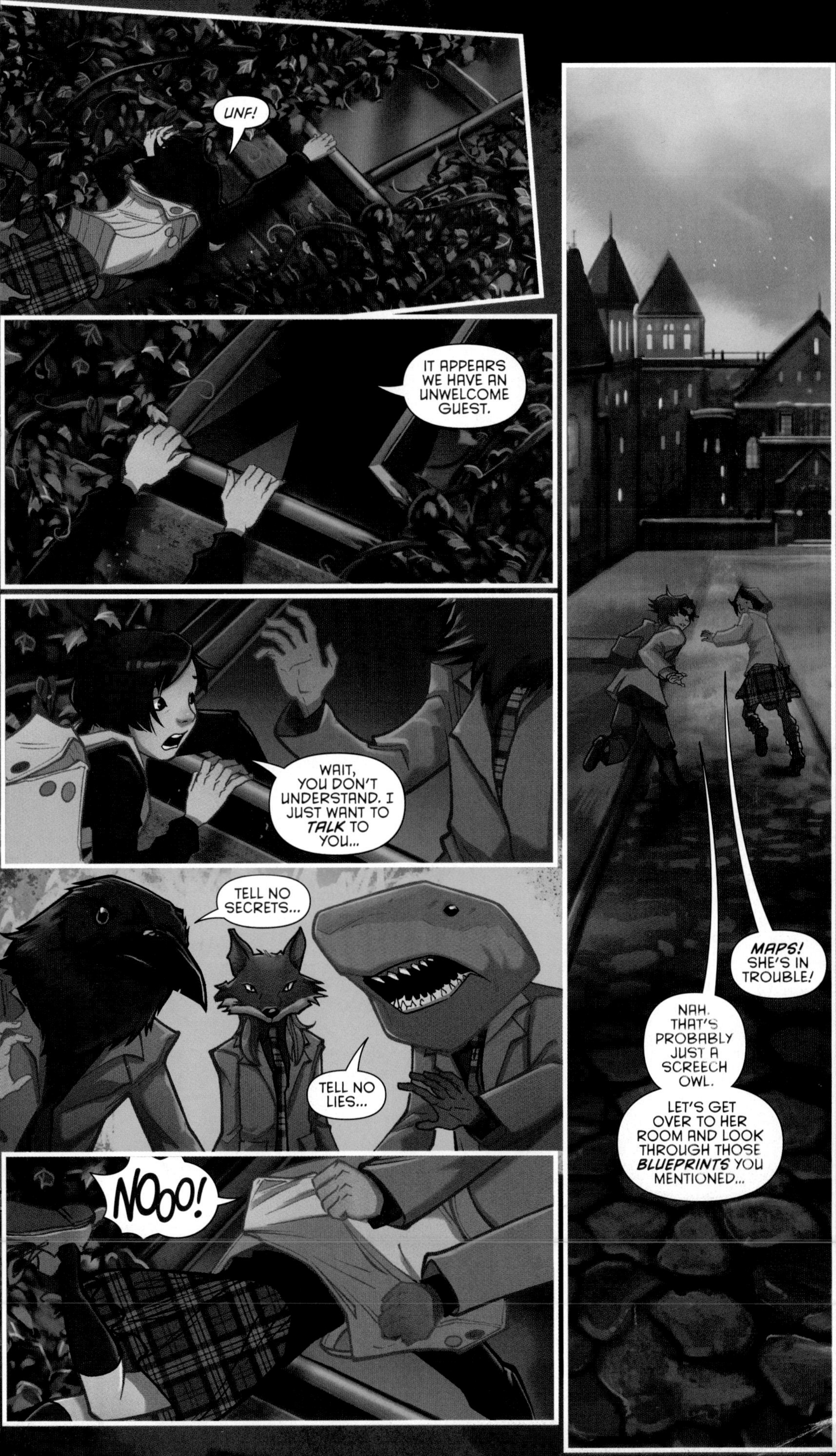
UNF!
IT APPEARS WE HAVE AN UNWELCOME GUEST.
WAIT, YOU DON'T UNDERSTAND. I JUST WANT TO *TALK* TO YOU...
TELL NO SECRETS...
TELL NO LIES...
NOOO!
MAPS! SHE'S IN TROUBLE!
NAH. THAT'S PROBABLY JUST A SCREECH OWL.
LET'S GET OVER TO HER ROOM AND LOOK THROUGH THOSE *BLUEPRINTS* YOU MENTIONED...

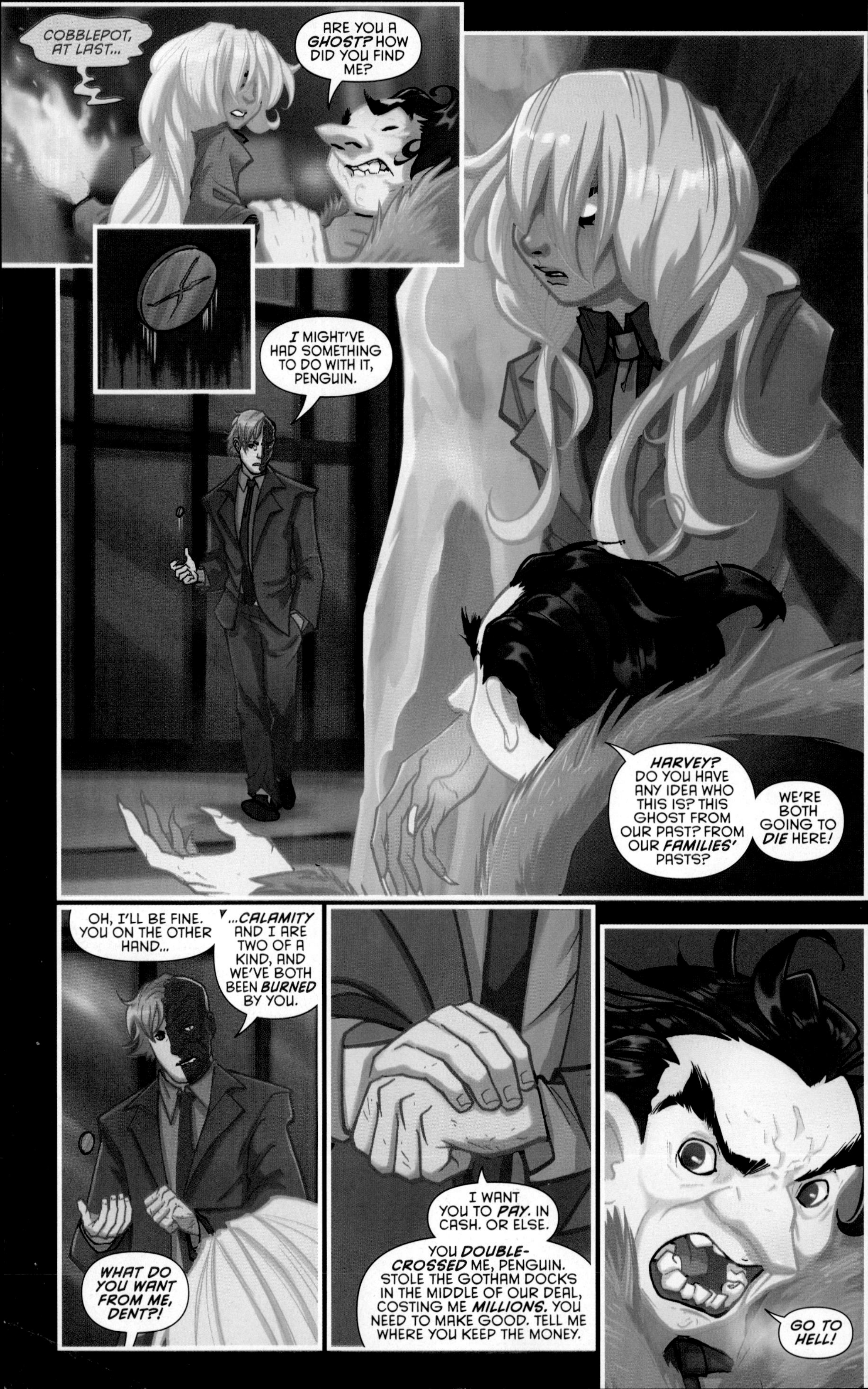
COBBLEPOT, AT LAST...
ARE YOU A GHOST? HOW DID YOU FIND ME?
I MIGHT'VE HAD SOMETHING TO DO WITH IT, PENGUIN.
HARVEY? DO YOU HAVE ANY IDEA WHO THIS IS? THIS GHOST FROM OUR PAST? FROM OUR FAMILIES' PASTS?
WE'RE BOTH GOING TO DIE HERE!
OH, I'LL BE FINE. YOU ON THE OTHER HAND...
...CALAMITY AND I ARE TWO OF A KIND, AND WE'VE BOTH BEEN BURNED BY YOU.
WHAT DO YOU WANT FROM ME, DENT?!
I WANT YOU TO PAY. IN CASH. OR ELSE.
YOU DOUBLE-CROSSED ME, PENGUIN. STOLE THE GOTHAM DOCKS IN THE MIDDLE OF OUR DEAL, COSTING ME MILLIONS. YOU NEED TO MAKE GOOD. TELL ME WHERE YOU KEEP THE MONEY.
GO TO HELL!

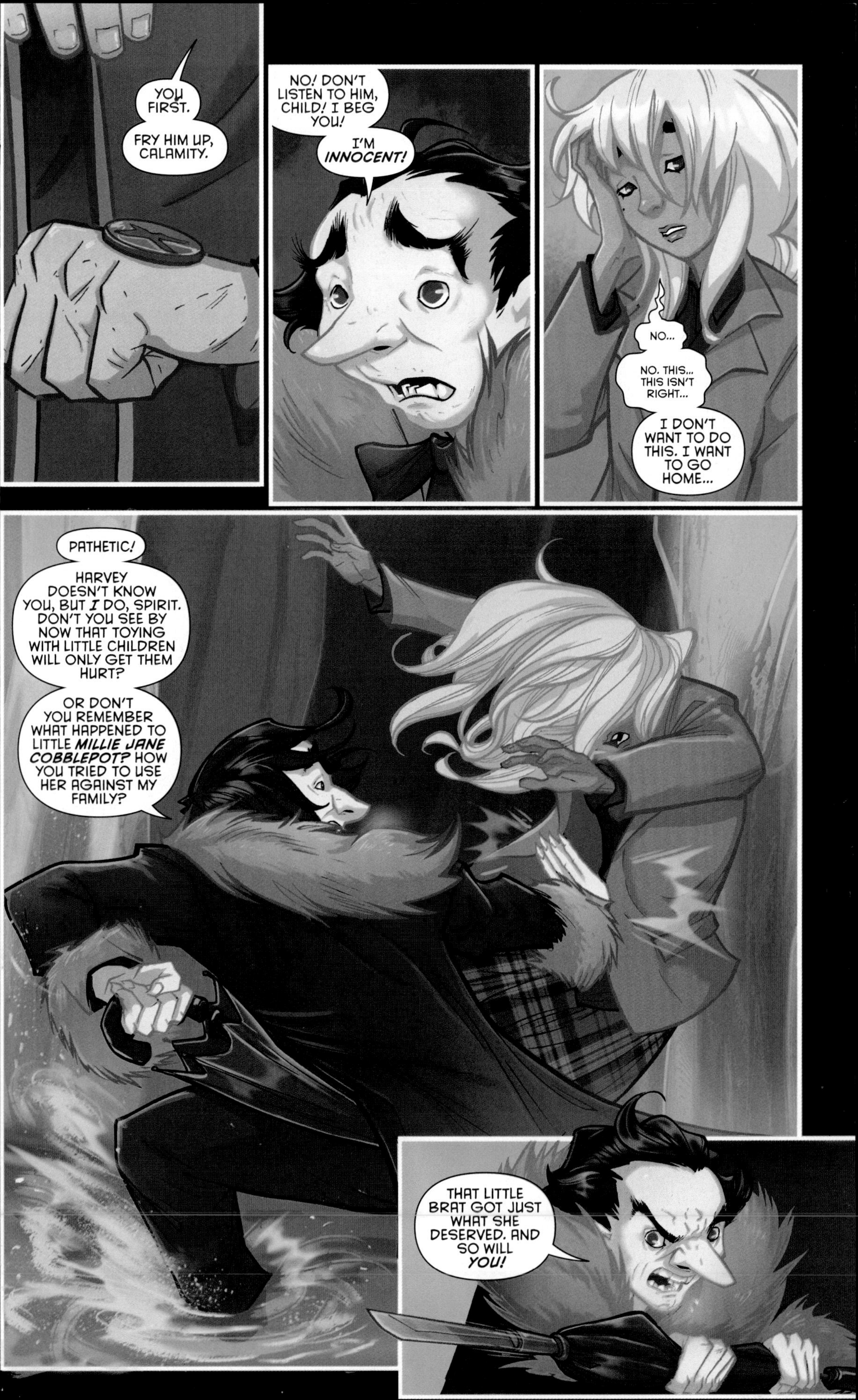
YOU FIRST.
FRY HIM UP, CALAMITY.
NO! DON'T LISTEN TO HIM, CHILD! I BEG YOU!
I'M *INNOCENT!*
NO...
NO. THIS... THIS ISN'T RIGHT...
I DON'T WANT TO DO THIS. I WANT TO GO HOME...
PATHETIC!
HARVEY DOESN'T KNOW YOU, BUT *I* DO, SPIRIT. DON'T YOU SEE BY NOW THAT TOYING WITH LITTLE CHILDREN WILL ONLY GET THEM HURT?
OR DON'T YOU REMEMBER WHAT HAPPENED TO LITTLE *MILLIE JANE COBBLEPOT?* HOW YOU TRIED TO USE HER AGAINST MY FAMILY?
THAT LITTLE BRAT GOT JUST WHAT SHE DESERVED. AND SO WILL *YOU!*

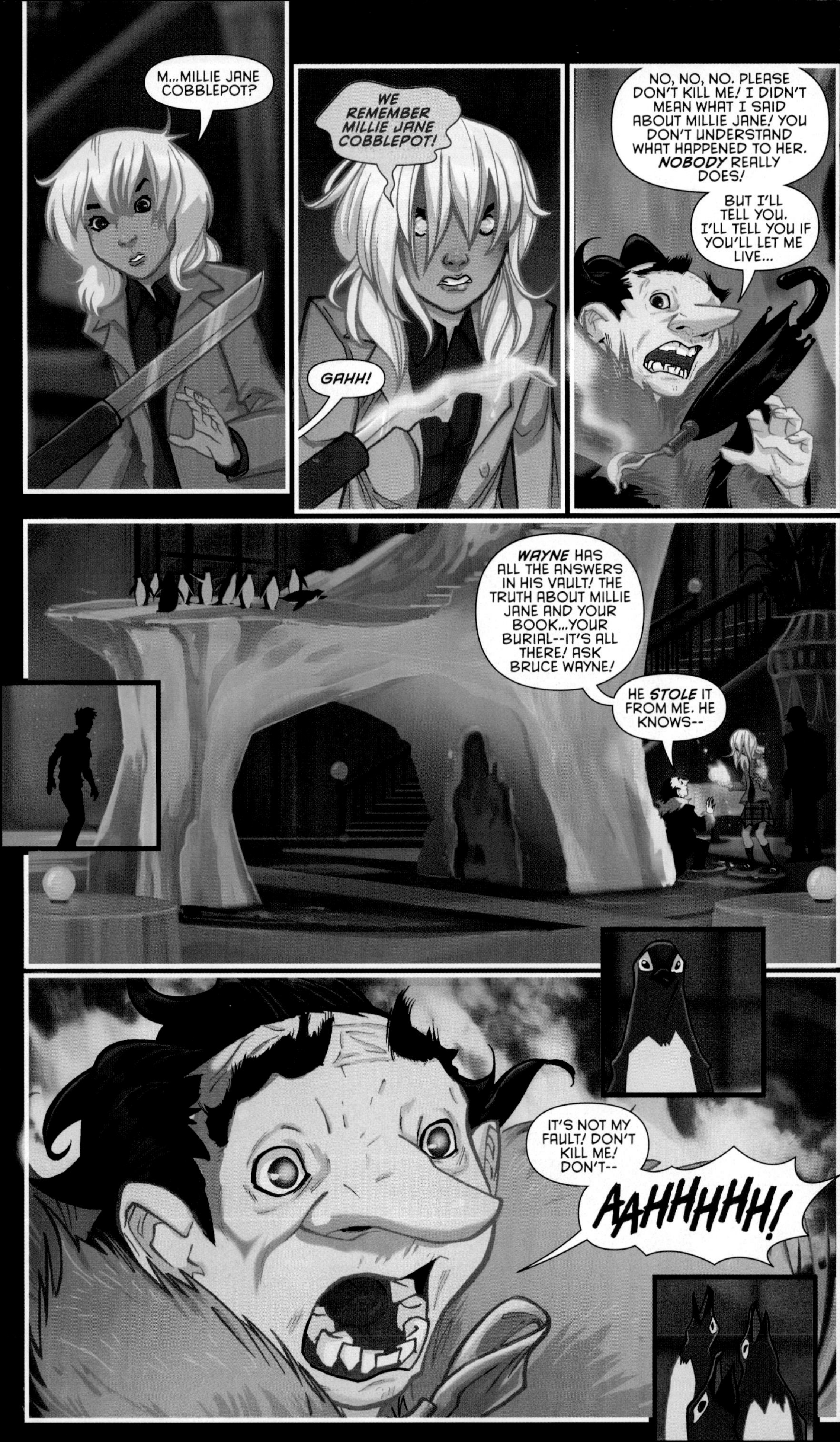

M...MILLIE JANE COBBLEPOT?
WE REMEMBER MILLIE JANE COBBLEPOT!
GAHH!
NO, NO, NO. PLEASE DON'T KILL ME! I DIDN'T MEAN WHAT I SAID ABOUT MILLIE JANE! YOU DON'T UNDERSTAND WHAT HAPPENED TO HER. NOBODY REALLY DOES!
BUT I'LL TELL YOU. I'LL TELL YOU IF YOU'LL LET ME LIVE...
WAYNE HAS ALL THE ANSWERS IN HIS VAULT! THE TRUTH ABOUT MILLIE JANE AND YOUR BOOK...YOUR BURIAL--IT'S ALL THERE! ASK BRUCE WAYNE!
HE STOLE IT FROM ME. HE KNOWS--
IT'S NOT MY FAULT! DON'T KILL ME! DON'T--
AAHHHHH!

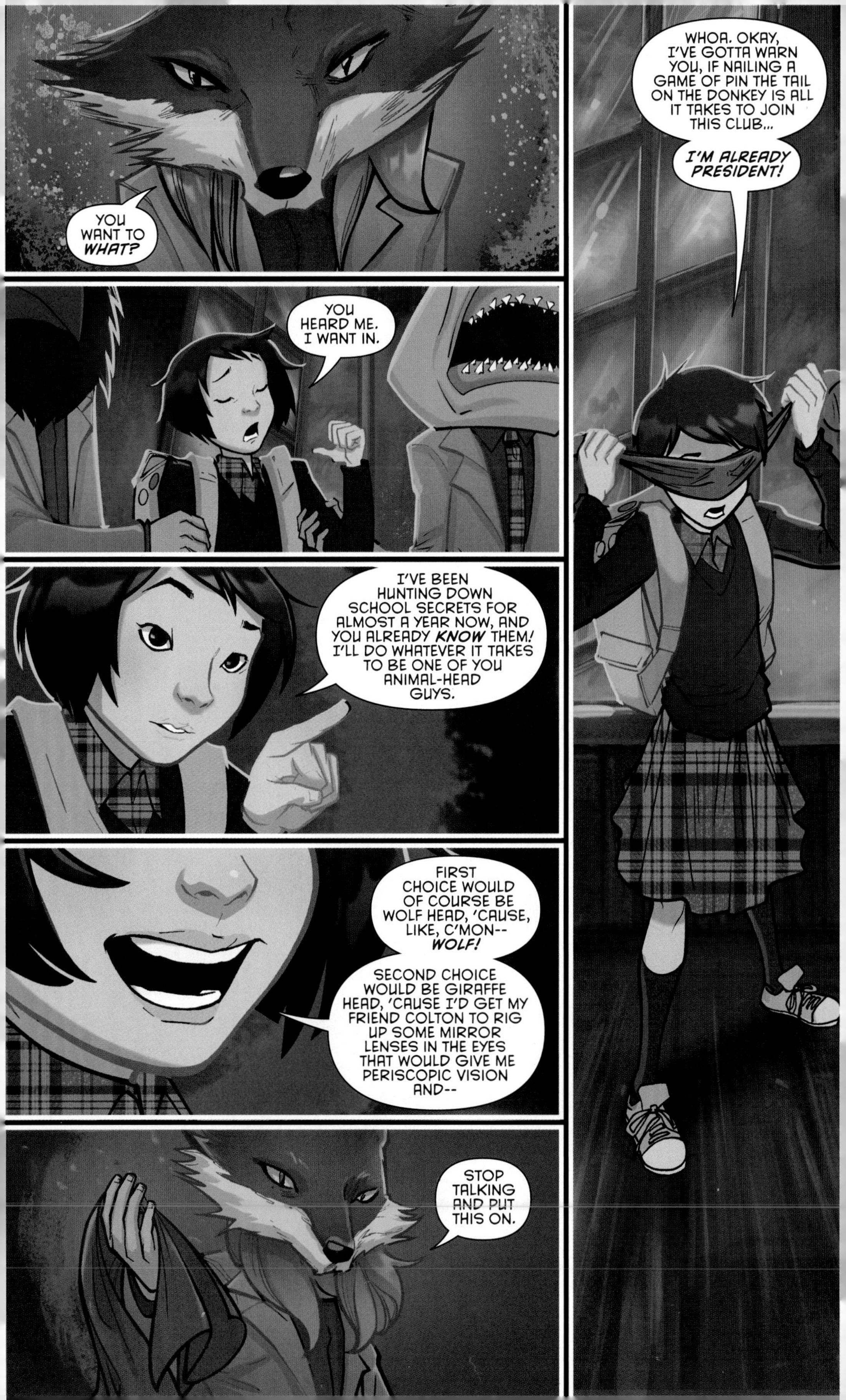
YOU WANT TO *WHAT?*
YOU HEARD ME. I WANT IN.
I'VE BEEN HUNTING DOWN SCHOOL SECRETS FOR ALMOST A YEAR NOW, AND YOU ALREADY *KNOW* THEM! I'LL DO WHATEVER IT TAKES TO BE ONE OF YOU ANIMAL-HEAD GUYS.
FIRST CHOICE WOULD OF COURSE BE WOLF HEAD, 'CAUSE, LIKE, C'MON-- *WOLF!*
SECOND CHOICE WOULD BE GIRAFFE HEAD, 'CAUSE I'D GET MY FRIEND COLTON TO RIG UP SOME MIRROR LENSES IN THE EYES THAT WOULD GIVE ME PERISCOPIC VISION AND--
STOP TALKING AND PUT THIS ON.
WHOA. OKAY, I'VE GOTTA WARN YOU, IF NAILING A GAME OF PIN THE TAIL ON THE DONKEY IS ALL IT TAKES TO JOIN THIS CLUB...
I'M ALREADY PRESIDENT!

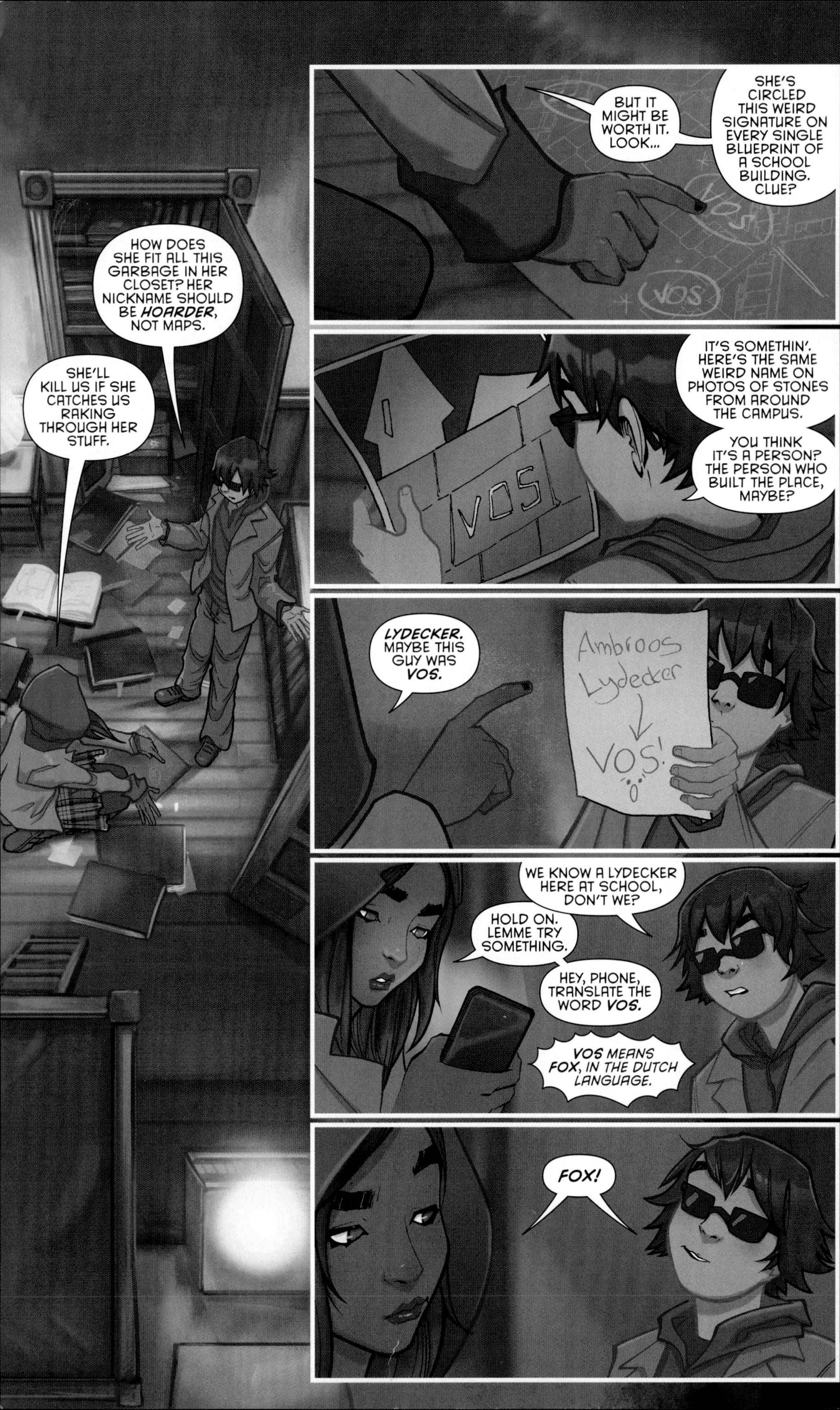
HOW DOES SHE FIT ALL THIS GARBAGE IN HER CLOSET? HER NICKNAME SHOULD BE HOARDER, NOT MAPS.
SHE'LL KILL US IF SHE CATCHES US RAKING THROUGH HER STUFF.
BUT IT MIGHT BE WORTH IT. LOOK...
SHE'S CIRCLED THIS WEIRD SIGNATURE ON EVERY SINGLE BLUEPRINT OF A SCHOOL BUILDING. CLUE?
VOS
VOS
VOS
IT'S SOMETHIN'. HERE'S THE SAME WEIRD NAME ON PHOTOS OF STONES FROM AROUND THE CAMPUS.
YOU THINK IT'S A PERSON? THE PERSON WHO BUILT THE PLACE, MAYBE?
VOS
LYDECKER. MAYBE THIS GUY WAS VOS.
Ambroos Lydecker
VOS!
WE KNOW A LYDECKER HERE AT SCHOOL, DON'T WE?
HOLD ON. LEMME TRY SOMETHING.
HEY, PHONE, TRANSLATE THE WORD VOS.
VOS MEANS FOX, IN THE DUTCH LANGUAGE.
FOX!

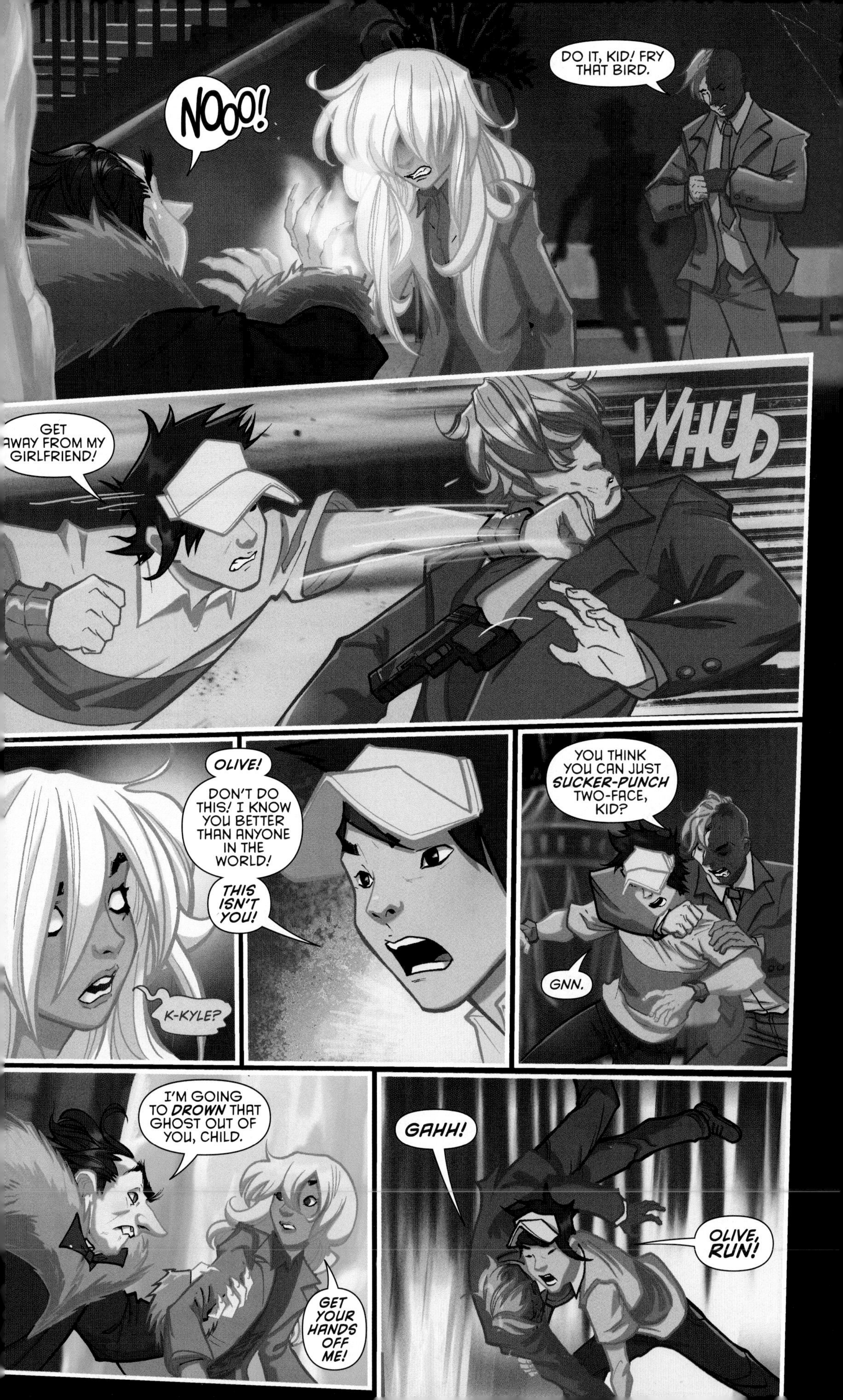
NOOO!
DO IT, KID! FRY THAT BIRD.
GET AWAY FROM MY GIRLFRIEND!
WHUD
OLIVE!
DON'T DO THIS! I KNOW YOU BETTER THAN ANYONE IN THE WORLD!
THIS ISN'T YOU!
K-KYLE?
YOU THINK YOU CAN JUST SUCKER-PUNCH TWO-FACE, KID?
GNN.
I'M GOING TO DROWN THAT GHOST OUT OF YOU, CHILD.
GET YOUR HANDS OFF ME!
GAHH!
OLIVE, RUN!

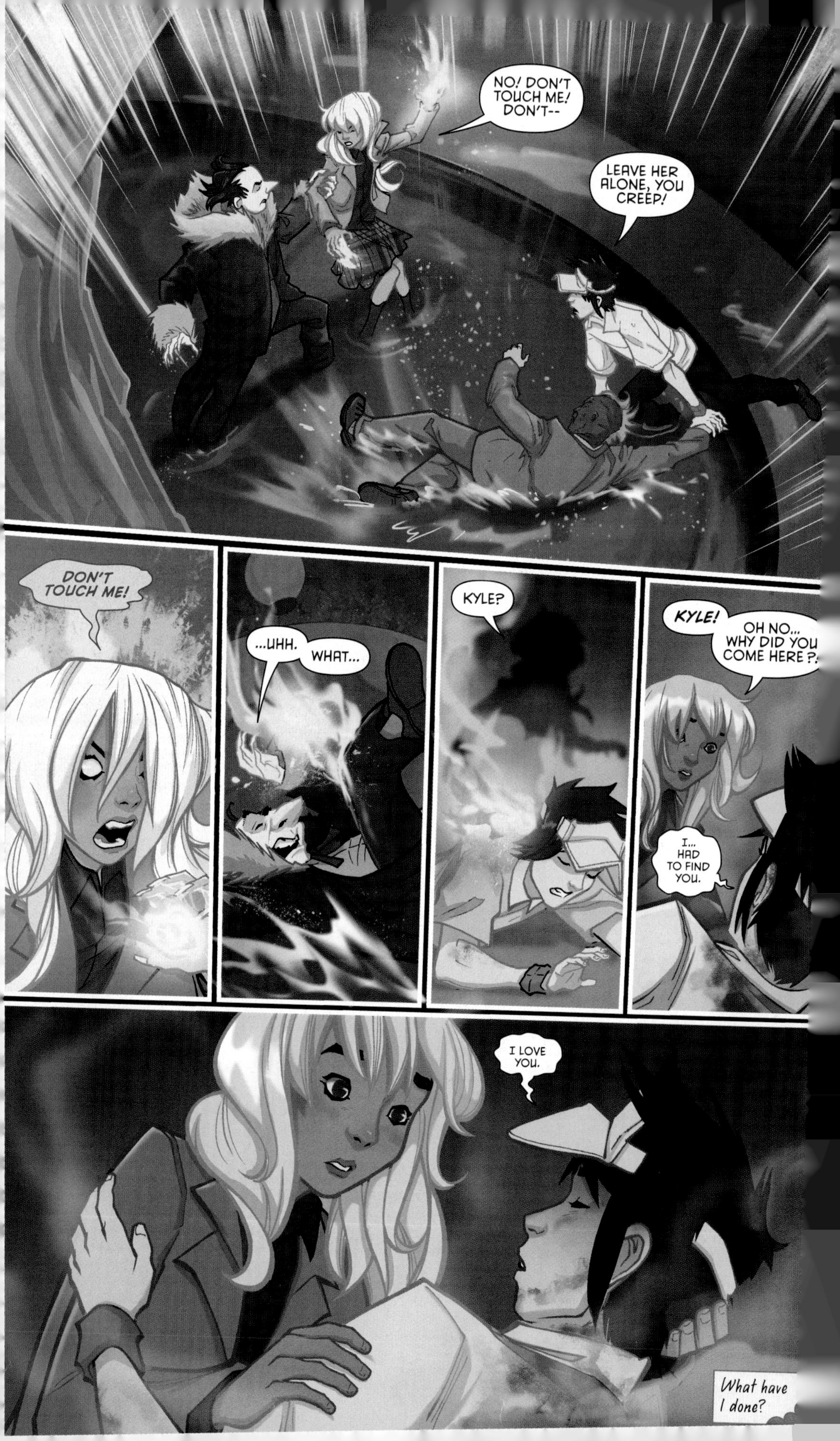
NO! DON'T TOUCH ME! DON'T--
LEAVE HER ALONE, YOU CREEP!
DON'T TOUCH ME!
...UHH.
WHAT...
KYLE?
KYLE!
OH NO... WHY DID YOU COME HERE?!
I... HAD TO FIND YOU.
I LOVE YOU.
What have I done?

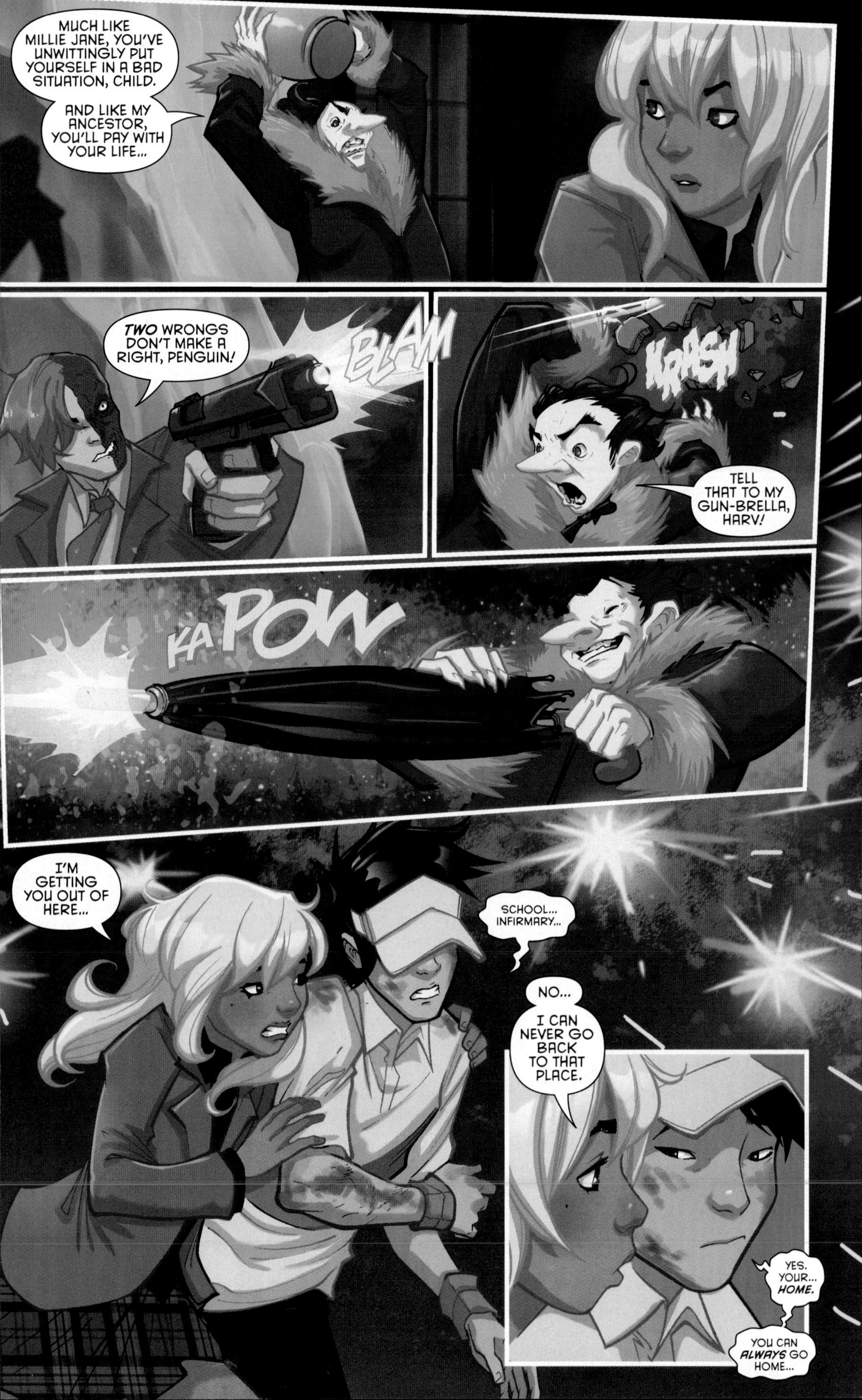
MUCH LIKE MILLIE JANE, YOU'VE UNWITTINGLY PUT YOURSELF IN A BAD SITUATION, CHILD.
AND LIKE MY ANCESTOR, YOU'LL PAY WITH YOUR LIFE...
TWO WRONGS DON'T MAKE A RIGHT, PENGUIN!
BLAM
KRASH
TELL THAT TO MY GUN-BRELLA, HARV!
KA POW
I'M GETTING YOU OUT OF HERE...
SCHOOL... INFIRMARY...
NO...
I CAN NEVER GO BACK TO THAT PLACE.
YES. YOUR... ***HOME.***
YOU CAN *ALWAYS* GO HOME...

ZIEZO, HERE WE ARE...

YES! RIGHT AGAIN, MAPS! I COULD TELL BY THE NUMBER OF STAIRS AND THE PATTERN OF THE BUILDING THAT WE WERE HEADING FOR THE TOP OF THE CHAPEL TOWER.

SO, NO TAIL ON THE DONKEY, I GUESS?

IF YOU WANT TO BE ONE OF US, YOU NEED TO PASS OUR *INITIATION.*

SEE THAT *FLAG* IN THE GARGOYLE'S MOUTH?

YOU WANT ME TO WALK OUT AND GRAB IT? NO PROBS, AMANDA.

I CAN DO THIS WITH MY EYES CLOSED.

WHA--? HOW DID YOU--?

DUH! I'M PRESIDENT OF THE DETECTIVE CLUB, REMEMBER? *DETECTIVE?*

YOUR ANCESTOR IS *AMBROOS LYDECKER,* THE GUY WHO DESIGNED THE ACADEMY BUILDINGS AND THE ORIGINAL ARKHAM ASYLUM AND, LIKE, *HALF* OF GOTHAM. HE WENT BY THE NAME *VOS,* OR "FOX" IN ENGLISH.

WHAT *I* CAN'T UNDERSTA IS WHY-

OH...L OKAY, THIS W JUST TRAF

DUMB MOVE, MAPS. SHOULDA SEEN THIS COMING

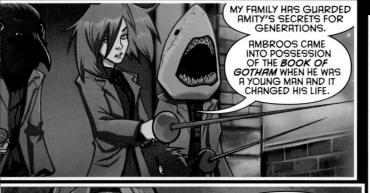

MY FAMILY HAS GUARDED AMITY'S SECRETS FOR GENERATIONS.

AMBROOS CAME INTO POSSESSION OF THE *BOOK OF GOTHAM* WHEN HE WAS A YOUNG MAN AND IT CHANGED HIS LIFE.

HE BUILT THIS ACADEMY, THIS *CITY*, TO HONOR AND PROTECT HER. TO ENSURE SHE LIVED ON NO MATTER THE COST.

AS ALL LYDECKERS HAVE DONE SINCE.

AND YOU, MAPS MIZOGUCHI, ARE A *THREAT* TO AMITY THAT NEEDS TO BE DEALT WITH.

BUT...BUT YOU'RE OLIVE'S FRIEND, TOO. HOW CAN YOU JUST--

AND IT'S OUR DUTY TO ENSURE THAT SHE HAS THE *POWER* SHE NEEDS TO SET GOTHAM BACK ON THE RIGHT TRACK.

THERE *IS NO* OLIVE SILVERLOCK ANYMORE, MAPS. SHE'S A VESSEL FOR AMITY ARKHAM.

AFTER ALL THESE YEARS, AMITY HAS *RETURNED* TO US.

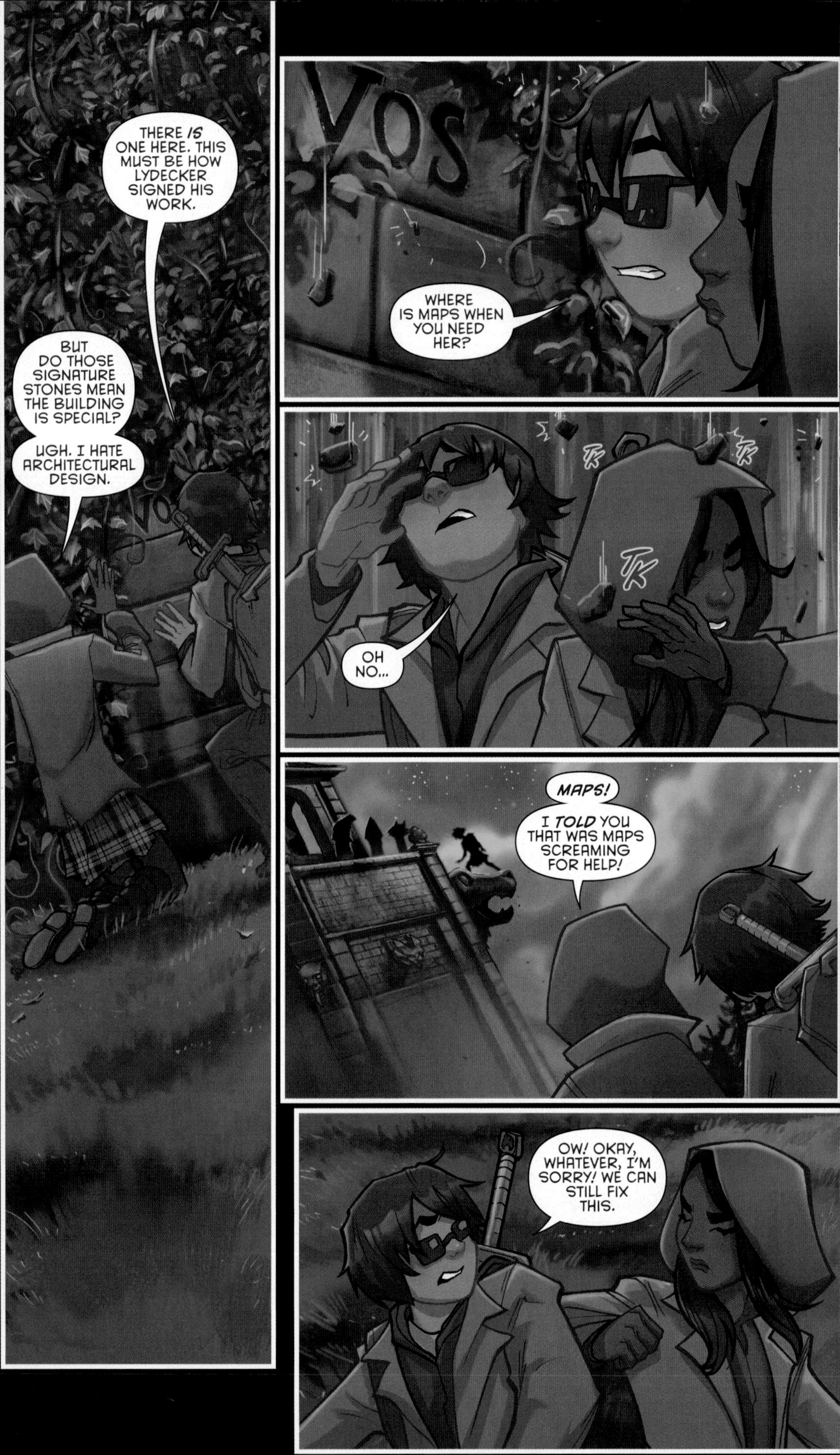
THERE *IS* ONE HERE. THIS MUST BE HOW LYDECKER SIGNED HIS WORK.
BUT DO THOSE SIGNATURE STONES MEAN THE BUILDING IS SPECIAL?
UGH. I HATE ARCHITECTURAL DESIGN.
VOS
WHERE IS MAPS WHEN YOU NEED HER?
TK
TK
TK
OH NO...
MAPS!
I *TOLD* YOU THAT WAS MAPS SCREAMING FOR HELP!
OW! OKAY, WHATEVER, I'M SORRY! WE CAN STILL FIX THIS.

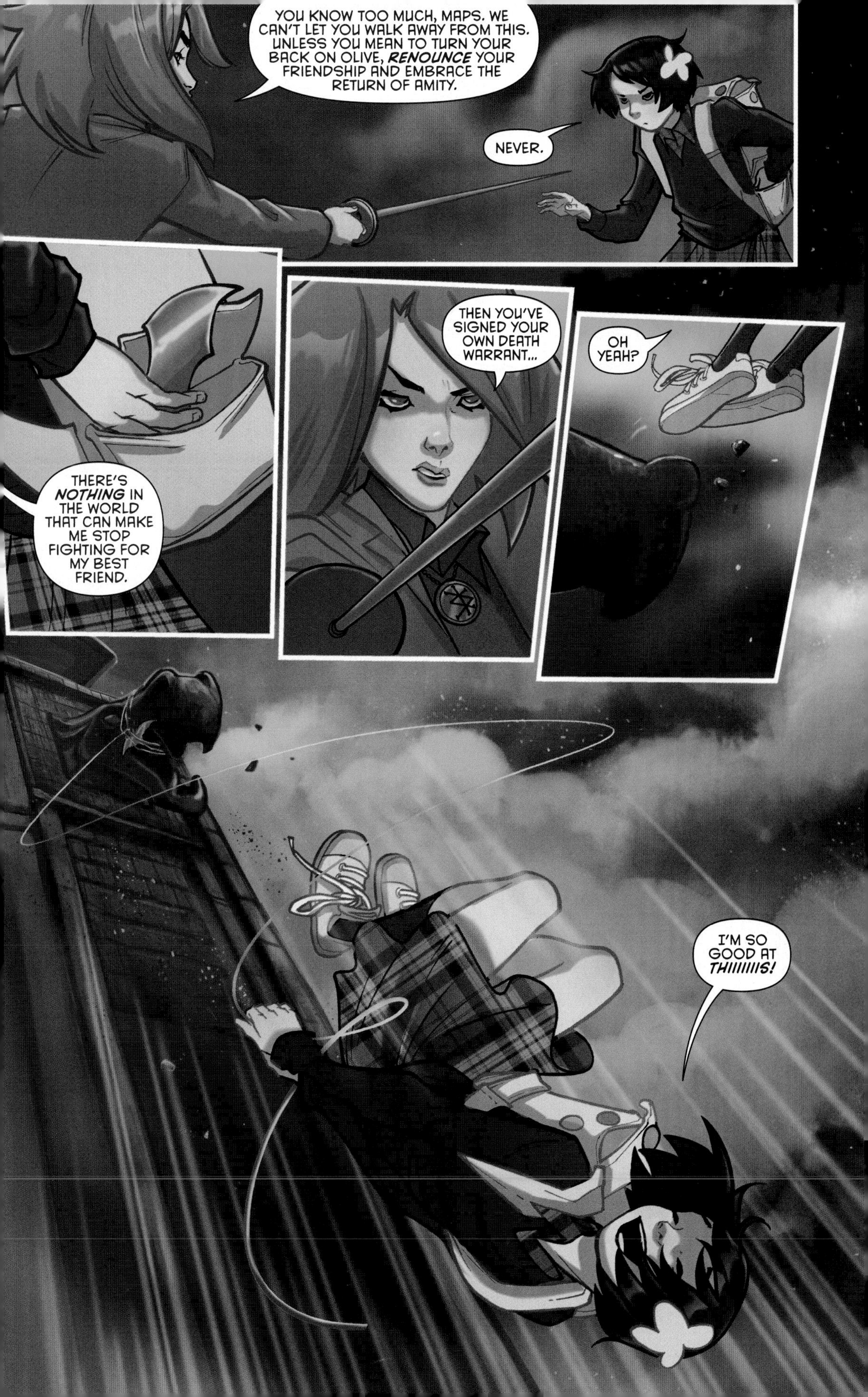
YOU KNOW TOO MUCH, MAPS. WE CAN'T LET YOU WALK AWAY FROM THIS. UNLESS YOU MEAN TO TURN YOUR BACK ON OLIVE, ***RENOUNCE*** YOUR FRIENDSHIP AND EMBRACE THE RETURN OF AMITY.
NEVER.
THERE'S ***NOTHING*** IN THE WORLD THAT CAN MAKE ME STOP FIGHTING FOR MY BEST FRIEND.
THEN YOU'VE SIGNED YOUR OWN DEATH WARRANT...
OH YEAH?
I'M SO GOOD AT ***THIIIIIIS!***

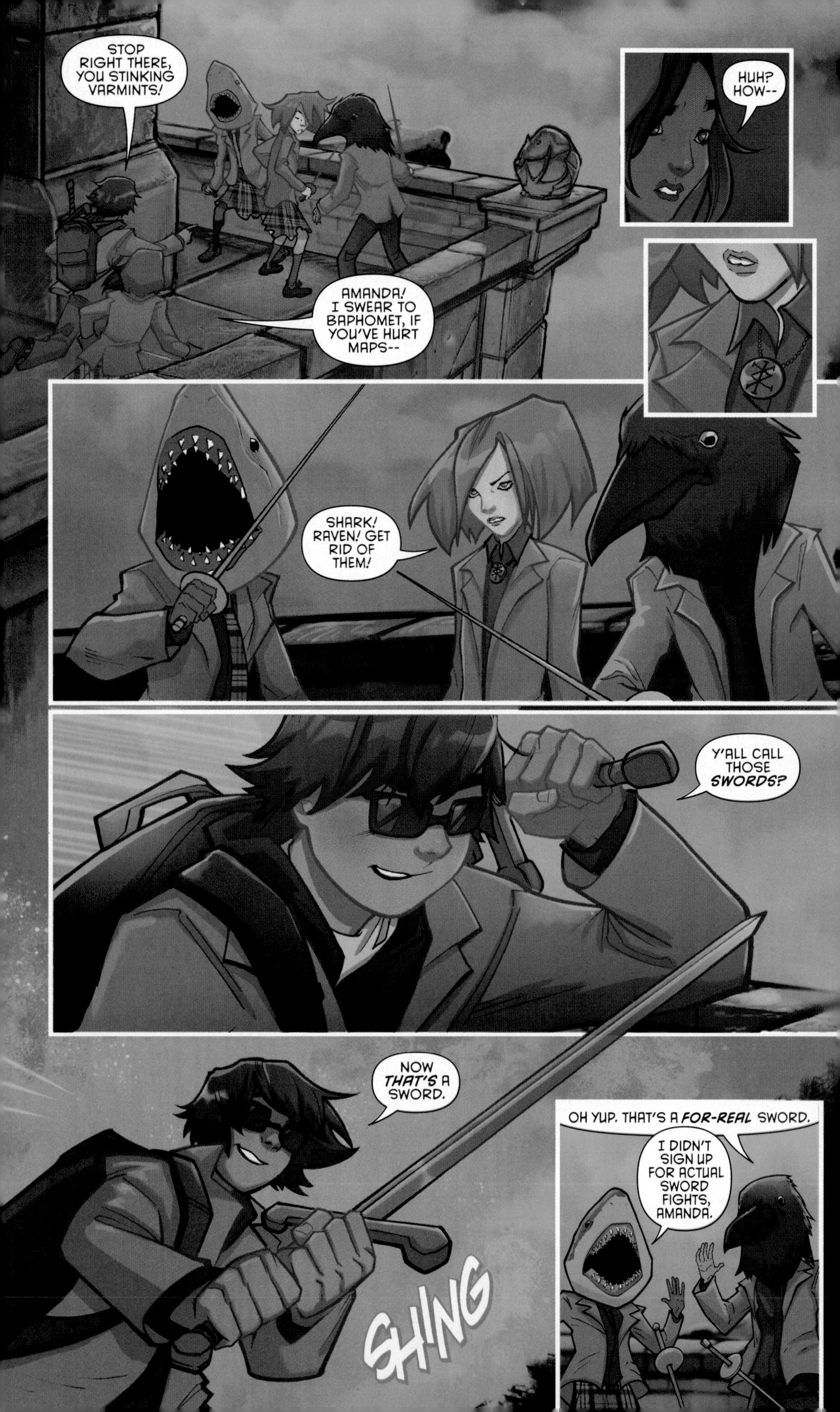
STOP RIGHT THERE, YOU STINKING VARMINTS!
AMANDA! I SWEAR TO BAPHOMET, IF YOU'VE HURT MAPS--
HUH? HOW--
SHARK! RAVEN! GET RID OF THEM!
Y'ALL CALL THOSE SWORDS?
NOW THAT'S A SWORD.
SHING
OH YUP. THAT'S A FOR-REAL SWORD.
I DIDN'T SIGN UP FOR ACTUAL SWORD FIGHTS, AMANDA.

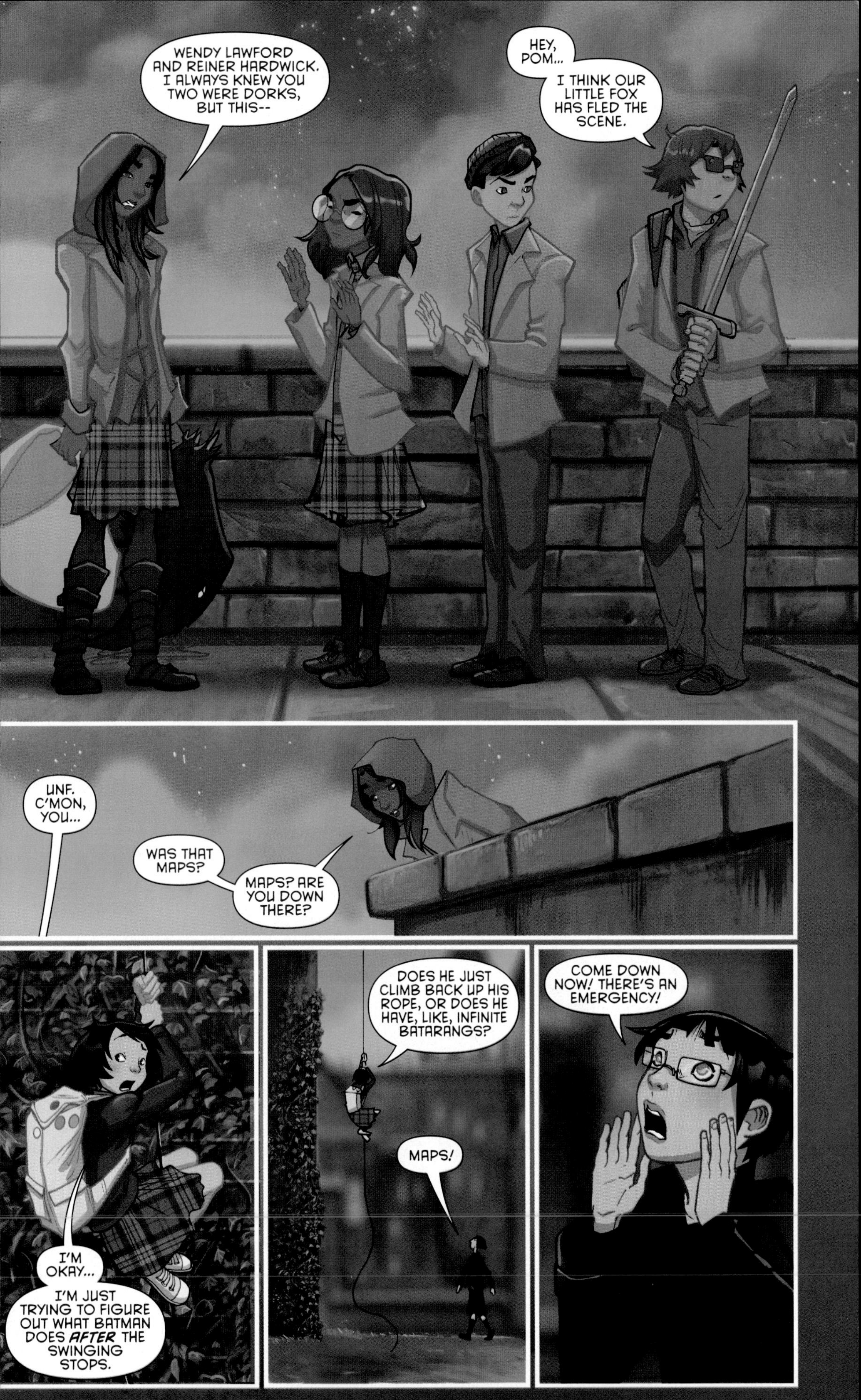
WENDY LAWFORD AND REINER HARDWICK. I ALWAYS KNEW YOU TWO WERE DORKS, BUT THIS--
HEY, POM...
I THINK OUR LITTLE FOX HAS FLED THE SCENE.
UNF. C'MON, YOU...
WAS THAT MAPS?
MAPS? ARE YOU DOWN THERE?
I'M OKAY...
I'M JUST TRYING TO FIGURE OUT WHAT BATMAN DOES *AFTER* THE SWINGING STOPS.
DOES HE JUST CLIMB BACK UP HIS ROPE, OR DOES HE HAVE, LIKE, INFINITE BATARANGS?
MAPS!
COME DOWN NOW! THERE'S AN EMERGENCY!

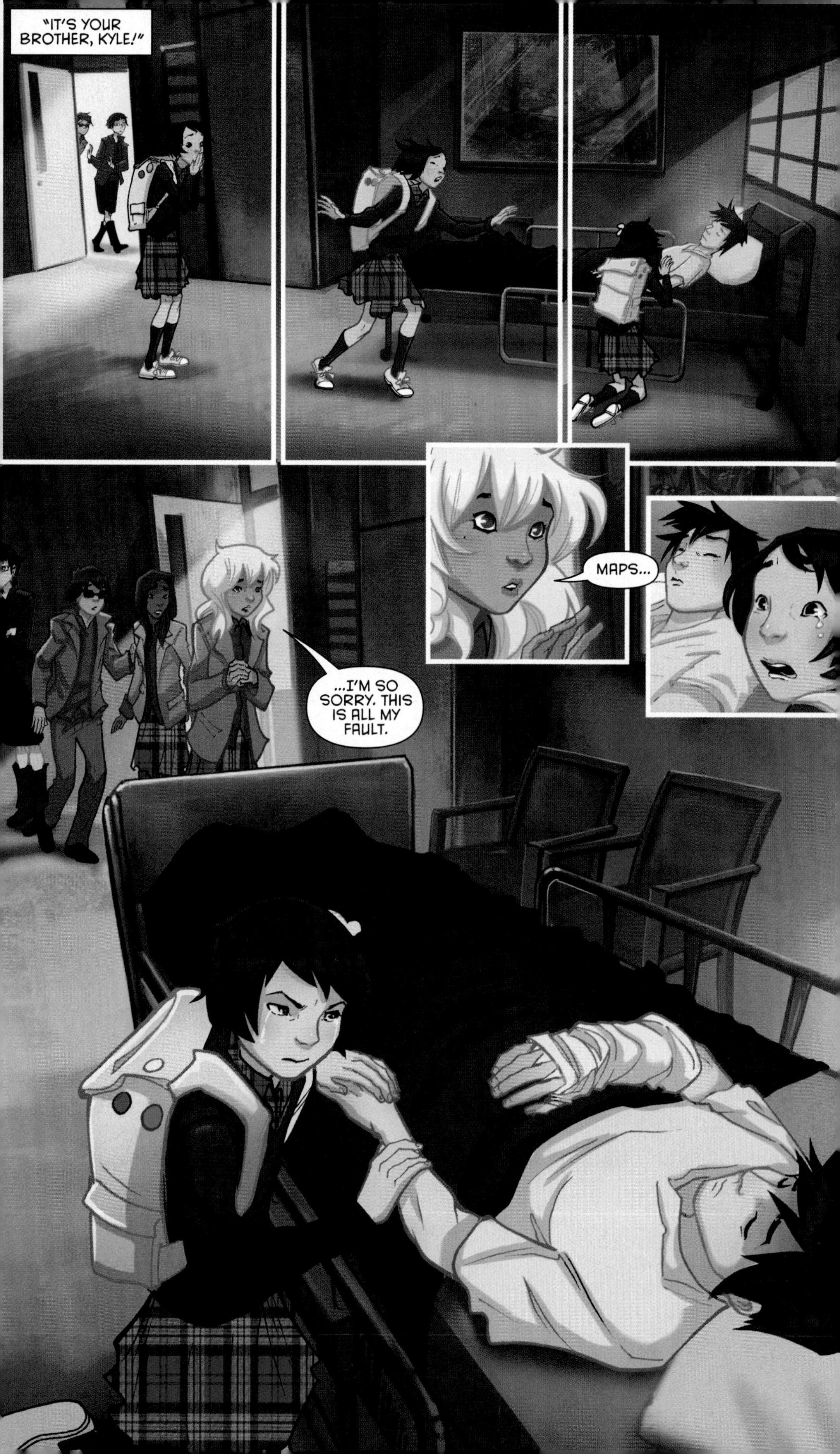
"IT'S YOUR BROTHER, KYLE!"
MAPS...
...I'M SO SORRY. THIS IS ALL MY FAULT.

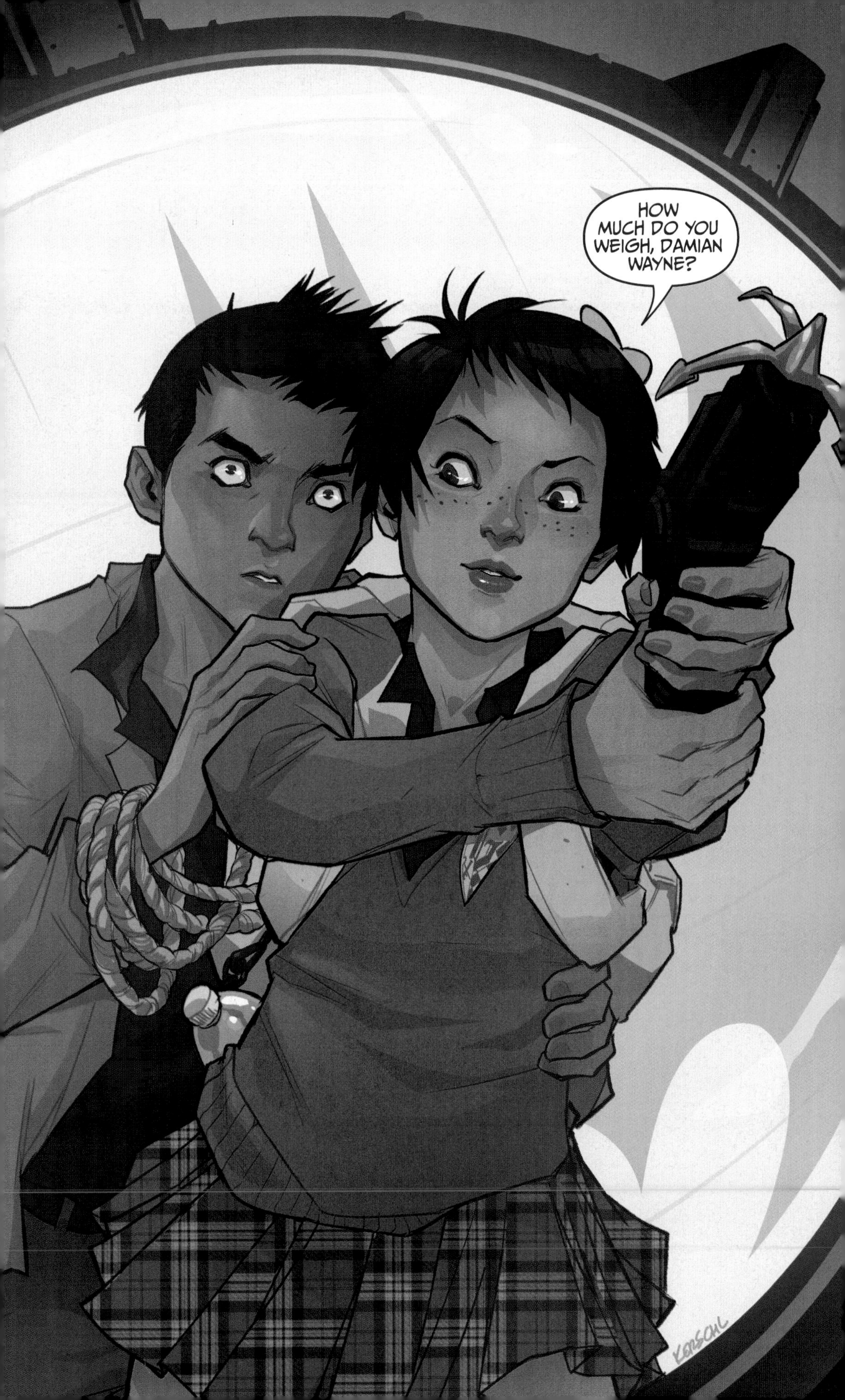
HOW MUCH DO YOU WEIGH, DAMIAN WAYNE?

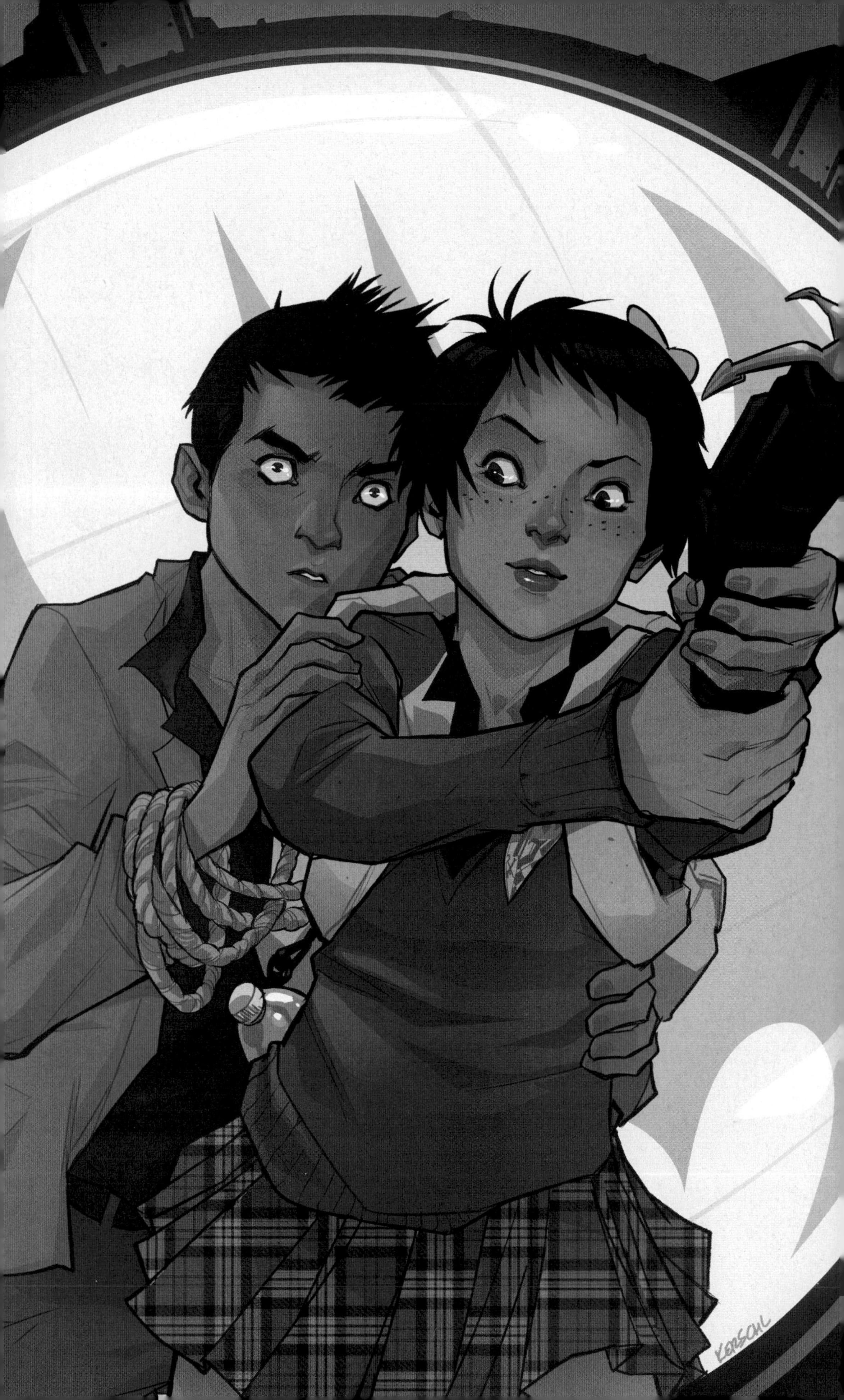

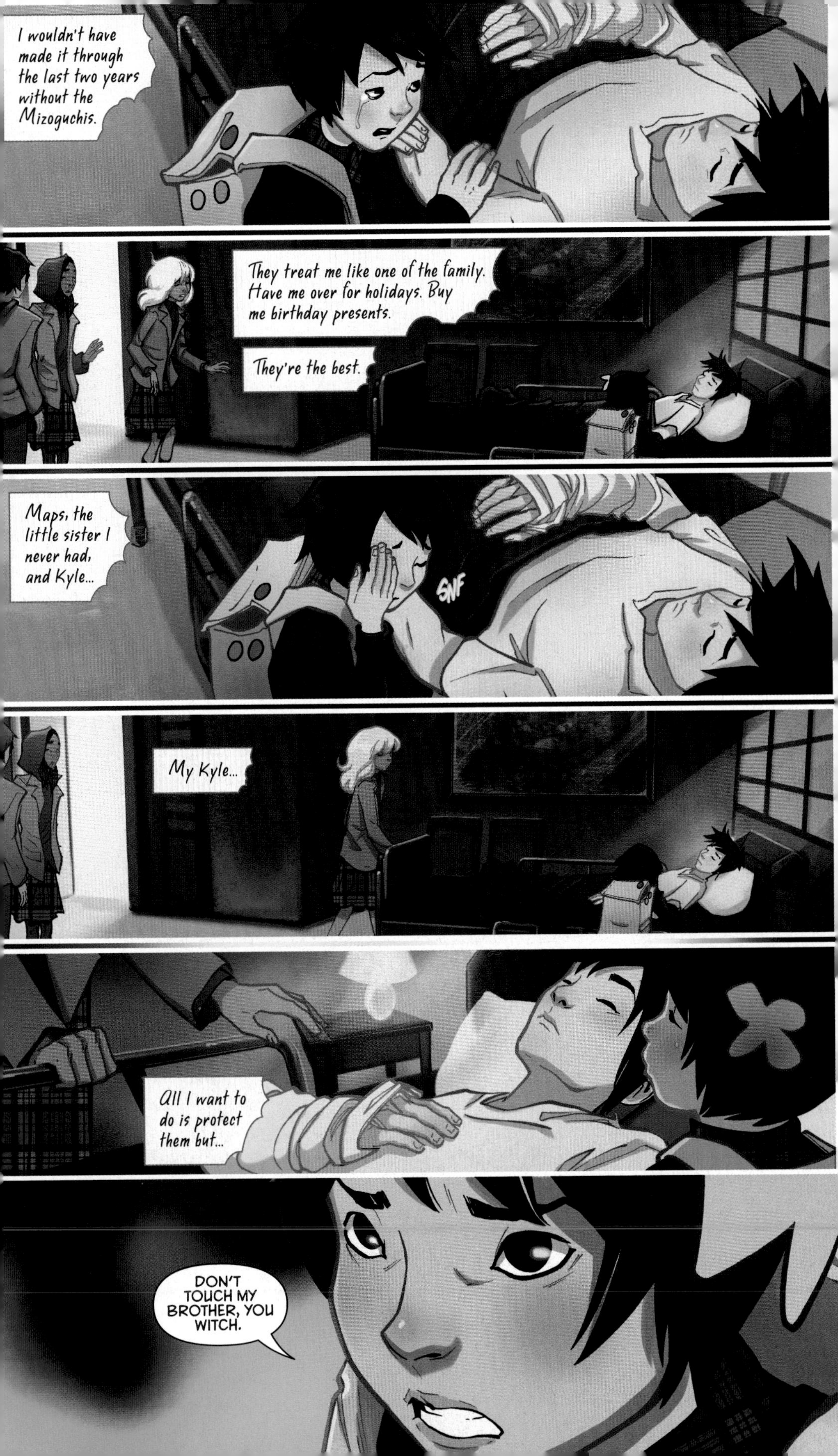

I wouldn't have made it through the last two years without the Mizoguchis.
They treat me like one of the family. Have me over for holidays. Buy me birthday presents.
They're the best.
Maps, the little sister I never had, and Kyle...
SNF
My Kyle...
All I want to do is protect them but...
DON'T TOUCH MY BROTHER, YOU WITCH.

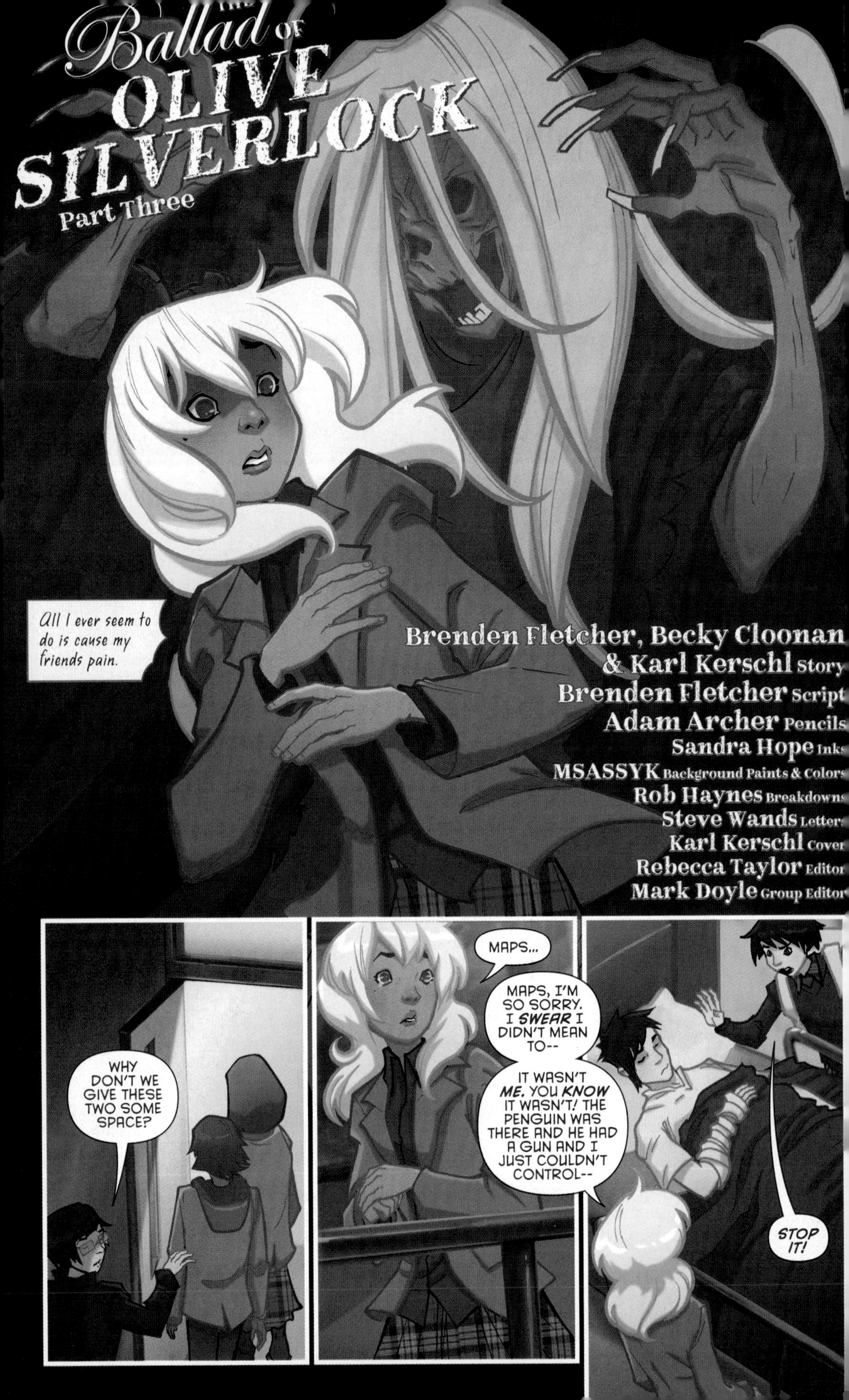

THE Ballad OF OLIVE SILVERLOCK
Part Three
All I ever seem to do is cause my friends pain.
Brenden Fletcher, Becky Cloonan & Karl Kerschl Story
Brenden Fletcher Script
Adam Archer Pencils
Sandra Hope Inks
MSASSYK Background Paints & Colors
Rob Haynes Breakdowns
Steve Wands Letters
Karl Kerschl Cover
Rebecca Taylor Editor
Mark Doyle Group Editor
WHY DON'T WE GIVE THESE TWO SOME SPACE?
MAPS...
MAPS, I'M SO SORRY. I SWEAR I DIDN'T MEAN TO--
IT WASN'T ME. YOU KNOW IT WASN'T! THE PENGUIN WAS THERE AND HE HAD A GUN AND I JUST COULDN'T CONTROL--
STOP IT!

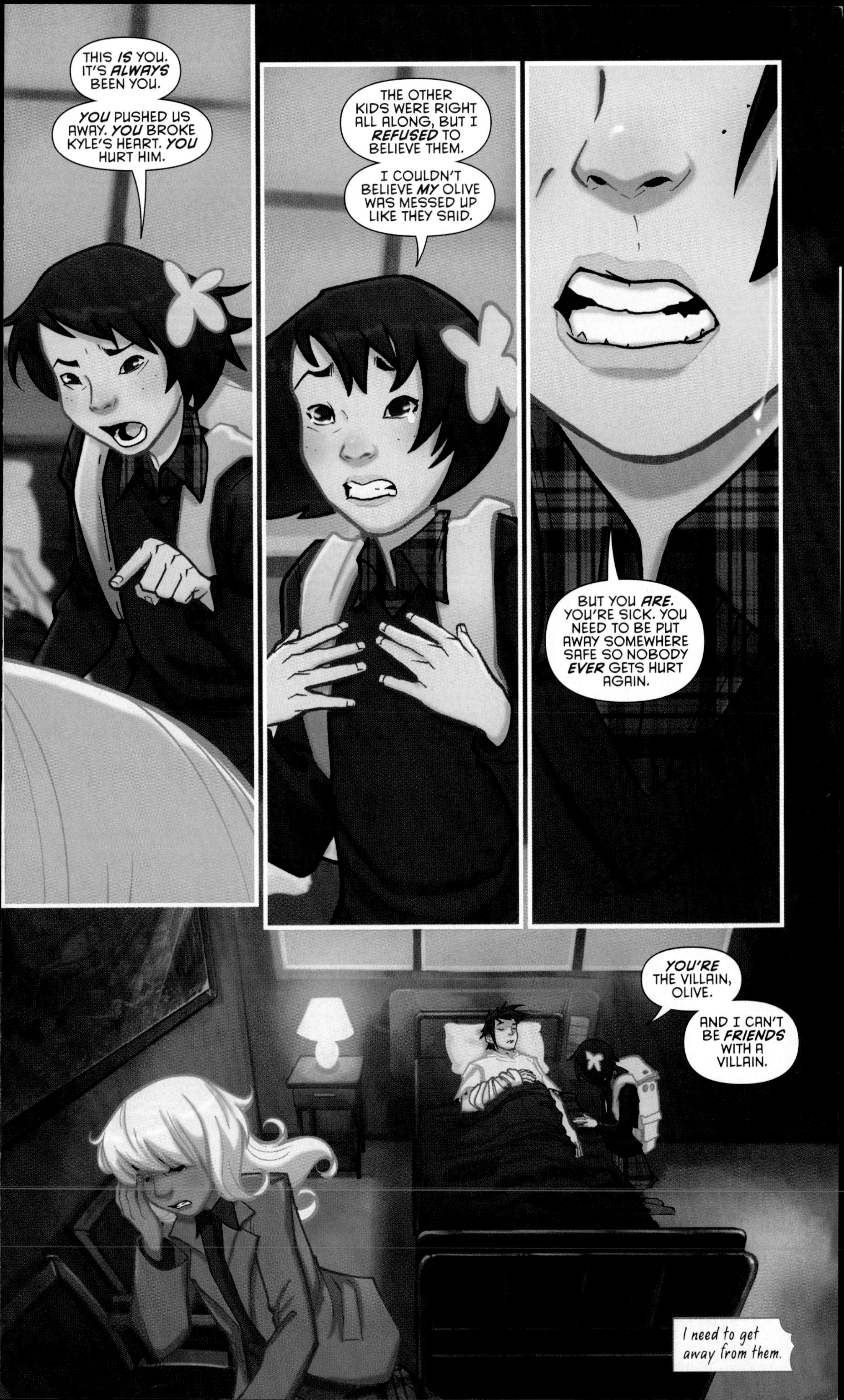

THIS *IS* YOU. IT'S *ALWAYS* BEEN YOU.
YOU PUSHED US AWAY. *YOU* BROKE KYLE'S HEART. *YOU* HURT HIM.
THE OTHER KIDS WERE RIGHT ALL ALONG, BUT I *REFUSED* TO BELIEVE THEM.
I COULDN'T BELIEVE *MY* OLIVE WAS MESSED UP LIKE THEY SAID.
BUT YOU *ARE*. YOU'RE SICK. YOU NEED TO BE PUT AWAY SOMEWHERE SAFE SO NOBODY *EVER* GETS HURT AGAIN.
YOU'RE THE VILLAIN, OLIVE.
AND I CAN'T BE *FRIENDS* WITH A VILLAIN.
I need to get away from them.

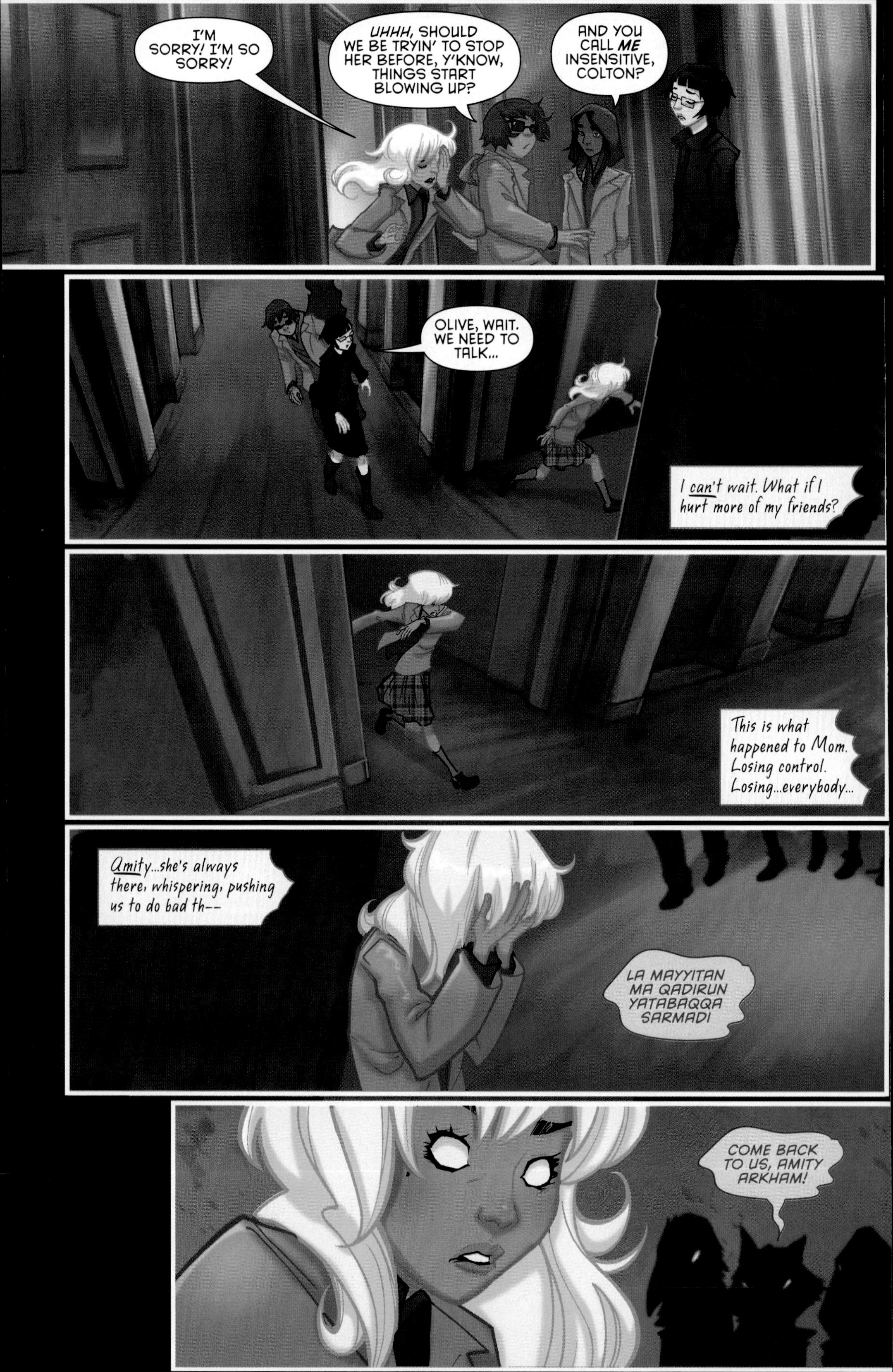
I'M SORRY! I'M SO SORRY!
UHHH, SHOULD WE BE TRYIN' TO STOP HER BEFORE, Y'KNOW, THINGS START BLOWING UP?
AND YOU CALL ME INSENSITIVE, COLTON?
OLIVE, WAIT. WE NEED TO TALK...
I can't wait. What if I hurt more of my friends?
This is what happened to Mom. Losing control. Losing...everybody...
Amity...she's always there, whispering, pushing us to do bad th--
LA MAYYITAN MA QADIRUN YATABAQQA SARMADI
COME BACK TO US, AMITY ARKHAM!

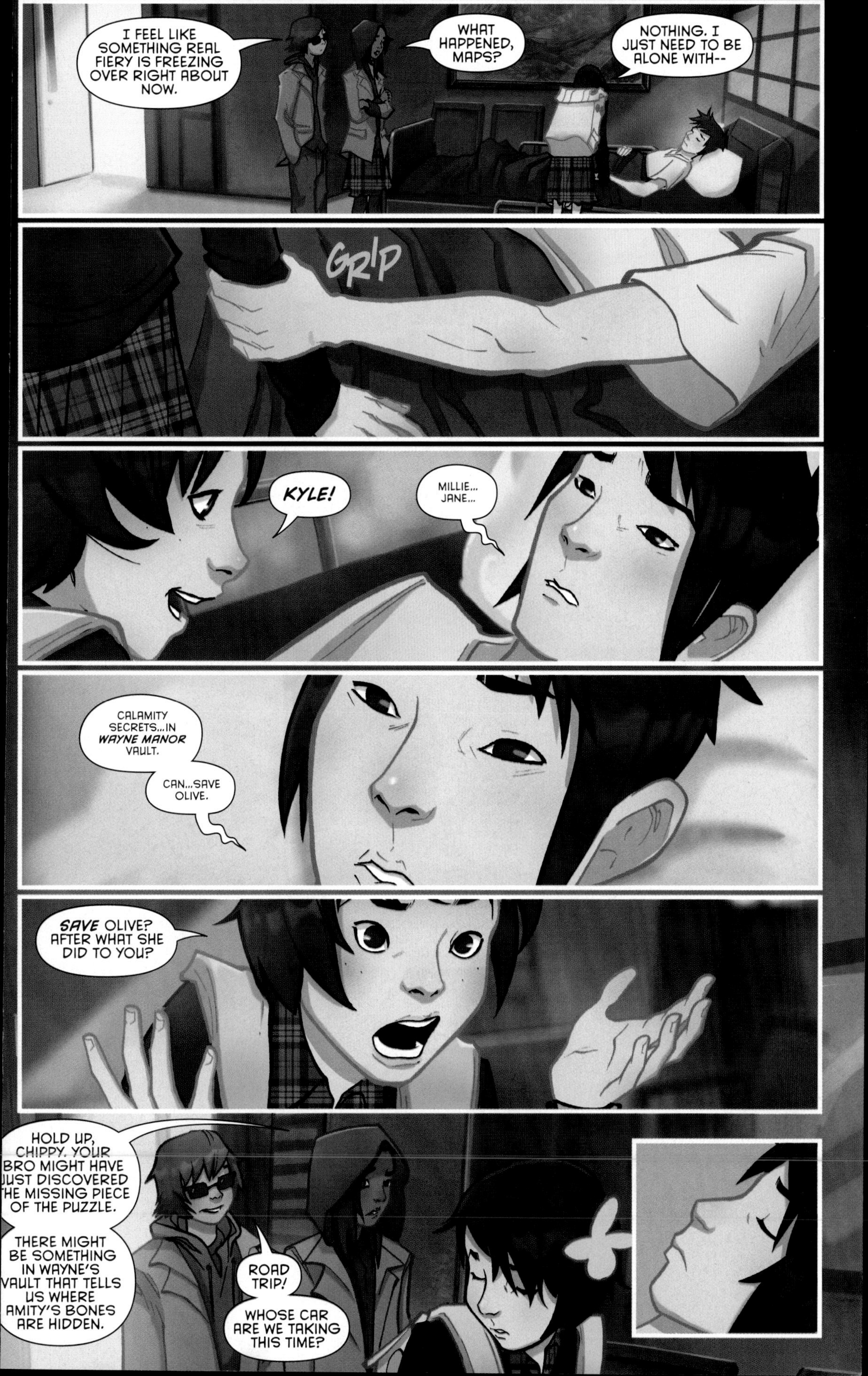
I FEEL LIKE SOMETHING REAL FIERY IS FREEZING OVER RIGHT ABOUT NOW.
WHAT HAPPENED, MAPS?
NOTHING. I JUST NEED TO BE ALONE WITH--
GRIP
KYLE!
MILLIE... JANE...
CALAMITY SECRETS...IN WAYNE MANOR VAULT.
CAN...SAVE OLIVE.
SAVE OLIVE? AFTER WHAT SHE DID TO YOU?
HOLD UP, CHIPPY. YOUR BRO MIGHT HAVE JUST DISCOVERED THE MISSING PIECE OF THE PUZZLE.
THERE MIGHT BE SOMETHING IN WAYNE'S VAULT THAT TELLS US WHERE AMITY'S BONES ARE HIDDEN.
ROAD TRIP!
WHOSE CAR ARE WE TAKING THIS TIME?

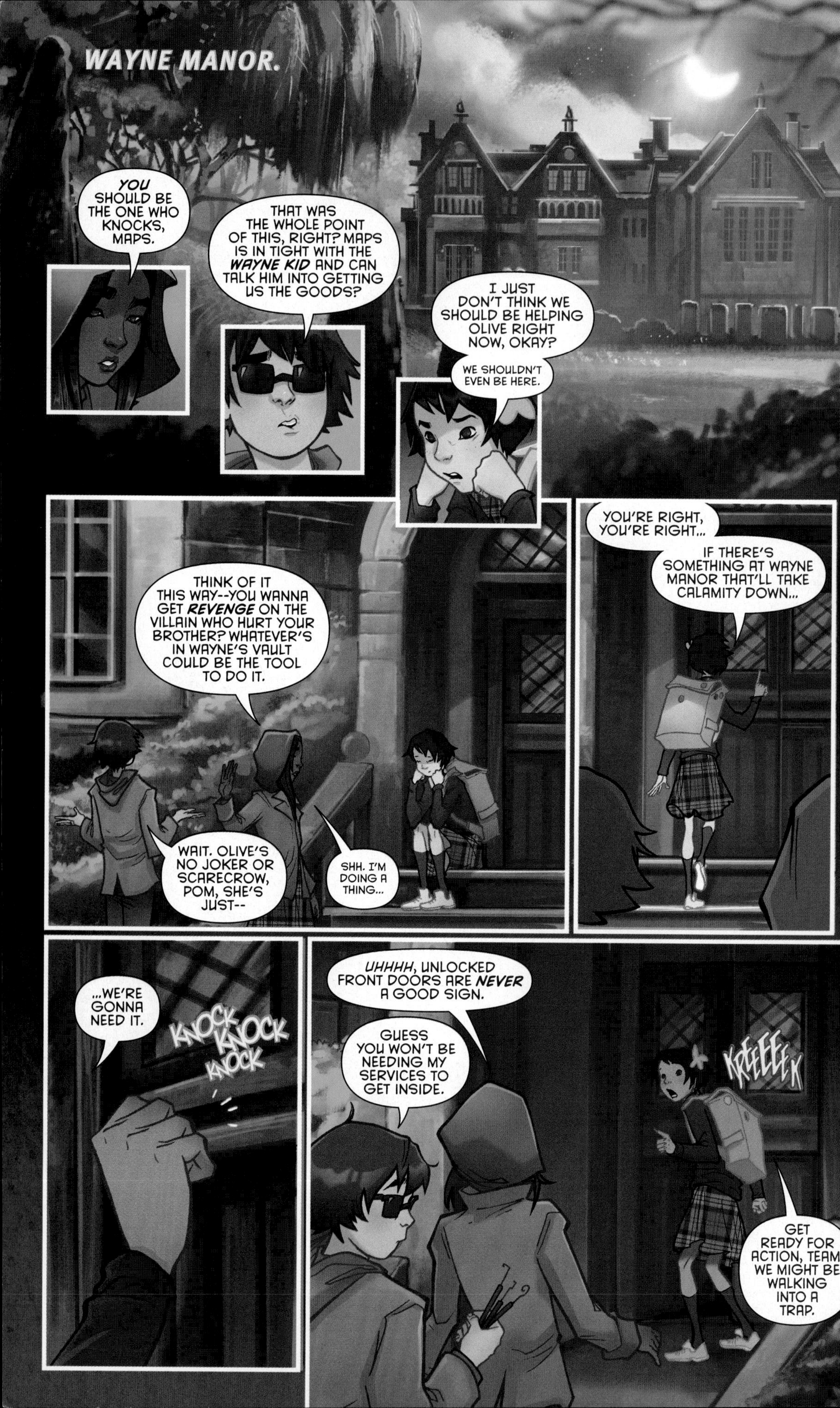
WAYNE MANOR.
YOU SHOULD BE THE ONE WHO KNOCKS, MAPS.
THAT WAS THE WHOLE POINT OF THIS, RIGHT? MAPS IS IN TIGHT WITH THE WAYNE KID AND CAN TALK HIM INTO GETTING US THE GOODS?
I JUST DON'T THINK WE SHOULD BE HELPING OLIVE RIGHT NOW, OKAY?
WE SHOULDN'T EVEN BE HERE.
THINK OF IT THIS WAY--YOU WANNA GET REVENGE ON THE VILLAIN WHO HURT YOUR BROTHER? WHATEVER'S IN WAYNE'S VAULT COULD BE THE TOOL TO DO IT.
WAIT. OLIVE'S NO JOKER OR SCARECROW, POM, SHE'S JUST--
SHH. I'M DOING A THING...
YOU'RE RIGHT, YOU'RE RIGHT...
IF THERE'S SOMETHING AT WAYNE MANOR THAT'LL TAKE CALAMITY DOWN...
...WE'RE GONNA NEED IT.
KNOCK KNOCK KNOCK
UHHHH, UNLOCKED FRONT DOORS ARE NEVER A GOOD SIGN.
GUESS YOU WON'T BE NEEDING MY SERVICES TO GET INSIDE.
KREEEEEK
GET READY FOR ACTION, TEAM WE MIGHT BE WALKING INTO A TRAP.

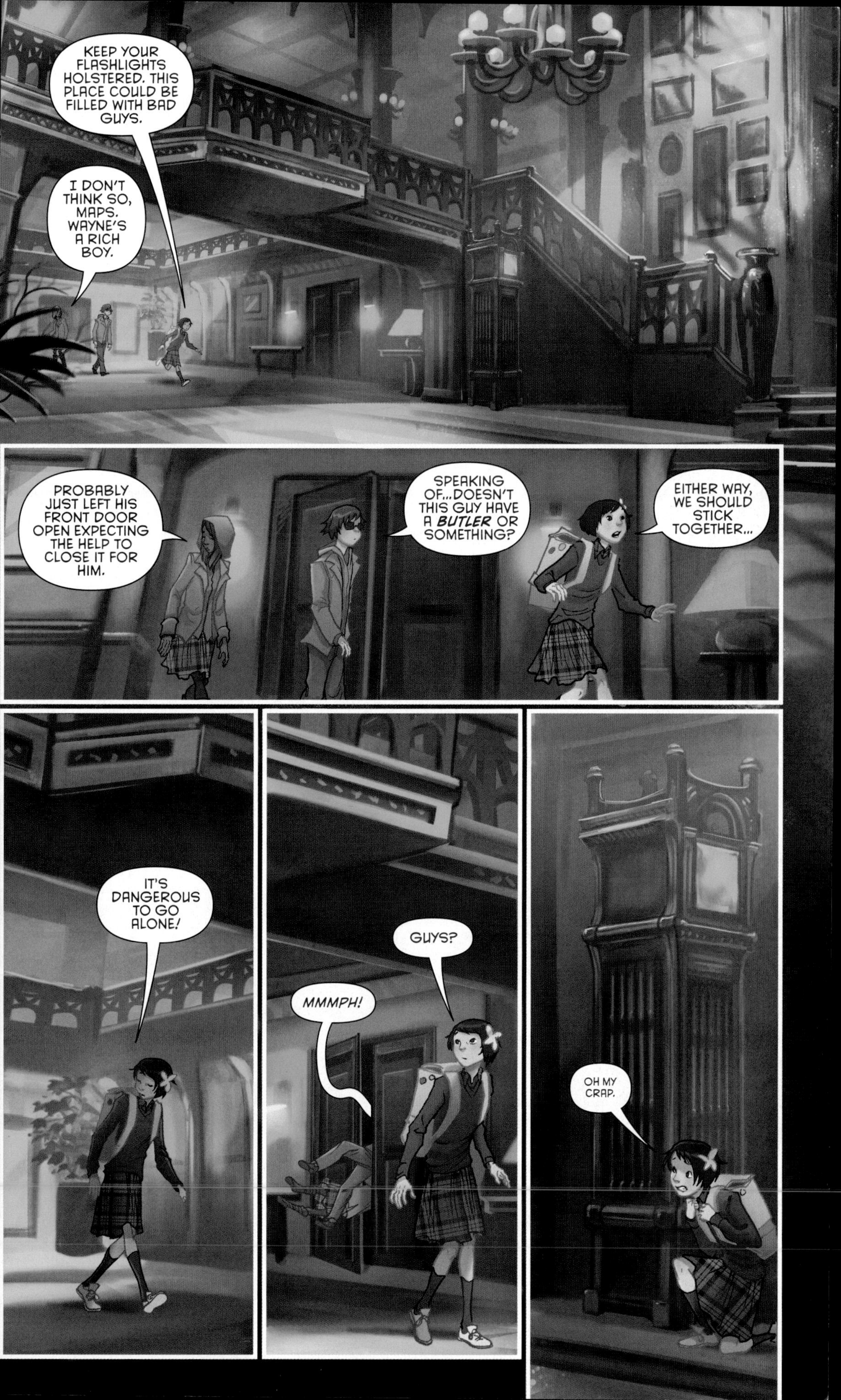
KEEP YOUR FLASHLIGHTS HOLSTERED. THIS PLACE COULD BE FILLED WITH BAD GUYS.
I DON'T THINK SO, MAPS. WAYNE'S A RICH BOY.
PROBABLY JUST LEFT HIS FRONT DOOR OPEN EXPECTING THE HELP TO CLOSE IT FOR HIM.
SPEAKING OF...DOESN'T THIS GUY HAVE A *BUTLER* OR SOMETHING?
EITHER WAY, WE SHOULD STICK TOGETHER...
IT'S DANGEROUS TO GO ALONE!
GUYS?
MMMPH!
OH MY CRAP.

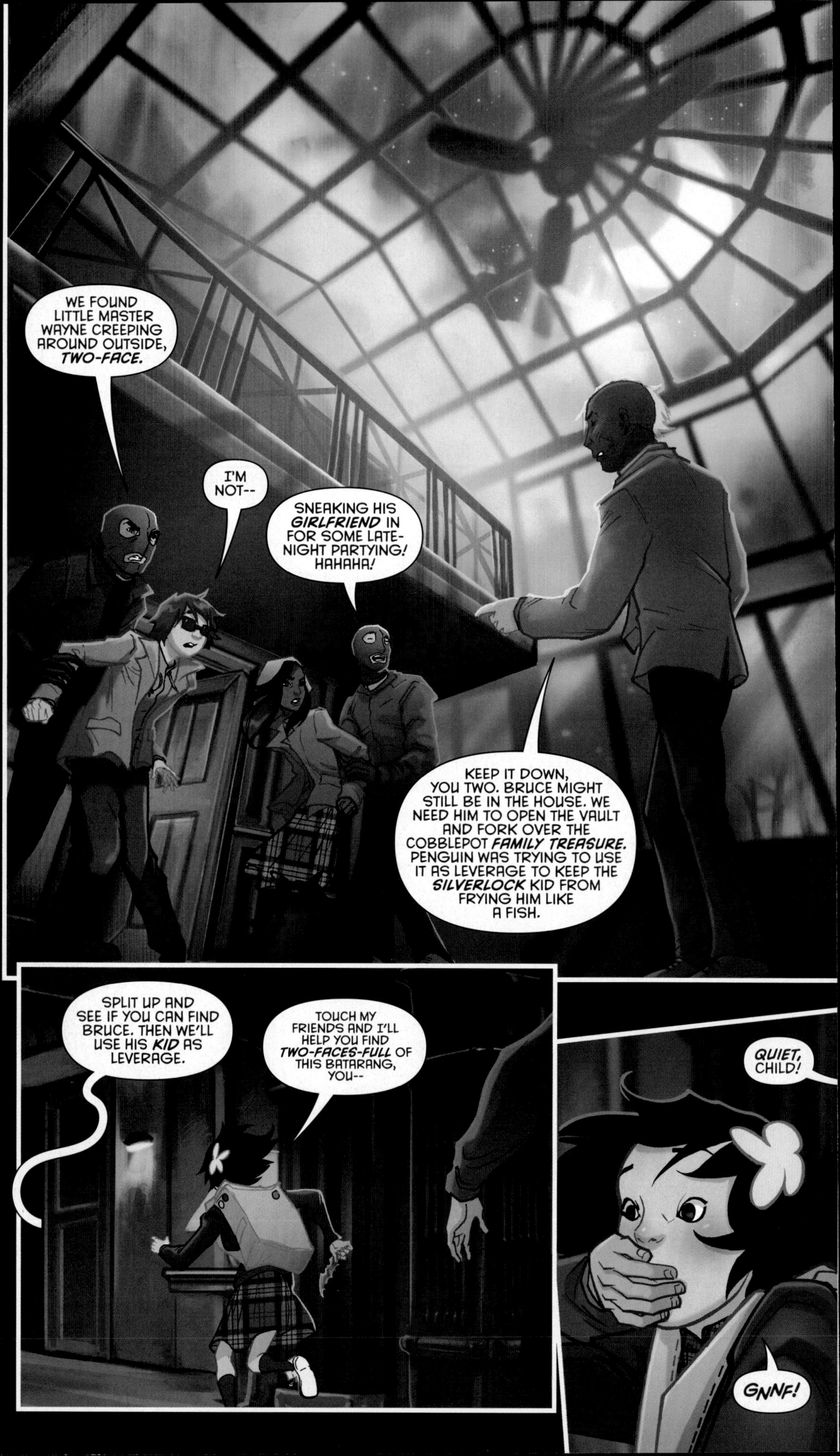

WE FOUND LITTLE MASTER WAYNE CREEPING AROUND OUTSIDE, TWO-FACE.
I'M NOT--
SNEAKING HIS GIRLFRIEND IN FOR SOME LATE-NIGHT PARTYING! HAHAHA!
KEEP IT DOWN, YOU TWO. BRUCE MIGHT STILL BE IN THE HOUSE. WE NEED HIM TO OPEN THE VAULT AND FORK OVER THE COBBLEPOT FAMILY TREASURE. PENGUIN WAS TRYING TO USE IT AS LEVERAGE TO KEEP THE SILVERLOCK KID FROM FRYING HIM LIKE A FISH.
SPLIT UP AND SEE IF YOU CAN FIND BRUCE. THEN WE'LL USE HIS KID AS LEVERAGE.
TOUCH MY FRIENDS AND I'LL HELP YOU FIND TWO-FACES-FULL OF THIS BATARANG, YOU--
QUIET, CHILD!
GNNF!

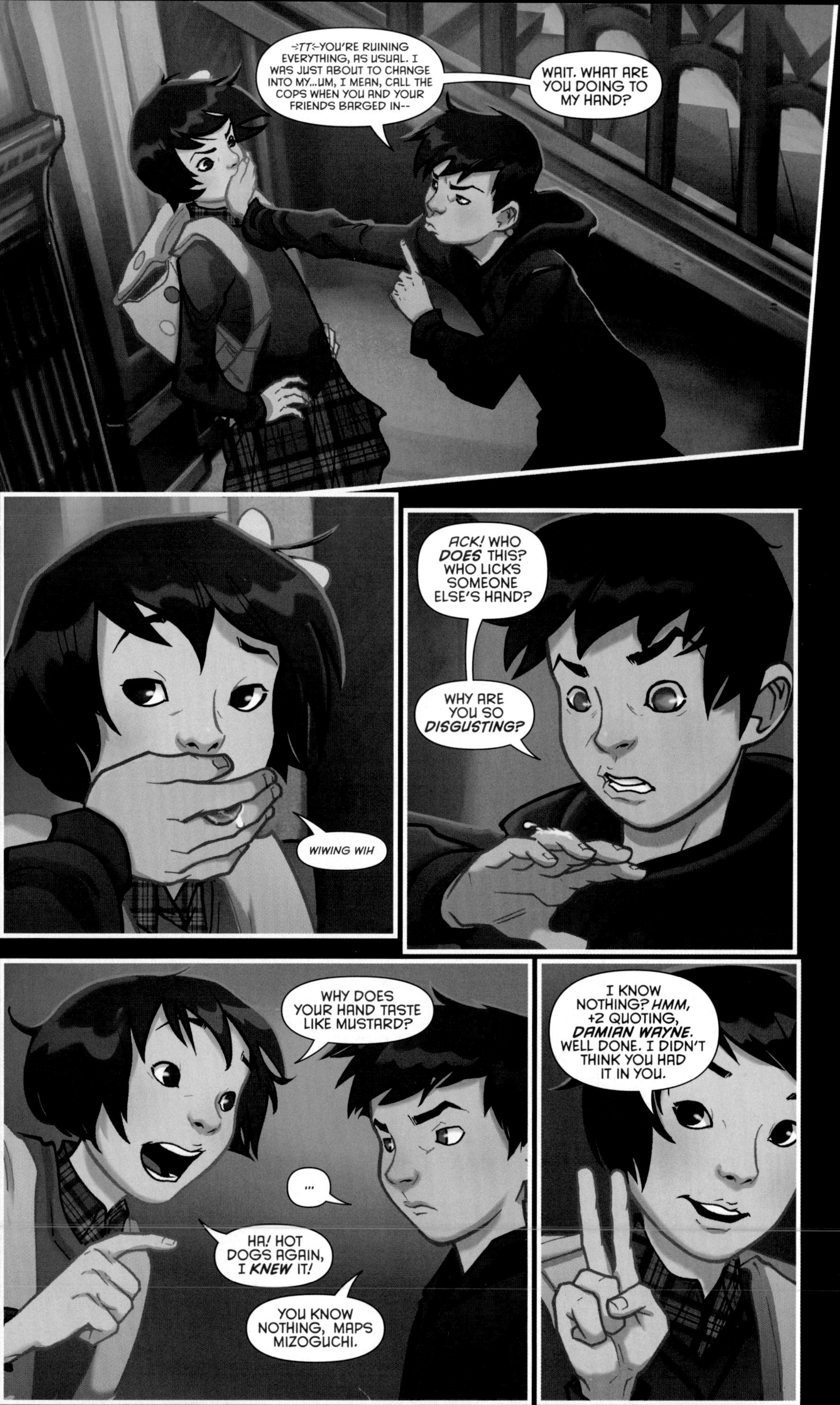

TT--YOU'RE RUINING EVERYTHING, AS USUAL. I WAS JUST ABOUT TO CHANGE INTO MY...UM, I MEAN, CALL THE COPS WHEN YOU AND YOUR FRIENDS BARGED IN--
WAIT. WHAT ARE YOU DOING TO MY HAND?
WIWING WIH
ACK! WHO *DOES* THIS? WHO LICKS SOMEONE ELSE'S HAND?
WHY ARE YOU SO *DISGUSTING?*
WHY DOES YOUR HAND TASTE LIKE MUSTARD?
...
HA! HOT DOGS AGAIN, I *KNEW* IT!
YOU KNOW NOTHING, MAPS MIZOGUCHI.
I KNOW NOTHING? *HMM,* +2 QUOTING, *DAMIAN WAYNE.* WELL DONE. I DIDN'T THINK YOU HAD IT IN YOU.

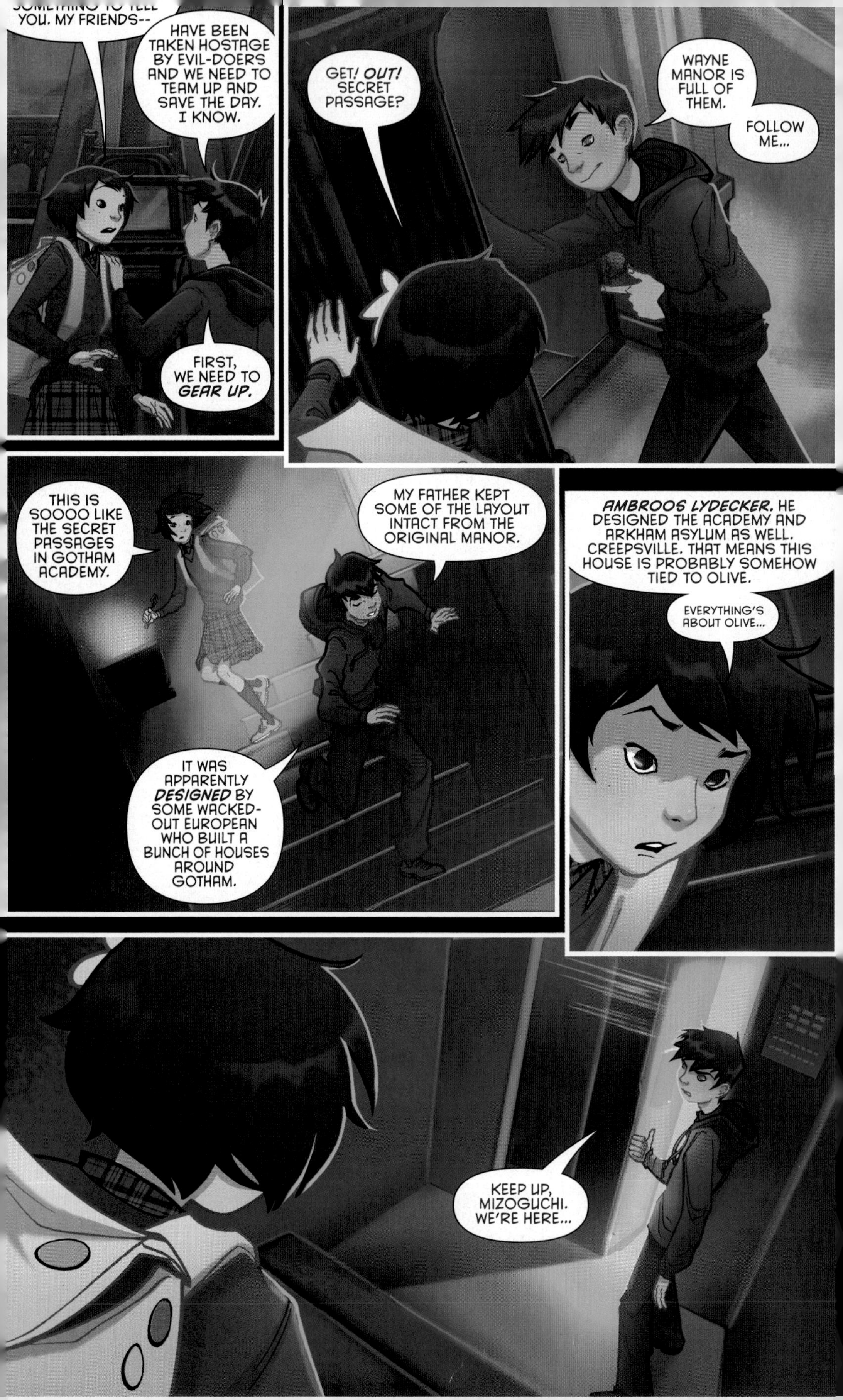
SOMETHING TO TELL YOU. MY FRIENDS--
HAVE BEEN TAKEN HOSTAGE BY EVIL-DOERS AND WE NEED TO TEAM UP AND SAVE THE DAY. I KNOW.
FIRST, WE NEED TO GEAR UP.
GET! OUT! SECRET PASSAGE?
WAYNE MANOR IS FULL OF THEM.
FOLLOW ME...
THIS IS SOOOO LIKE THE SECRET PASSAGES IN GOTHAM ACADEMY.
MY FATHER KEPT SOME OF THE LAYOUT INTACT FROM THE ORIGINAL MANOR.
IT WAS APPARENTLY DESIGNED BY SOME WACKED-OUT EUROPEAN WHO BUILT A BUNCH OF HOUSES AROUND GOTHAM.
AMBROOS LYDECKER. HE DESIGNED THE ACADEMY AND ARKHAM ASYLUM AS WELL. CREEPSVILLE. THAT MEANS THIS HOUSE IS PROBABLY SOMEHOW TIED TO OLIVE.
EVERYTHING'S ABOUT OLIVE...
KEEP UP, MIZOGUCHI. WE'RE HERE...

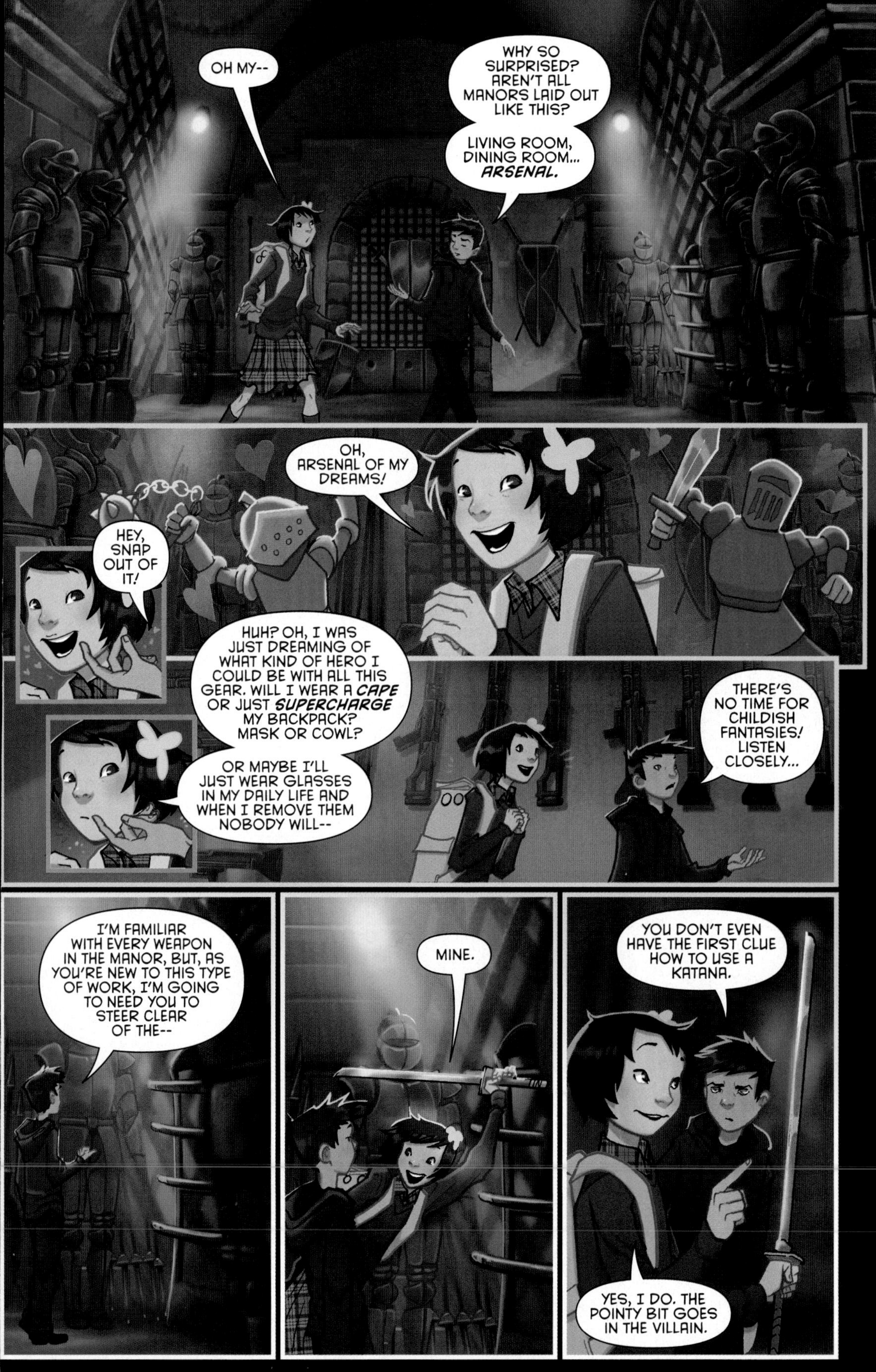
OH MY--
WHY SO SURPRISED? AREN'T ALL MANORS LAID OUT LIKE THIS?
LIVING ROOM, DINING ROOM... ARSENAL.
OH, ARSENAL OF MY DREAMS!
HEY, SNAP OUT OF IT!
HUH? OH, I WAS JUST DREAMING OF WHAT KIND OF HERO I COULD BE WITH ALL THIS GEAR. WILL I WEAR A CAPE OR JUST SUPERCHARGE MY BACKPACK? MASK OR COWL?
OR MAYBE I'LL JUST WEAR GLASSES IN MY DAILY LIFE AND WHEN I REMOVE THEM NOBODY WILL--
THERE'S NO TIME FOR CHILDISH FANTASIES! LISTEN CLOSELY...
I'M FAMILIAR WITH EVERY WEAPON IN THE MANOR, BUT, AS YOU'RE NEW TO THIS TYPE OF WORK, I'M GOING TO NEED YOU TO STEER CLEAR OF THE--
MINE.
YOU DON'T EVEN HAVE THE FIRST CLUE HOW TO USE A KATANA.
YES, I DO. THE POINTY BIT GOES IN THE VILLAIN.

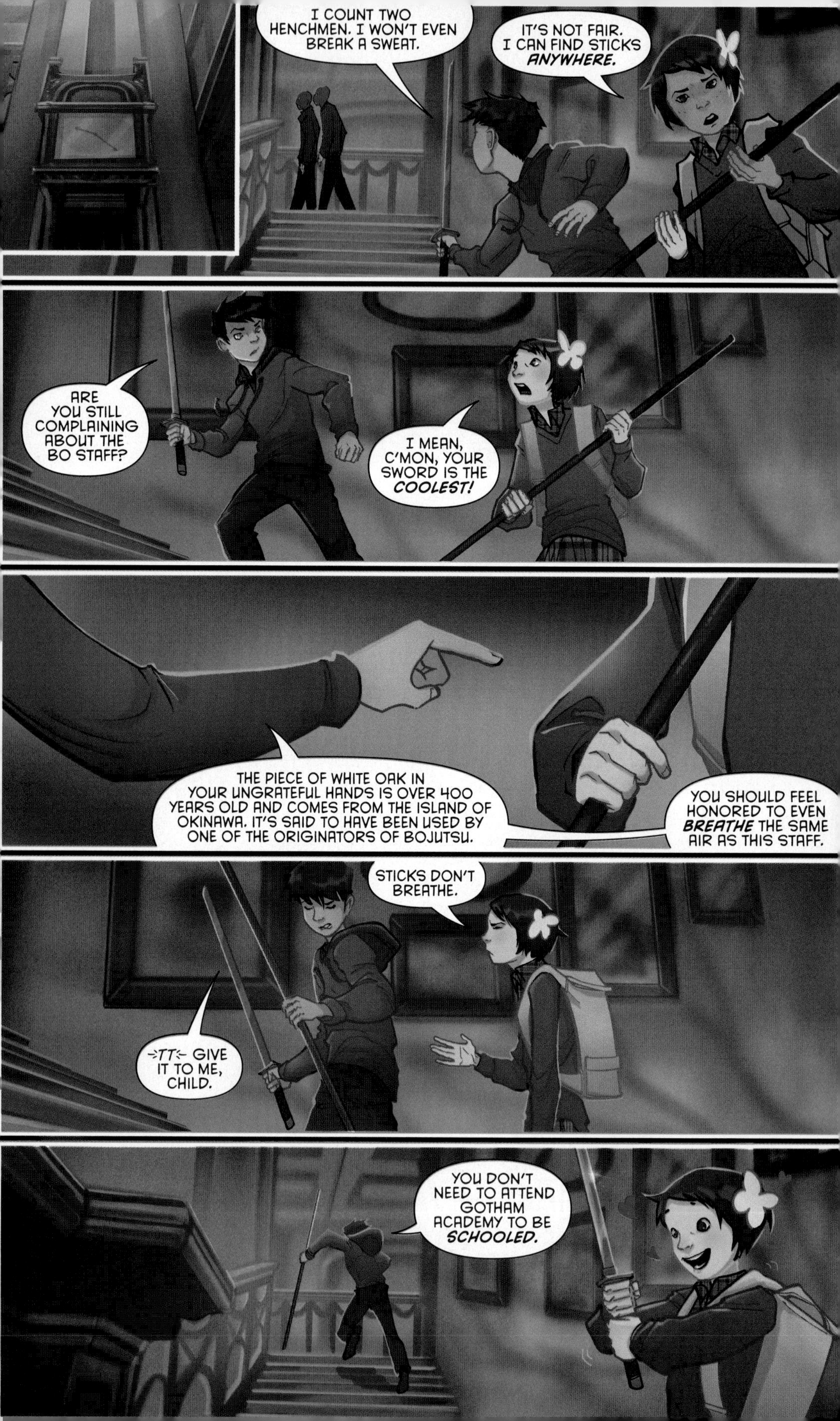
I COUNT TWO HENCHMEN. I WON'T EVEN BREAK A SWEAT.
IT'S NOT FAIR. I CAN FIND STICKS ANYWHERE.
ARE YOU STILL COMPLAINING ABOUT THE BO STAFF?
I MEAN, C'MON, YOUR SWORD IS THE COOLEST!
THE PIECE OF WHITE OAK IN YOUR UNGRATEFUL HANDS IS OVER 400 YEARS OLD AND COMES FROM THE ISLAND OF OKINAWA. IT'S SAID TO HAVE BEEN USED BY ONE OF THE ORIGINATORS OF BOJUTSU.
YOU SHOULD FEEL HONORED TO EVEN BREATHE THE SAME AIR AS THIS STAFF.
STICKS DON'T BREATHE.
TT GIVE IT TO ME, CHILD.
YOU DON'T NEED TO ATTEND GOTHAM ACADEMY TO BE SCHOOLED.

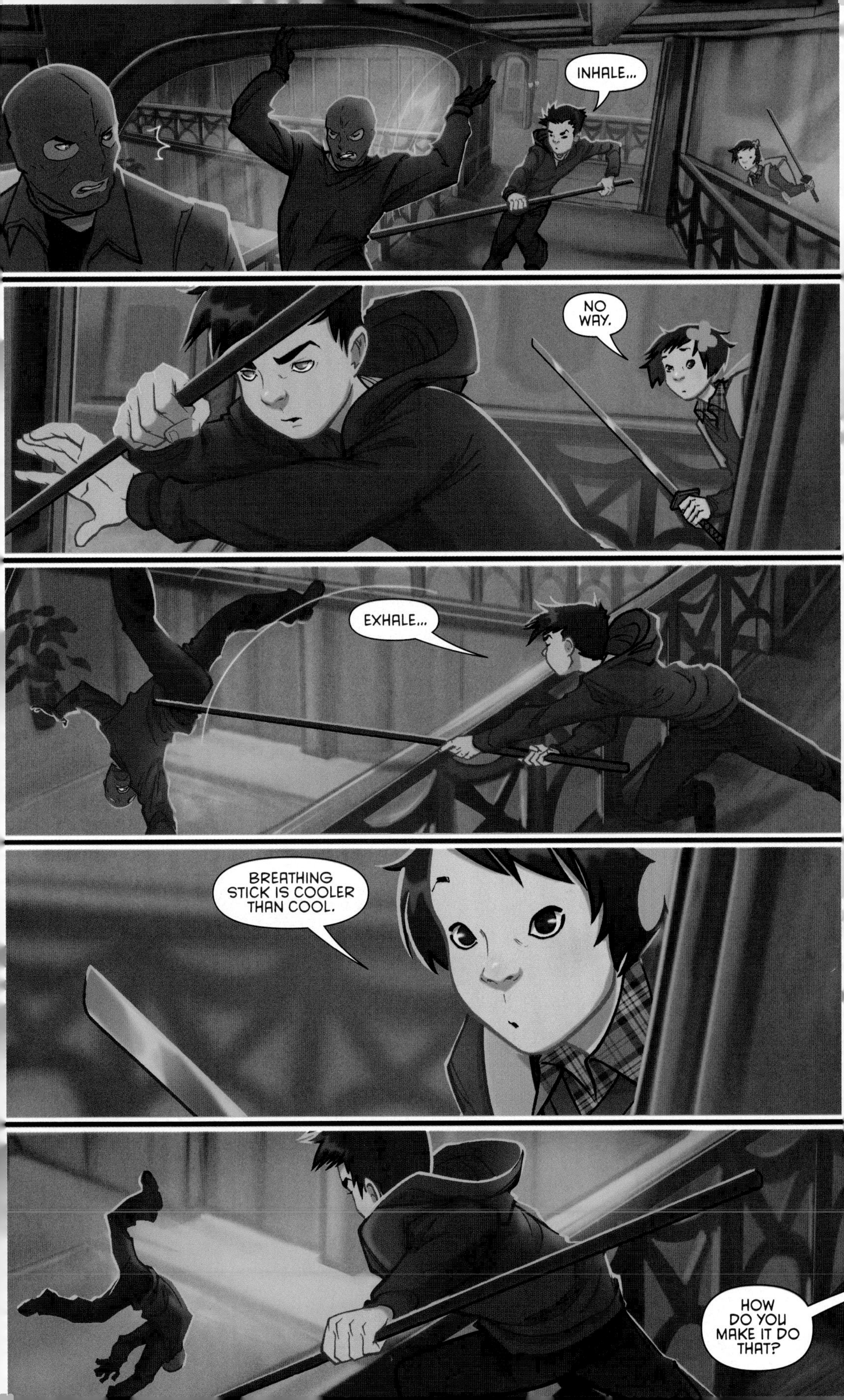
INHALE...
NO WAY.
EXHALE...
BREATHING STICK IS COOLER THAN COOL.
HOW DO YOU MAKE IT DO THAT?

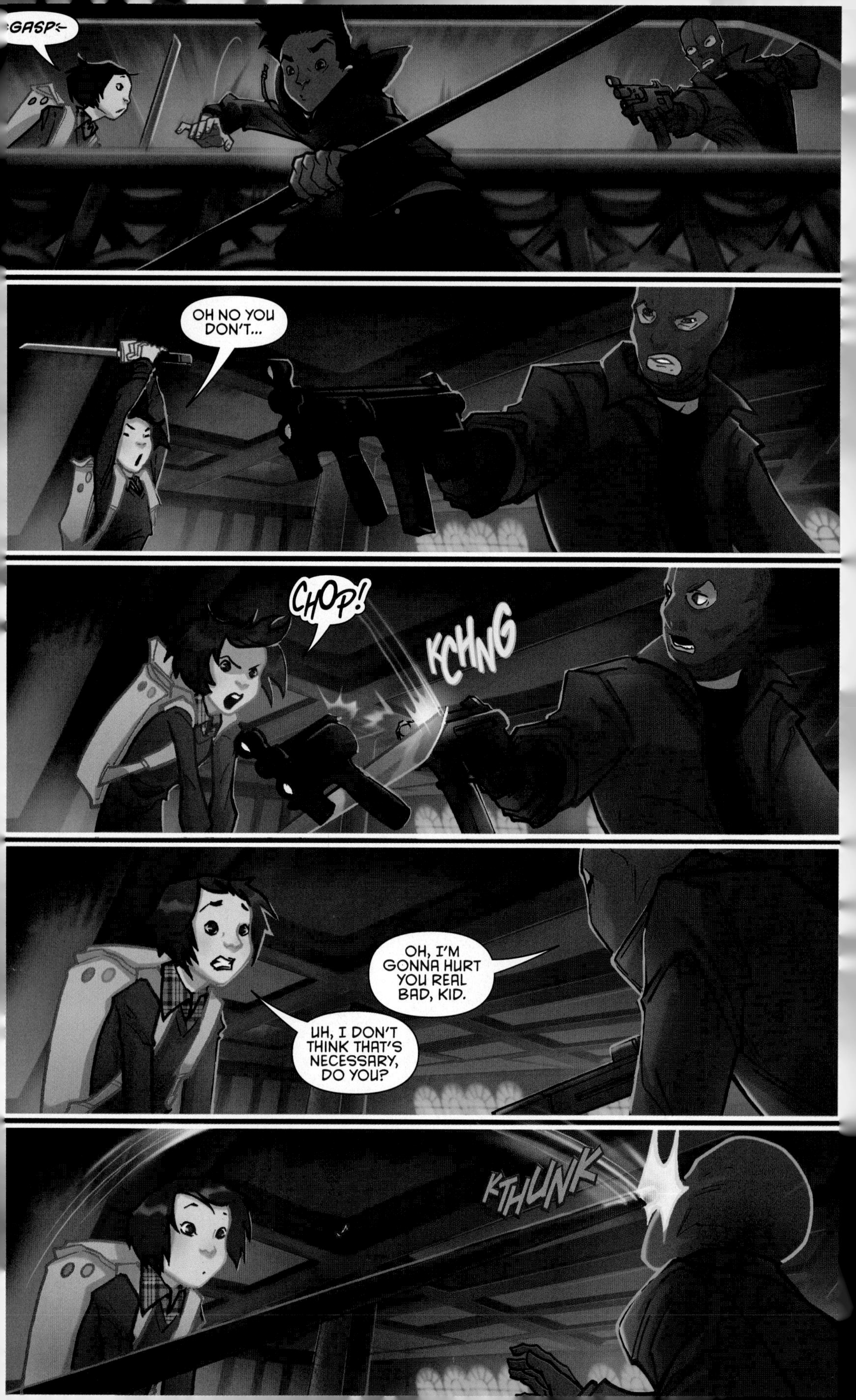

GASP
OH NO YOU DON'T...
CHOP!
KCHNG
OH, I'M GONNA HURT YOU REAL BAD, KID.
UH, I DON'T THINK THAT'S NECESSARY, DO YOU?
KTHUNK

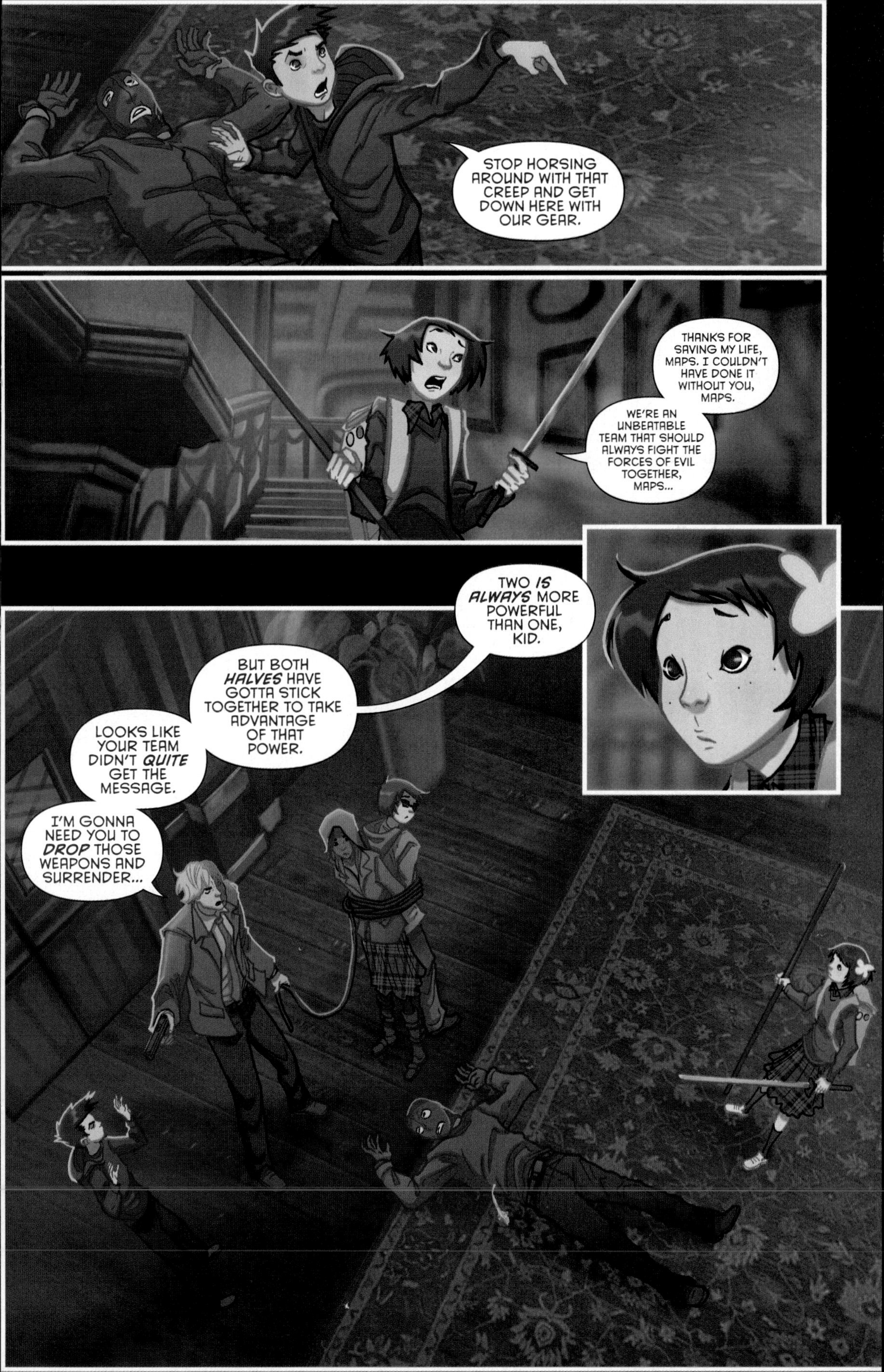
STOP HORSING AROUND WITH THAT CREEP AND GET DOWN HERE WITH OUR GEAR.
THANKS FOR SAVING MY LIFE, MAPS. I COULDN'T HAVE DONE IT WITHOUT YOU, MAPS.
WE'RE AN UNBEATABLE TEAM THAT SHOULD ALWAYS FIGHT THE FORCES OF EVIL TOGETHER, MAPS...
TWO *IS* *ALWAYS* MORE POWERFUL THAN ONE, KID.
BUT BOTH *HALVES* HAVE GOTTA STICK TOGETHER TO TAKE ADVANTAGE OF THAT POWER.
LOOKS LIKE YOUR TEAM DIDN'T *QUITE* GET THE MESSAGE.
I'M GONNA NEED YOU TO *DROP* THOSE WEAPONS AND SURRENDER...

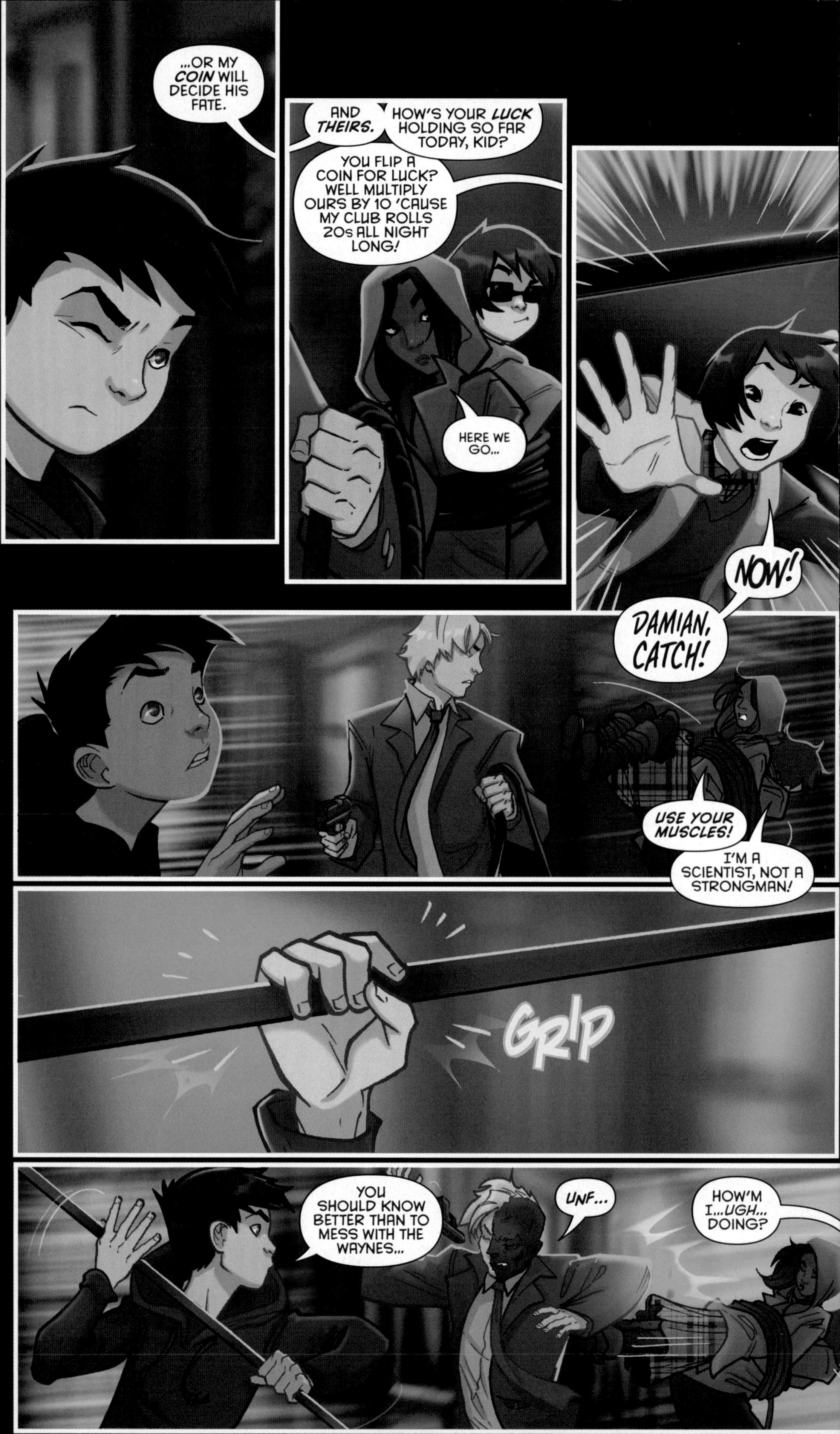

...OR MY COIN WILL DECIDE HIS FATE.
AND THEIRS.
HOW'S YOUR LUCK HOLDING SO FAR TODAY, KID?
YOU FLIP A COIN FOR LUCK? WELL MULTIPLY OURS BY 10 'CAUSE MY CLUB ROLLS 20s ALL NIGHT LONG!
HERE WE GO...
NOW!
DAMIAN, CATCH!
USE YOUR MUSCLES!
I'M A SCIENTIST, NOT A STRONGMAN!
GRIP
YOU SHOULD KNOW BETTER THAN TO MESS WITH THE WAYNES...
UNF...
HOW'M I...UGH... DOING?

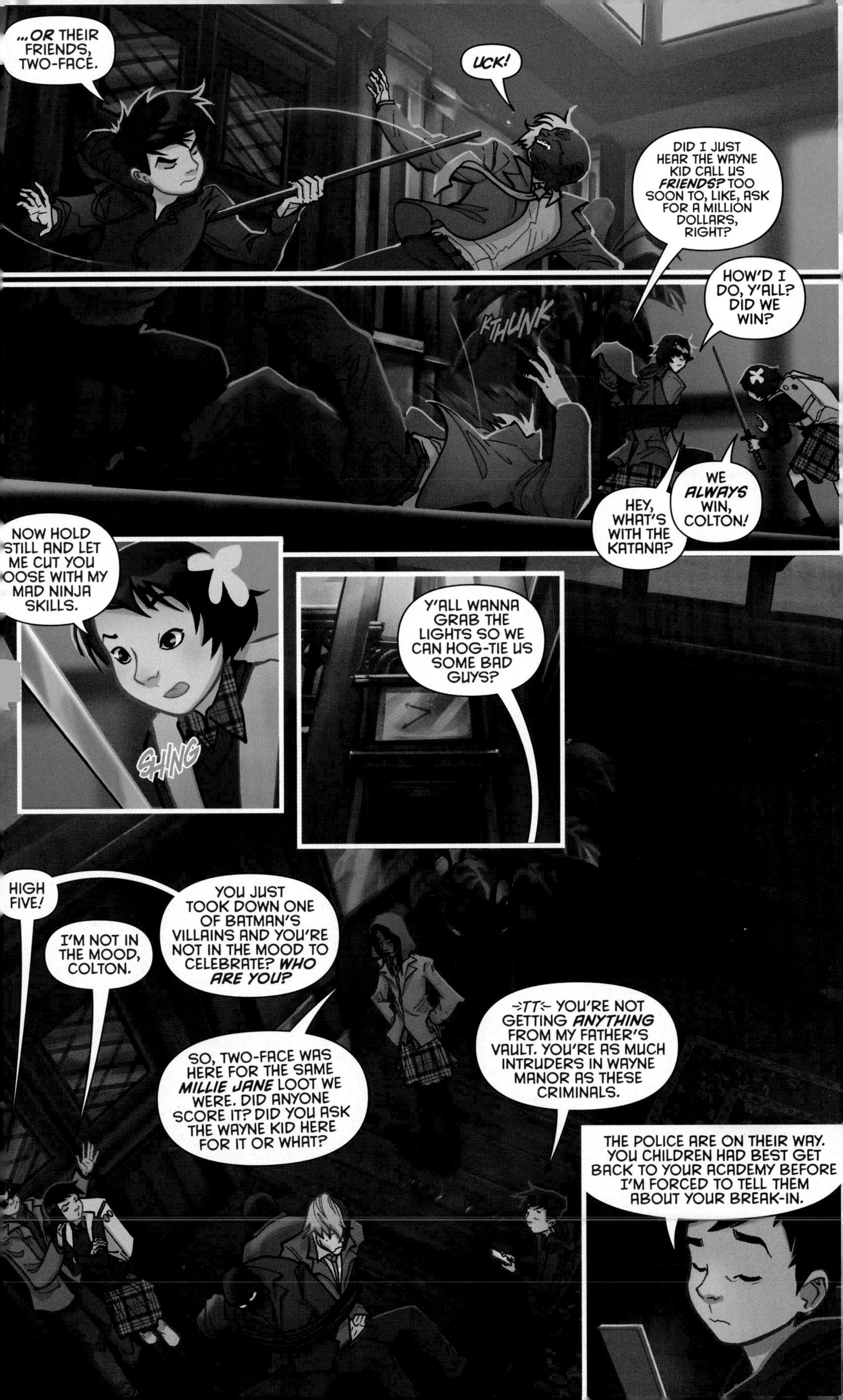
...OR THEIR FRIENDS, TWO-FACE.
UCK!
DID I JUST HEAR THE WAYNE KID CALL US FRIENDS? TOO SOON TO, LIKE, ASK FOR A MILLION DOLLARS, RIGHT?
HOW'D I DO, Y'ALL? DID WE WIN?
K'THUNK
WE ALWAYS WIN, COLTON!
HEY, WHAT'S WITH THE KATANA?
NOW HOLD STILL AND LET ME CUT YOU OOSE WITH MY MAD NINJA SKILLS.
SHING
Y'ALL WANNA GRAB THE LIGHTS SO WE CAN HOG-TIE US SOME BAD GUYS?
HIGH FIVE!
YOU JUST TOOK DOWN ONE OF BATMAN'S VILLAINS AND YOU'RE NOT IN THE MOOD TO CELEBRATE? WHO ARE YOU?
I'M NOT IN THE MOOD, COLTON.
SO, TWO-FACE WAS HERE FOR THE SAME MILLIE JANE LOOT WE WERE. DID ANYONE SCORE IT? DID YOU ASK THE WAYNE KID HERE FOR IT OR WHAT?
-TT- YOU'RE NOT GETTING ANYTHING FROM MY FATHER'S VAULT. YOU'RE AS MUCH INTRUDERS IN WAYNE MANOR AS THESE CRIMINALS.
THE POLICE ARE ON THEIR WAY. YOU CHILDREN HAD BEST GET BACK TO YOUR ACADEMY BEFORE I'M FORCED TO TELL THEM ABOUT YOUR BREAK-IN.

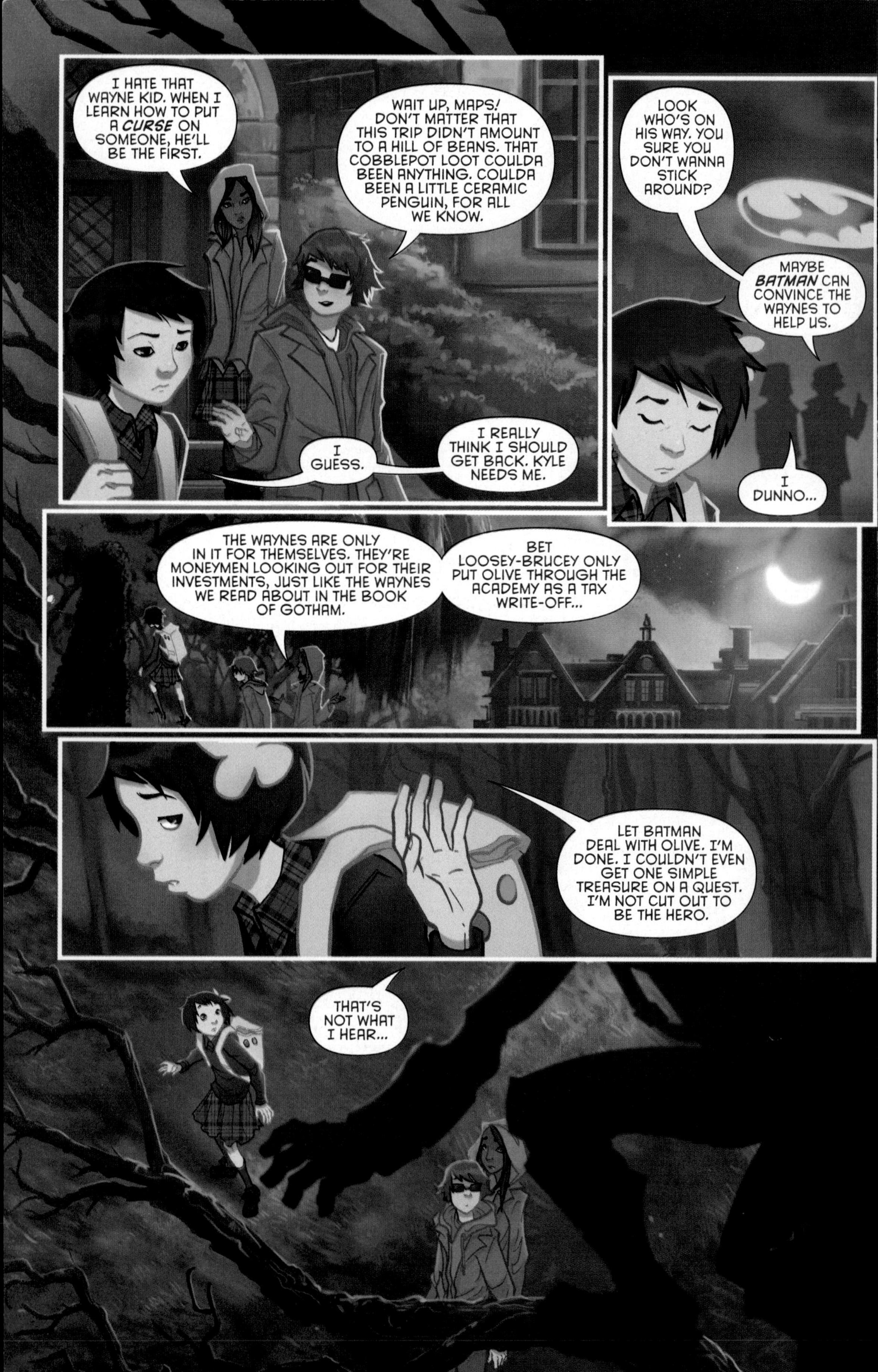
I HATE THAT WAYNE KID. WHEN I LEARN HOW TO PUT A CURSE ON SOMEONE, HE'LL BE THE FIRST.
WAIT UP, MAPS! DON'T MATTER THAT THIS TRIP DIDN'T AMOUNT TO A HILL OF BEANS. THAT COBBLEPOT LOOT COULDA BEEN ANYTHING. COULDA BEEN A LITTLE CERAMIC PENGUIN, FOR ALL WE KNOW.
I GUESS.
I REALLY THINK I SHOULD GET BACK. KYLE NEEDS ME.
LOOK WHO'S ON HIS WAY. YOU SURE YOU DON'T WANNA STICK AROUND?
MAYBE BATMAN CAN CONVINCE THE WAYNES TO HELP US.
I DUNNO...
THE WAYNES ARE ONLY IN IT FOR THEMSELVES. THEY'RE MONEYMEN LOOKING OUT FOR THEIR INVESTMENTS, JUST LIKE THE WAYNES WE READ ABOUT IN THE BOOK OF GOTHAM.
BET LOOSEY-BRUCEY ONLY PUT OLIVE THROUGH THE ACADEMY AS A TAX WRITE-OFF...
LET BATMAN DEAL WITH OLIVE. I'M DONE. I COULDN'T EVEN GET ONE SIMPLE TREASURE ON A QUEST. I'M NOT CUT OUT TO BE THE HERO.
THAT'S NOT WHAT I HEAR...

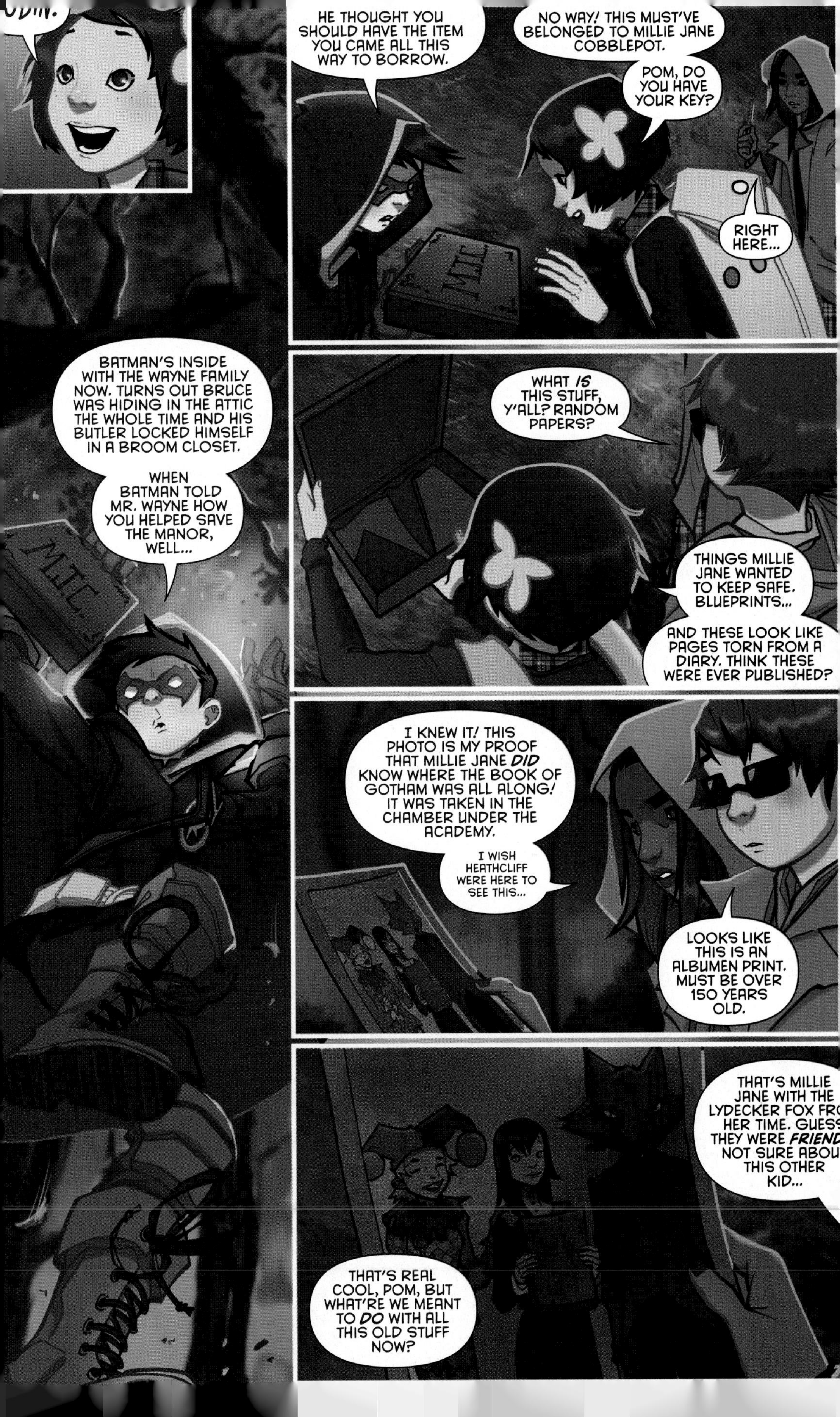
BATMAN'S INSIDE WITH THE WAYNE FAMILY NOW. TURNS OUT BRUCE WAS HIDING IN THE ATTIC THE WHOLE TIME AND HIS BUTLER LOCKED HIMSELF IN A BROOM CLOSET.
WHEN BATMAN TOLD MR. WAYNE HOW YOU HELPED SAVE THE MANOR, WELL...
M.J.C.
HE THOUGHT YOU SHOULD HAVE THE ITEM YOU CAME ALL THIS WAY TO BORROW.
NO WAY! THIS MUST'VE BELONGED TO MILLIE JANE COBBLEPOT.
POM, DO YOU HAVE YOUR KEY?
RIGHT HERE...
WHAT *IS* THIS STUFF, Y'ALL? RANDOM PAPERS?
THINGS MILLIE JANE WANTED TO KEEP SAFE. BLUEPRINTS...
AND THESE LOOK LIKE PAGES TORN FROM A DIARY. THINK THESE WERE EVER PUBLISHED?
I KNEW IT! THIS PHOTO IS MY PROOF THAT MILLIE JANE *DID* KNOW WHERE THE BOOK OF GOTHAM WAS ALL ALONG! IT WAS TAKEN IN THE CHAMBER UNDER THE ACADEMY.
I WISH HEATHCLIFF WERE HERE TO SEE THIS...
LOOKS LIKE THIS IS AN ALBUMEN PRINT. MUST BE OVER 150 YEARS OLD.
THAT'S REAL COOL, POM, BUT WHAT'RE WE MEANT TO *DO* WITH ALL THIS OLD STUFF NOW?

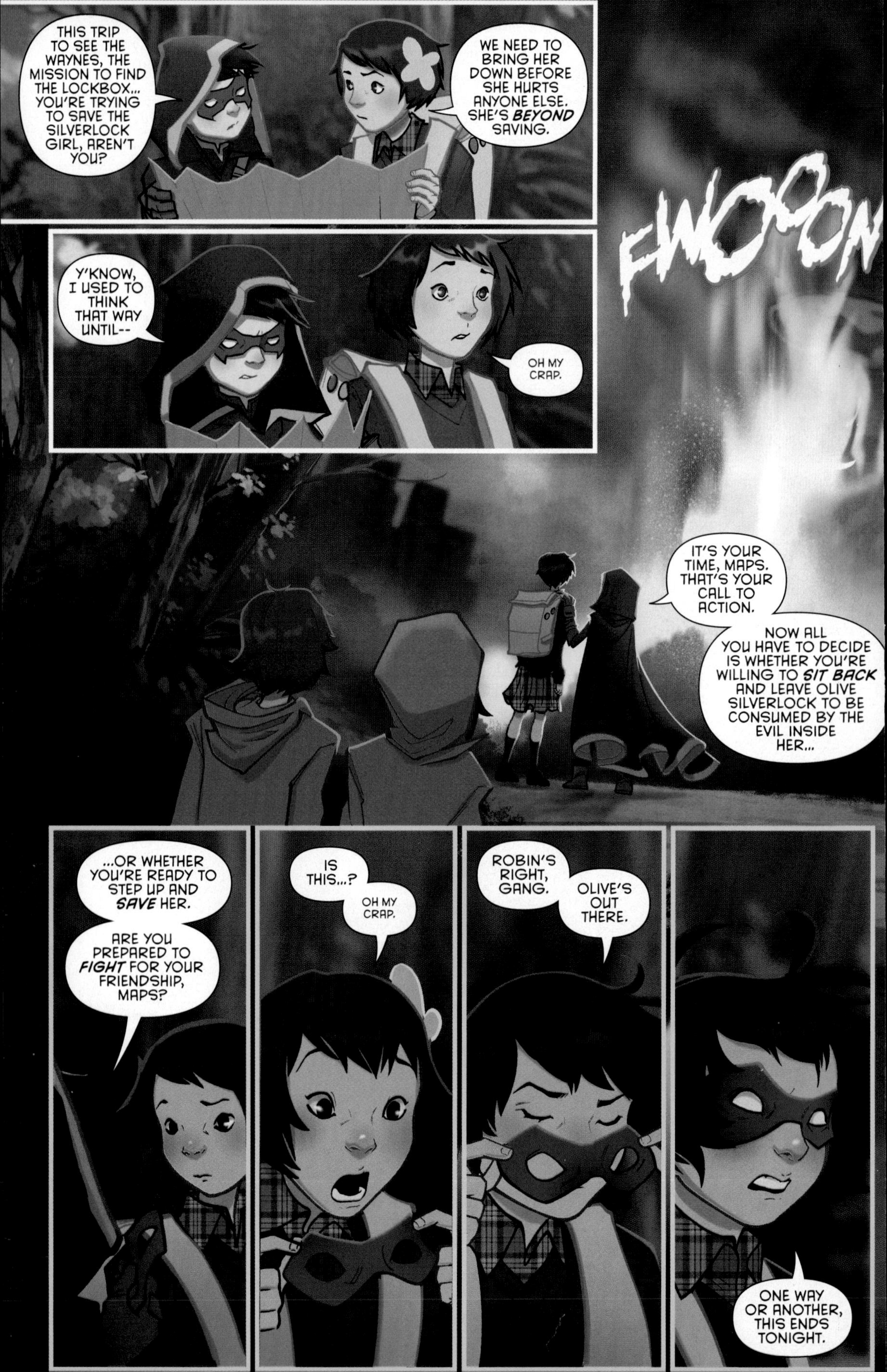
THIS TRIP TO SEE THE WAYNES, THE MISSION TO FIND THE LOCKBOX... YOU'RE TRYING TO SAVE THE SILVERLOCK GIRL, AREN'T YOU?
WE NEED TO BRING HER DOWN BEFORE SHE HURTS ANYONE ELSE. SHE'S *BEYOND* SAVING.
FWOOOON
Y'KNOW, I USED TO THINK THAT WAY UNTIL--
OH MY CRAP.
IT'S YOUR TIME, MAPS. THAT'S YOUR CALL TO ACTION.
NOW ALL YOU HAVE TO DECIDE IS WHETHER YOU'RE WILLING TO *SIT BACK* AND LEAVE OLIVE SILVERLOCK TO BE CONSUMED BY THE EVIL INSIDE HER...
...OR WHETHER YOU'RE READY TO STEP UP AND *SAVE* HER.
ARE YOU PREPARED TO *FIGHT* FOR YOUR FRIENDSHIP, MAPS?
IS THIS...?
OH MY CRAP.
ROBIN'S RIGHT, GANG.
OLIVE'S OUT THERE.
ONE WAY OR ANOTHER, THIS ENDS TONIGHT.

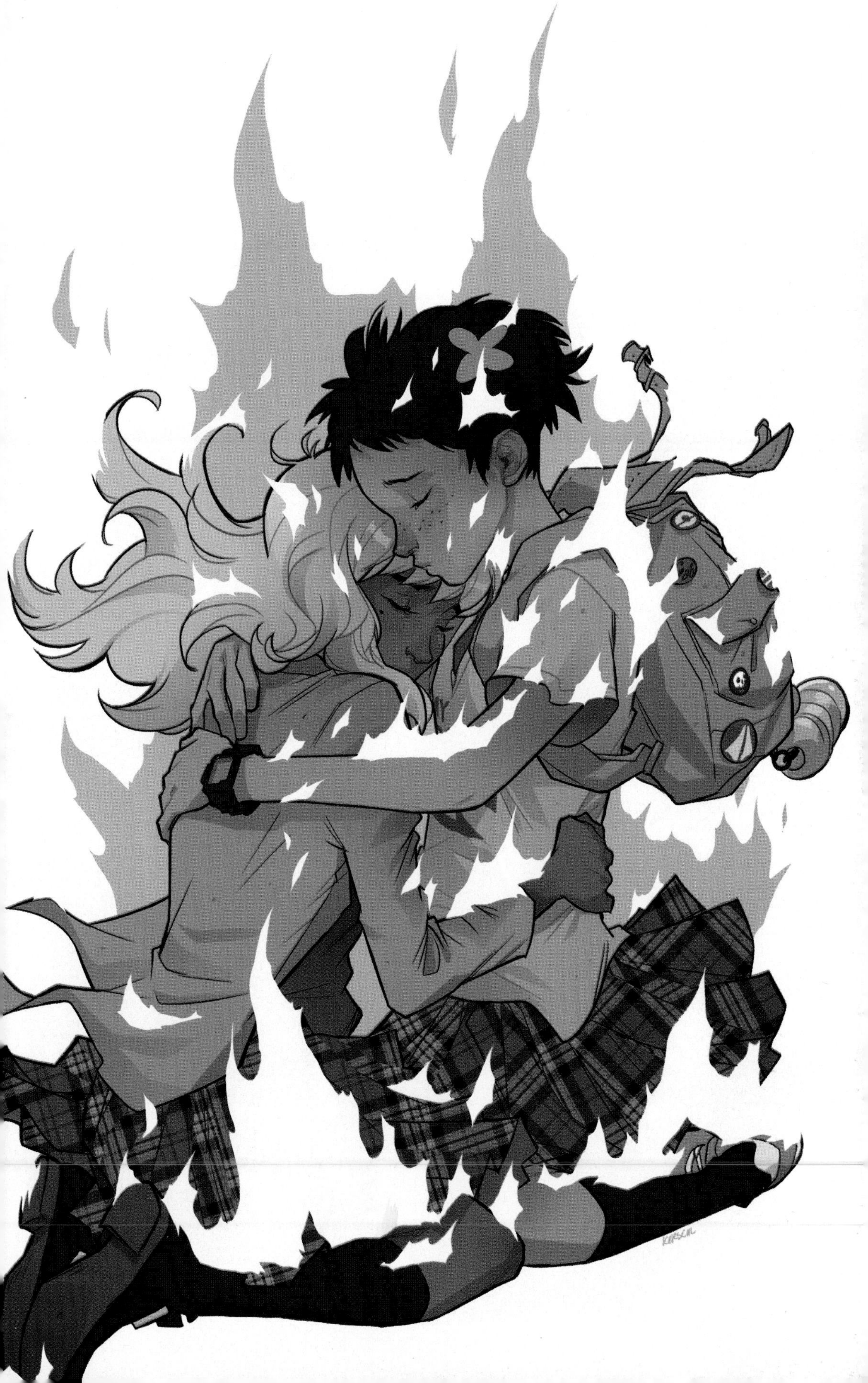

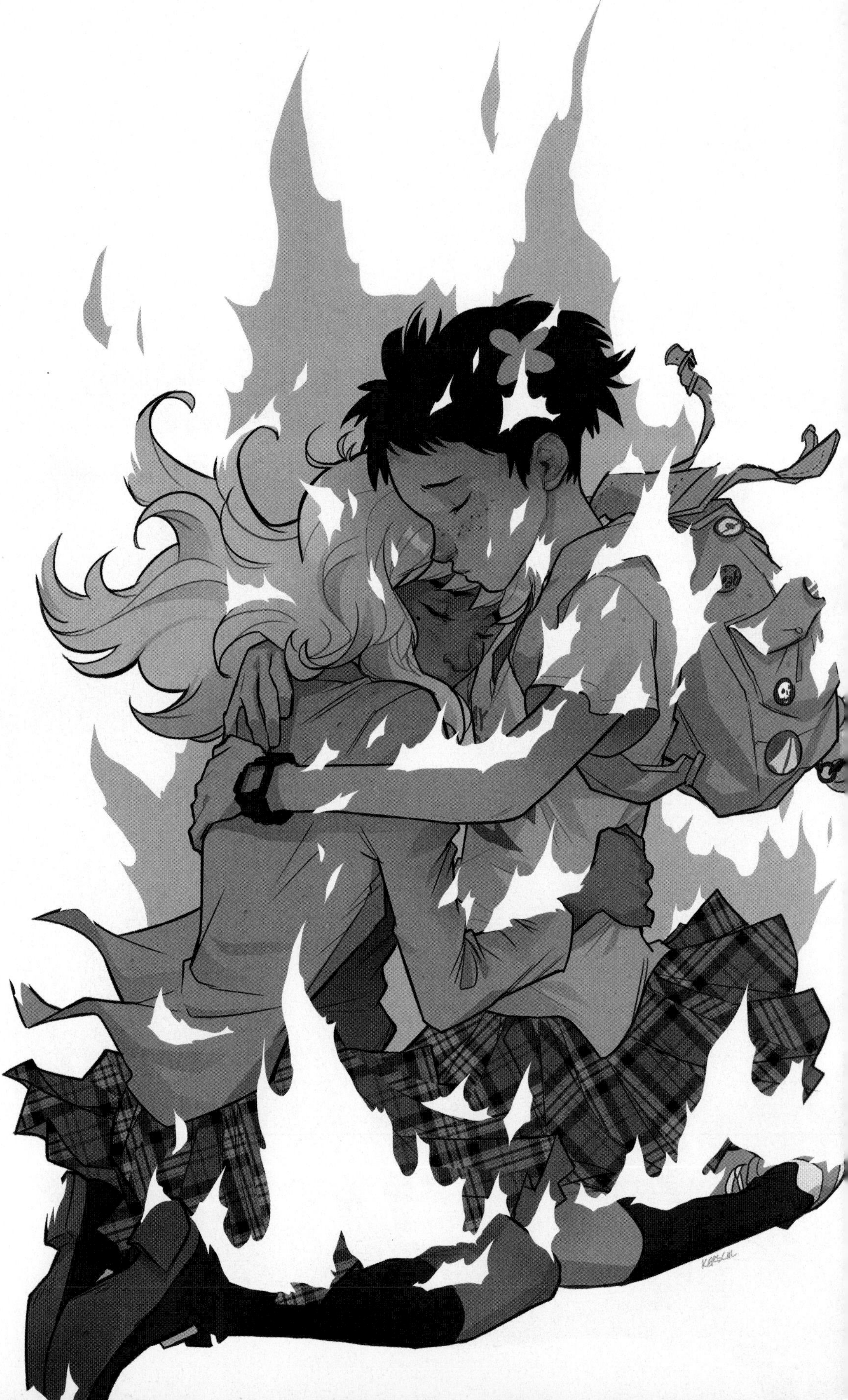

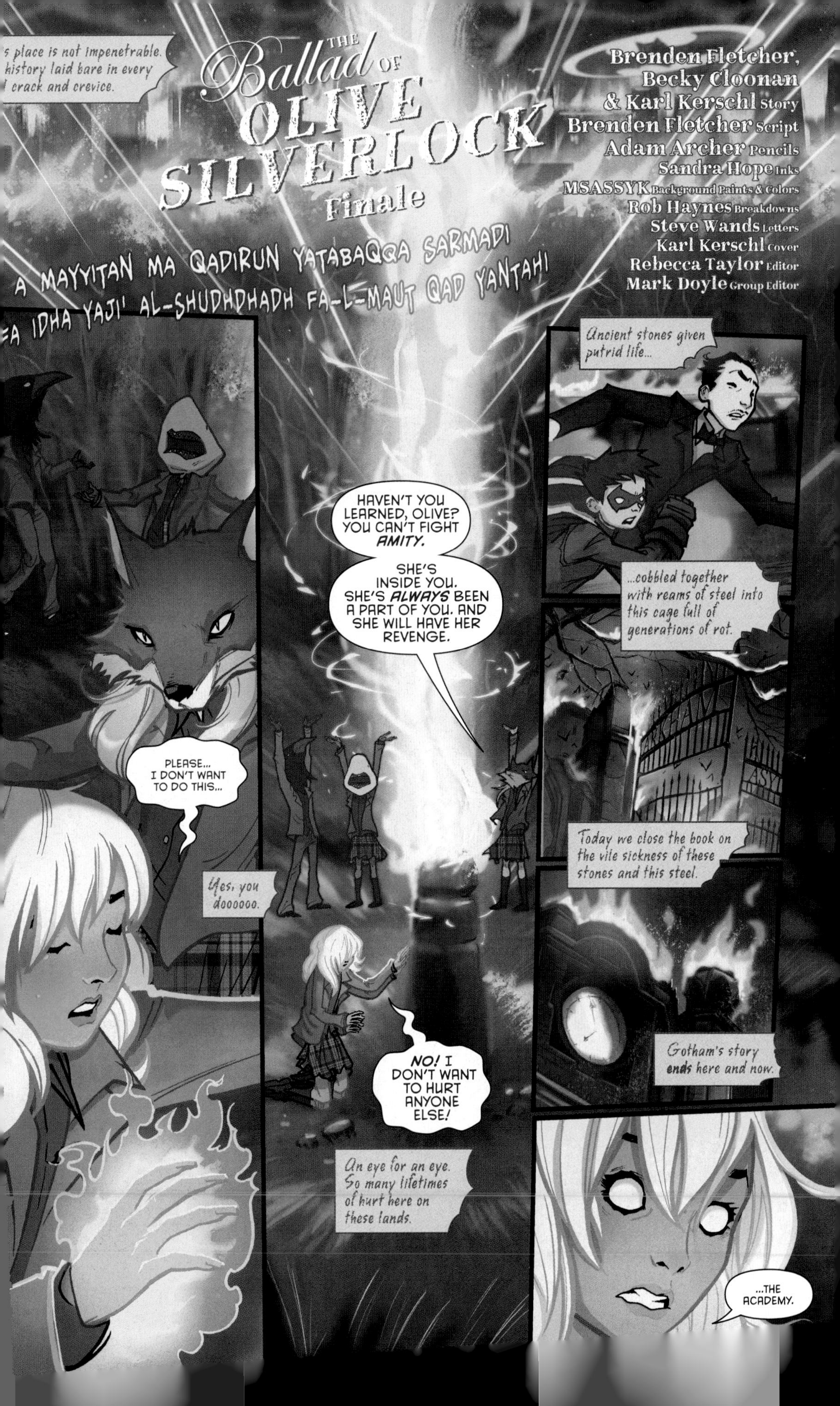

...s place is not impenetrable. ...history laid bare in every ...crack and crevice.
THE Ballad OF OLIVE SILVERLOCK Finale
Brenden Fletcher, Becky Cloonan & Karl Kerschl Story
Brenden Fletcher Script
Adam Archer Pencils
Sandra Hope Inks
MSASSYK Background Paints & Colors
Rob Haynes Breakdowns
Steve Wands Letters
Karl Kerschl Cover
Rebecca Taylor Editor
Mark Doyle Group Editor
A MAYYITAN MA QADIRUN YATABAQQA SARMADI
FA IDHA YAJI' AL-SHUDHDHADH FA-L-MAUT QAD YANTAHI
PLEASE... I DON'T WANT TO DO THIS...
Yes, you doooooo.
HAVEN'T YOU LEARNED, OLIVE? YOU CAN'T FIGHT AMITY.
SHE'S INSIDE YOU. SHE'S ALWAYS BEEN A PART OF YOU. AND SHE WILL HAVE HER REVENGE.
NO! I DON'T WANT TO HURT ANYONE ELSE!
An eye for an eye. So many lifetimes of hurt here on these lands.
Ancient stones given putrid life...
...cobbled together with reams of steel into this cage full of generations of rot.
Today we close the book on the vile sickness of these stones and this steel.
Gotham's story ends here and now.
...THE ACADEMY.

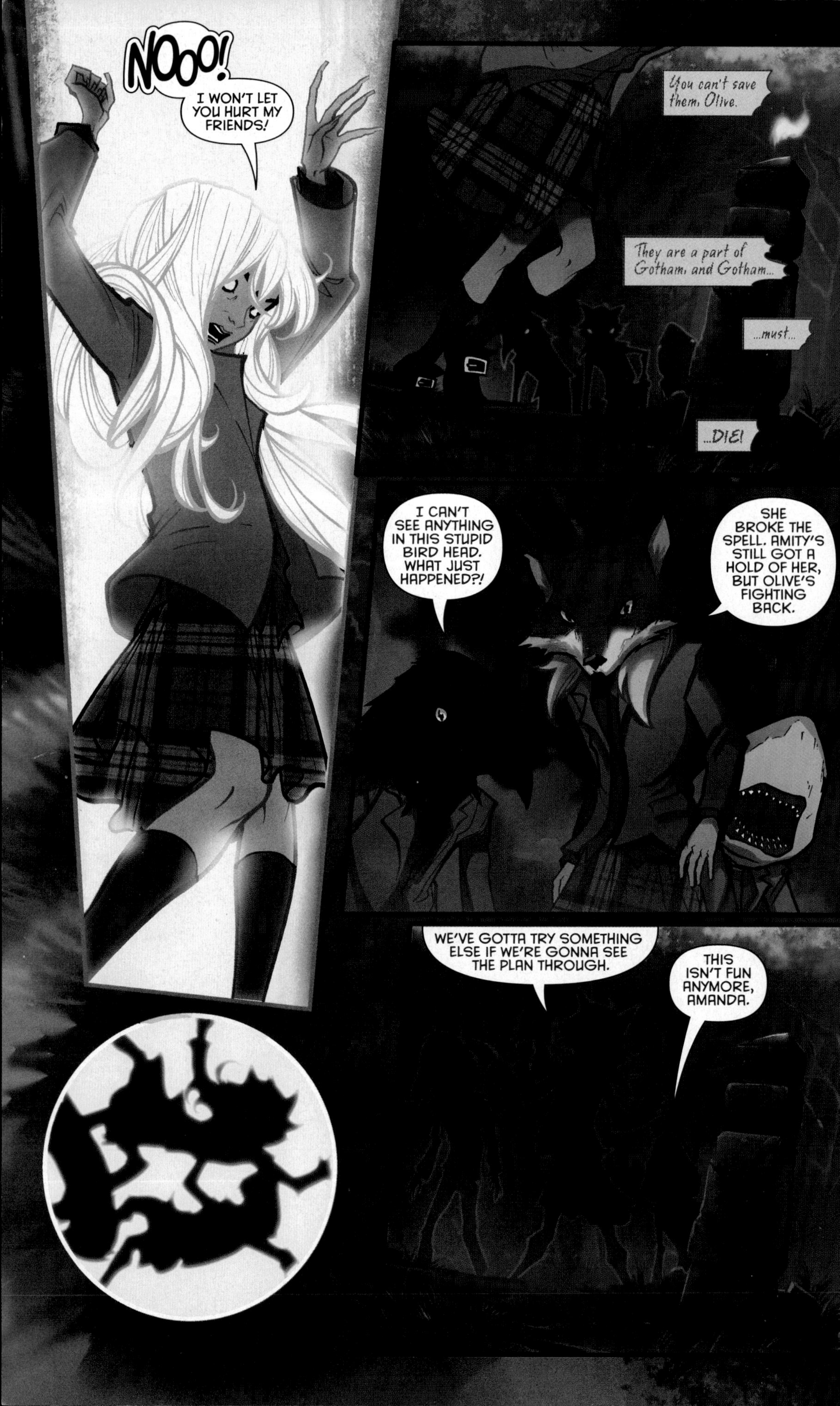
NOOO!
I WON'T LET YOU HURT MY FRIENDS!
You can't save them, Olive.
They are a part of Gotham, and Gotham...
...must...
...DIE!
I CAN'T SEE ANYTHING IN THIS STUPID BIRD HEAD. WHAT JUST HAPPENED?!
SHE BROKE THE SPELL. AMITY'S STILL GOT A HOLD OF HER, BUT OLIVE'S FIGHTING BACK.
WE'VE GOTTA TRY SOMETHING ELSE IF WE'RE GONNA SEE THE PLAN THROUGH.
THIS ISN'T FUN ANYMORE, AMANDA.

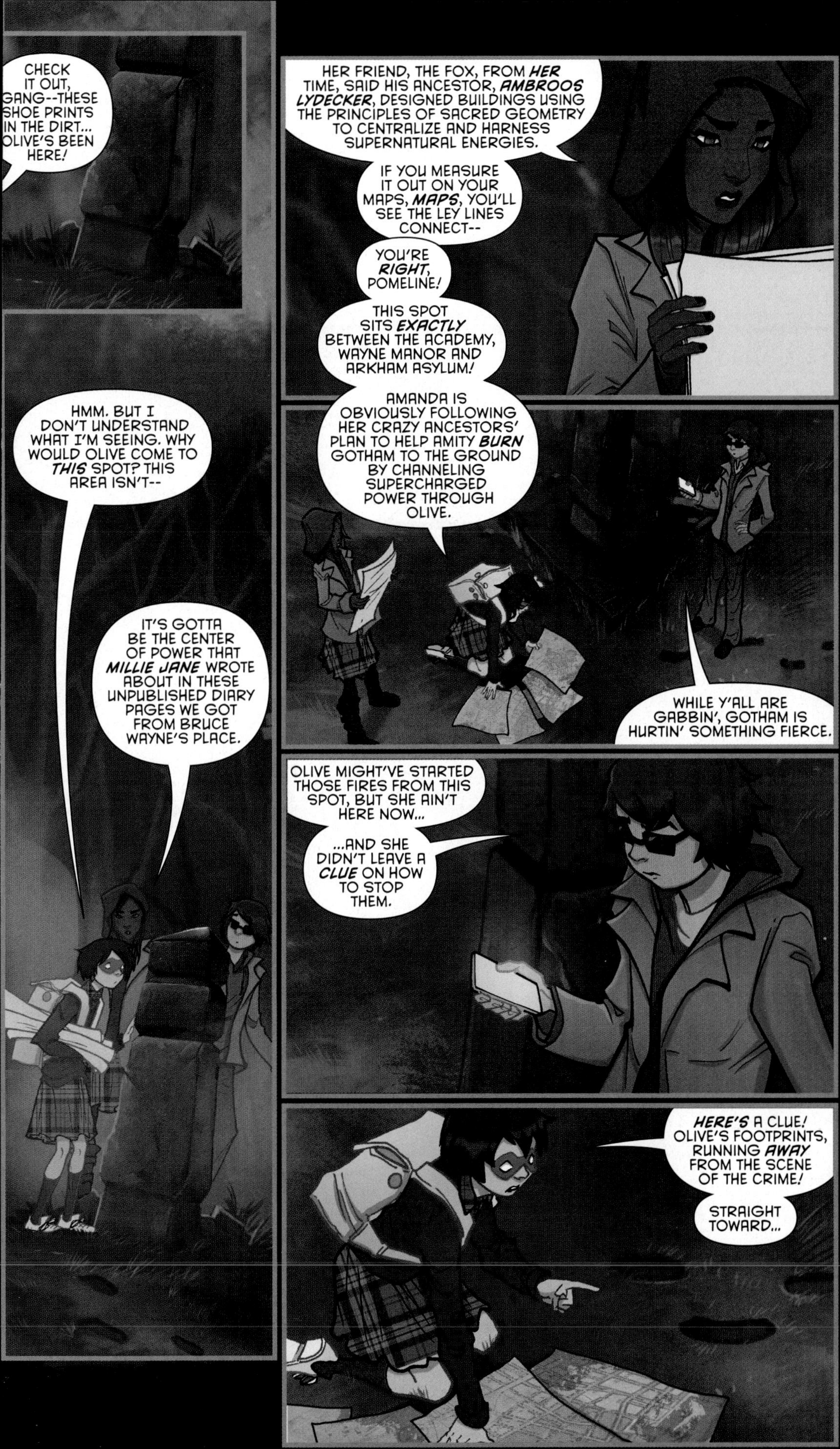
CHECK IT OUT, GANG--THESE SHOE PRINTS IN THE DIRT... OLIVE'S BEEN HERE!
HER FRIEND, THE FOX, FROM HER TIME, SAID HIS ANCESTOR, AMBROOS LYDECKER, DESIGNED BUILDINGS USING THE PRINCIPLES OF SACRED GEOMETRY TO CENTRALIZE AND HARNESS SUPERNATURAL ENERGIES.
IF YOU MEASURE IT OUT ON YOUR MAPS, MAPS, YOU'LL SEE THE LEY LINES CONNECT--
YOU'RE RIGHT, POMELINE!
THIS SPOT SITS EXACTLY BETWEEN THE ACADEMY, WAYNE MANOR AND ARKHAM ASYLUM!
HMM. BUT I DON'T UNDERSTAND WHAT I'M SEEING. WHY WOULD OLIVE COME TO THIS SPOT? THIS AREA ISN'T--
IT'S GOTTA BE THE CENTER OF POWER THAT MILLIE JANE WROTE ABOUT IN THESE UNPUBLISHED DIARY PAGES WE GOT FROM BRUCE WAYNE'S PLACE.
AMANDA IS OBVIOUSLY FOLLOWING HER CRAZY ANCESTORS' PLAN TO HELP AMITY BURN GOTHAM TO THE GROUND BY CHANNELING SUPERCHARGED POWER THROUGH OLIVE.
WHILE Y'ALL ARE GABBIN', GOTHAM IS HURTIN' SOMETHING FIERCE.
OLIVE MIGHT'VE STARTED THOSE FIRES FROM THIS SPOT, BUT SHE AIN'T HERE NOW...
...AND SHE DIDN'T LEAVE A CLUE ON HOW TO STOP THEM.
HERE'S A CLUE! OLIVE'S FOOTPRINTS, RUNNING AWAY FROM THE SCENE OF THE CRIME!
STRAIGHT TOWARD...

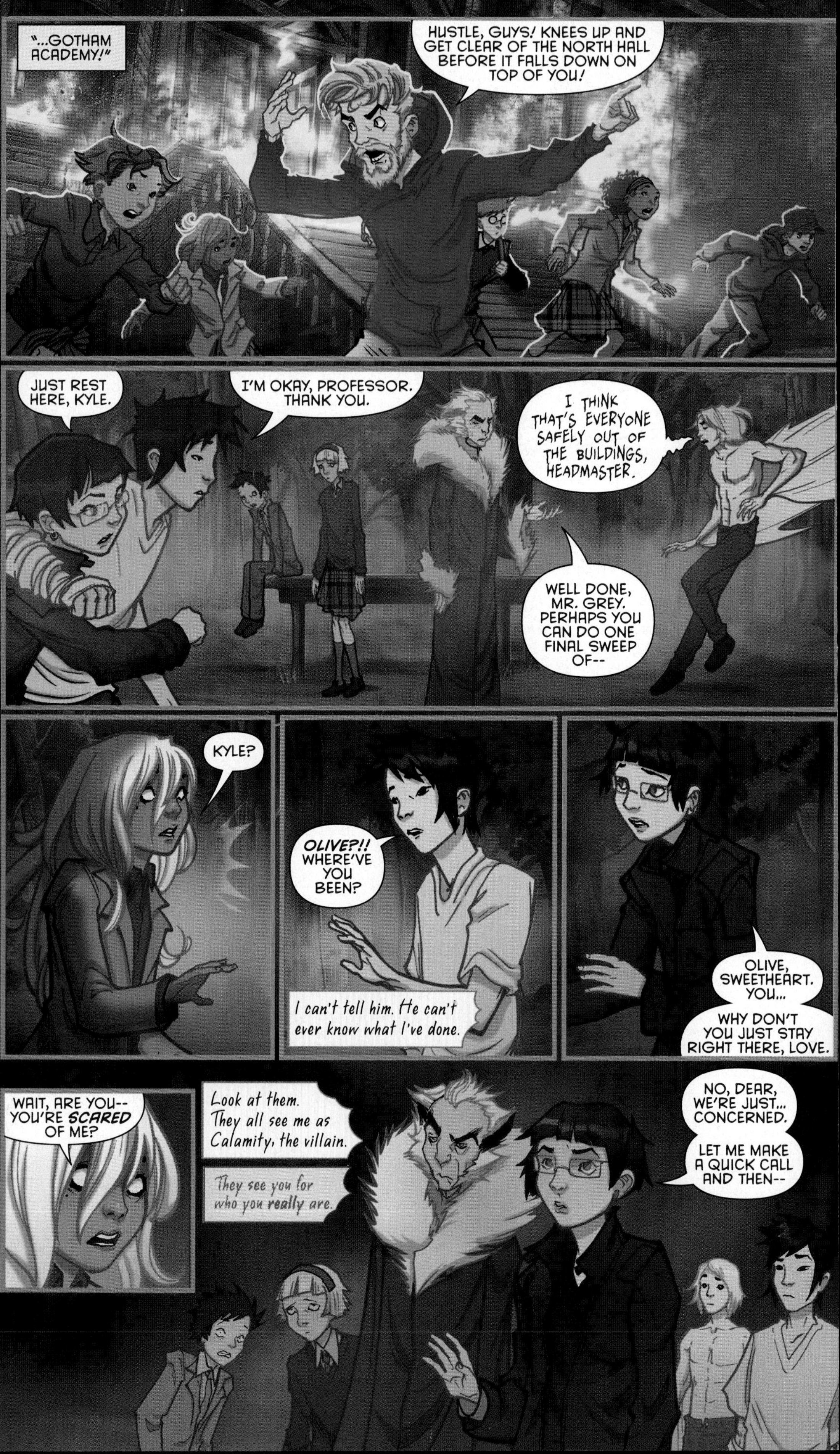
"...GOTHAM ACADEMY!"
HUSTLE, GUYS! KNEES UP AND GET CLEAR OF THE NORTH HALL BEFORE IT FALLS DOWN ON TOP OF YOU!
JUST REST HERE, KYLE.
I'M OKAY, PROFESSOR. THANK YOU.
I THINK THAT'S EVERYONE SAFELY OUT OF THE BUILDINGS, HEADMASTER.
WELL DONE, MR. GREY. PERHAPS YOU CAN DO ONE FINAL SWEEP OF--
KYLE?
OLIVE?!! WHERE'VE YOU BEEN?
I can't tell him. He can't ever know what I've done.
OLIVE, SWEETHEART. YOU...
WHY DON'T YOU JUST STAY RIGHT THERE, LOVE.
WAIT, ARE YOU-- YOU'RE SCARED OF ME?
Look at them. They all see me as Calamity, the villain.
They see you for who you really are.
NO, DEAR, WE'RE JUST... CONCERNED.
LET ME MAKE A QUICK CALL AND THEN--

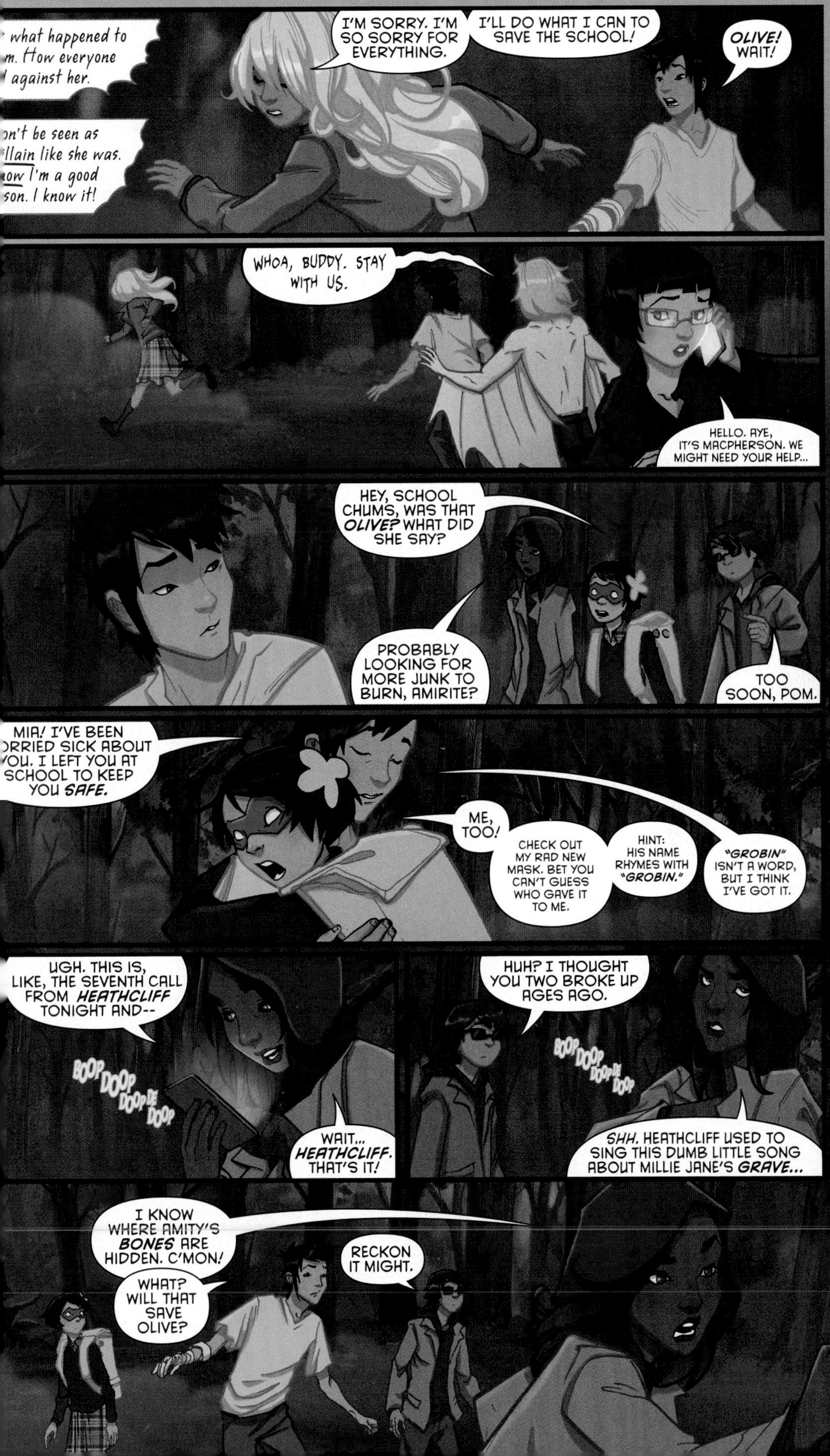

what happened to
m. How everyone
against her.
n't be seen as
llain like she was.
ow I'm a good
son. I know it!
I'M SORRY. I'M SO SORRY FOR EVERYTHING.
I'LL DO WHAT I CAN TO SAVE THE SCHOOL!
OLIVE! WAIT!
WHOA, BUDDY. STAY WITH US.
HELLO. AYE, IT'S MACPHERSON. WE MIGHT NEED YOUR HELP...
HEY, SCHOOL CHUMS, WAS THAT OLIVE? WHAT DID SHE SAY?
PROBABLY LOOKING FOR MORE JUNK TO BURN, AMIRITE?
TOO SOON, POM.
MIA! I'VE BEEN
RRIED SICK ABOUT
OU. I LEFT YOU AT SCHOOL TO KEEP YOU SAFE.
ME, TOO!
CHECK OUT MY RAD NEW MASK. BET YOU CAN'T GUESS WHO GAVE IT TO ME.
HINT: HIS NAME RHYMES WITH "GROBIN."
"GROBIN" ISN'T A WORD, BUT I THINK I'VE GOT IT.
UGH. THIS IS, LIKE, THE SEVENTH CALL FROM HEATHCLIFF TONIGHT AND--
BOOP DOOP DOOP DE DOOP
WAIT... HEATHCLIFF. THAT'S IT!
HUH? I THOUGHT YOU TWO BROKE UP AGES AGO.
BOOP DOOP DOOP DE DOOP
SHH. HEATHCLIFF USED TO SING THIS DUMB LITTLE SONG ABOUT MILLIE JANE'S GRAVE...
I KNOW WHERE AMITY'S BONES ARE HIDDEN. C'MON!
WHAT? WILL THAT SAVE OLIVE?
RECKON IT MIGHT.

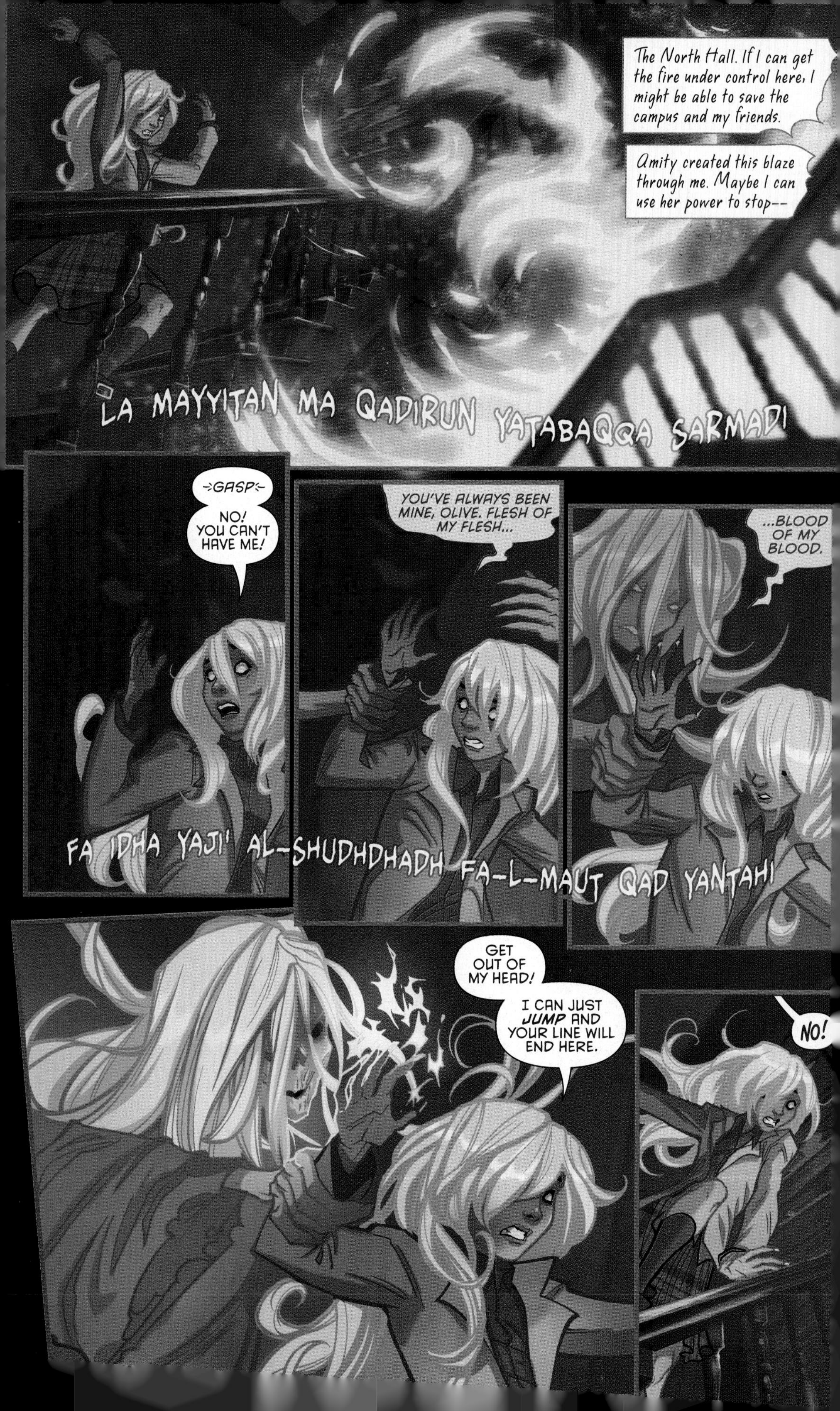

The North Hall. If I can get the fire under control here, I might be able to save the campus and my friends.
Amity created this blaze through me. Maybe I can use her power to stop--
LA MAYYITAN MA QADIRUN YATABAQQA SARMADI
-GASP-
NO! YOU CAN'T HAVE ME!
YOU'VE ALWAYS BEEN MINE, OLIVE. FLESH OF MY FLESH...
...BLOOD OF MY BLOOD.
FA IDHA YAJI' AL-SHUDHDHADH FA-L-MAUT QAD YANTAHI
GET OUT OF MY HEAD!
I CAN JUST JUMP AND YOUR LINE WILL END HERE.
NO!

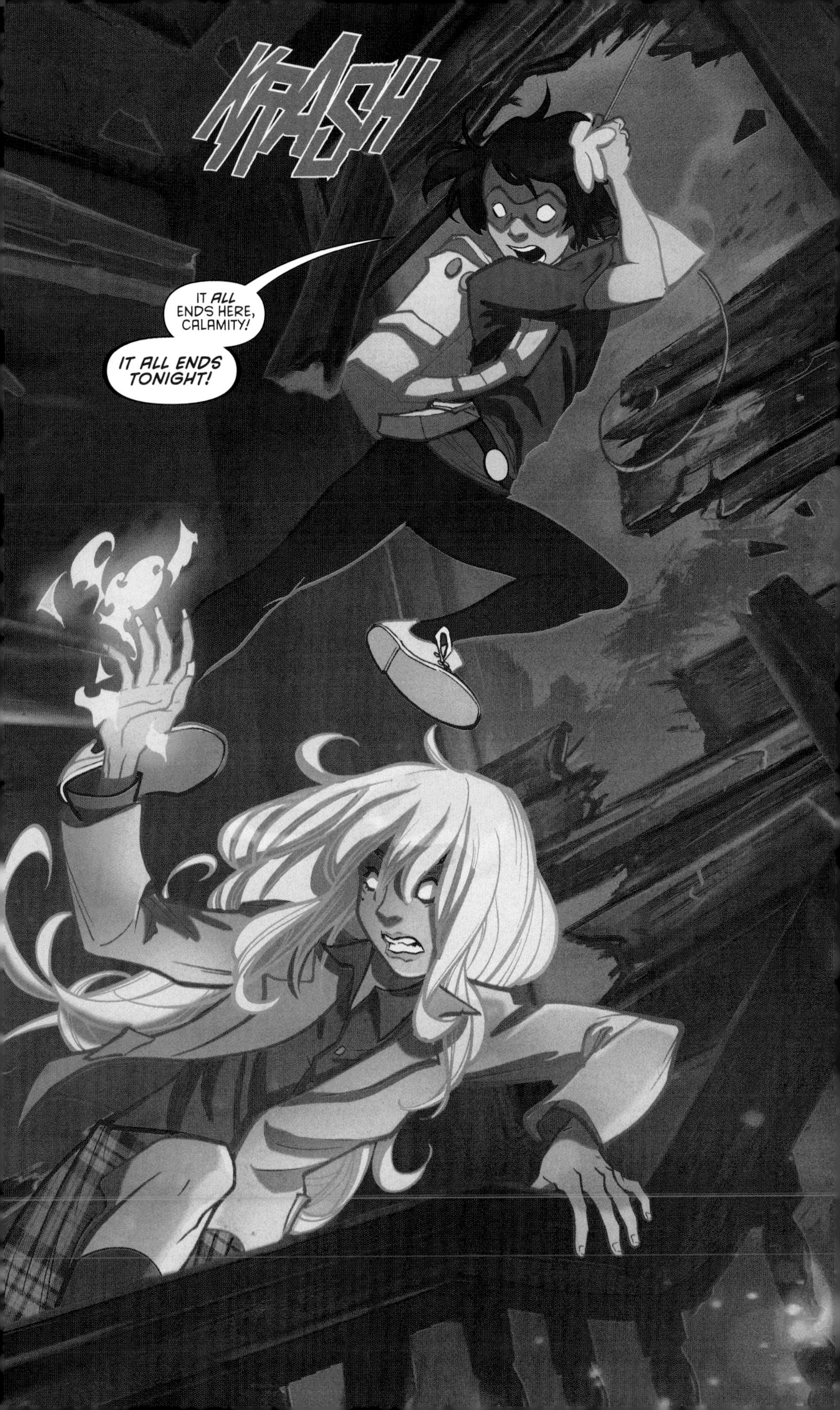
KRASH
IT ALL ENDS HERE, CALAMITY!
IT ALL ENDS TONIGHT!

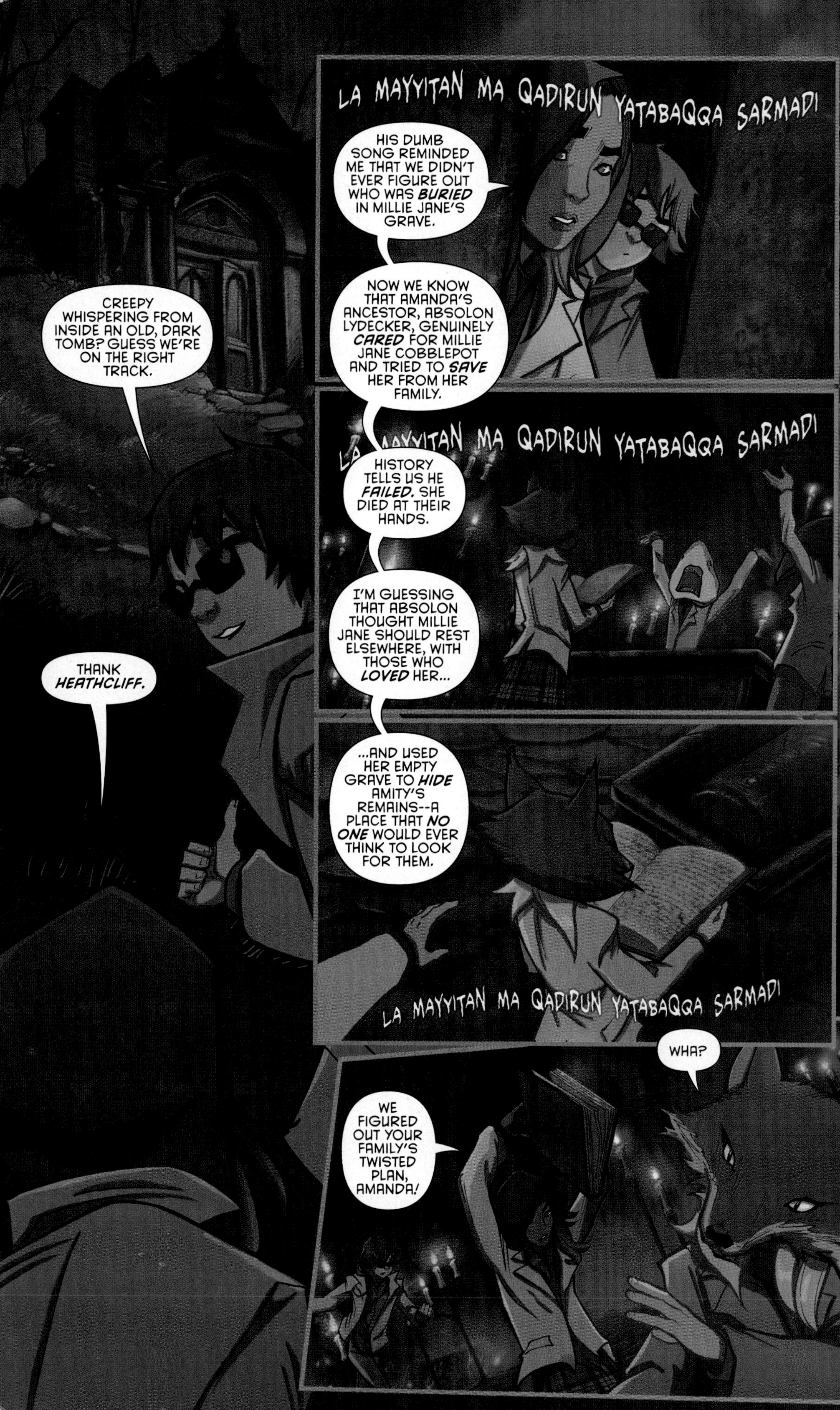

CREEPY WHISPERING FROM INSIDE AN OLD, DARK TOMB? GUESS WE'RE ON THE RIGHT TRACK.
THANK *HEATHCLIFF.*
LA MAYYITAN MA QADIRUN YATABAQQA SARMADI
HIS DUMB SONG REMINDED ME THAT WE DIDN'T EVER FIGURE OUT WHO WAS *BURIED* IN MILLIE JANE'S GRAVE.
NOW WE KNOW THAT AMANDA'S ANCESTOR, ABSOLON LYDECKER, GENUINELY *CARED* FOR MILLIE JANE COBBLEPOT AND TRIED TO *SAVE* HER FROM HER FAMILY.
LA MAYYITAN MA QADIRUN YATABAQQA SARMADI
HISTORY TELLS US HE *FAILED.* SHE DIED AT THEIR HANDS.
I'M GUESSING THAT ABSOLON THOUGHT MILLIE JANE SHOULD REST ELSEWHERE, WITH THOSE WHO *LOVED* HER...
...AND USED HER EMPTY GRAVE TO *HIDE* AMITY'S REMAINS--A PLACE THAT *NO ONE* WOULD EVER THINK TO LOOK FOR THEM.
LA MAYYITAN MA QADIRUN YATABAQQA SARMADI
WHA?
WE FIGURED OUT YOUR FAMILY'S TWISTED PLAN, AMANDA!

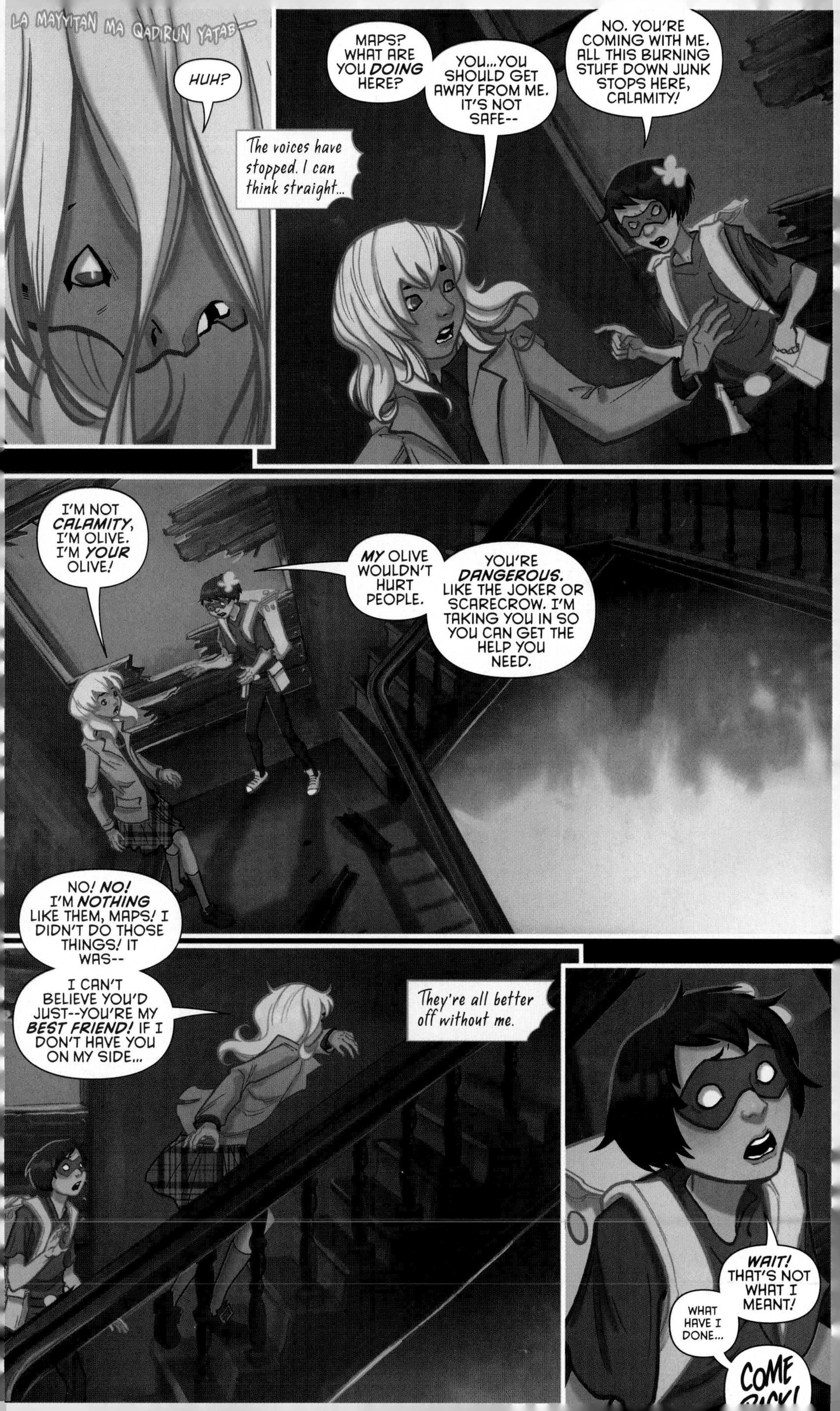
LA MAYYITAN MA QADIRUN YATAB--
HUH?
The voices have stopped. I can think straight...
MAPS? WHAT ARE YOU DOING HERE?
YOU...YOU SHOULD GET AWAY FROM ME. IT'S NOT SAFE--
NO. YOU'RE COMING WITH ME. ALL THIS BURNING STUFF DOWN JUNK STOPS HERE, CALAMITY!
I'M NOT CALAMITY, I'M OLIVE. I'M YOUR OLIVE!
MY OLIVE WOULDN'T HURT PEOPLE.
YOU'RE DANGEROUS. LIKE THE JOKER OR SCARECROW. I'M TAKING YOU IN SO YOU CAN GET THE HELP YOU NEED.
NO! NO! I'M NOTHING LIKE THEM, MAPS! I DIDN'T DO THOSE THINGS! IT WAS--
I CAN'T BELIEVE YOU'D JUST--YOU'RE MY BEST FRIEND! IF I DON'T HAVE YOU ON MY SIDE...
They're all better off without me.
WAIT! THAT'S NOT WHAT I MEANT!
WHAT HAVE I DONE...

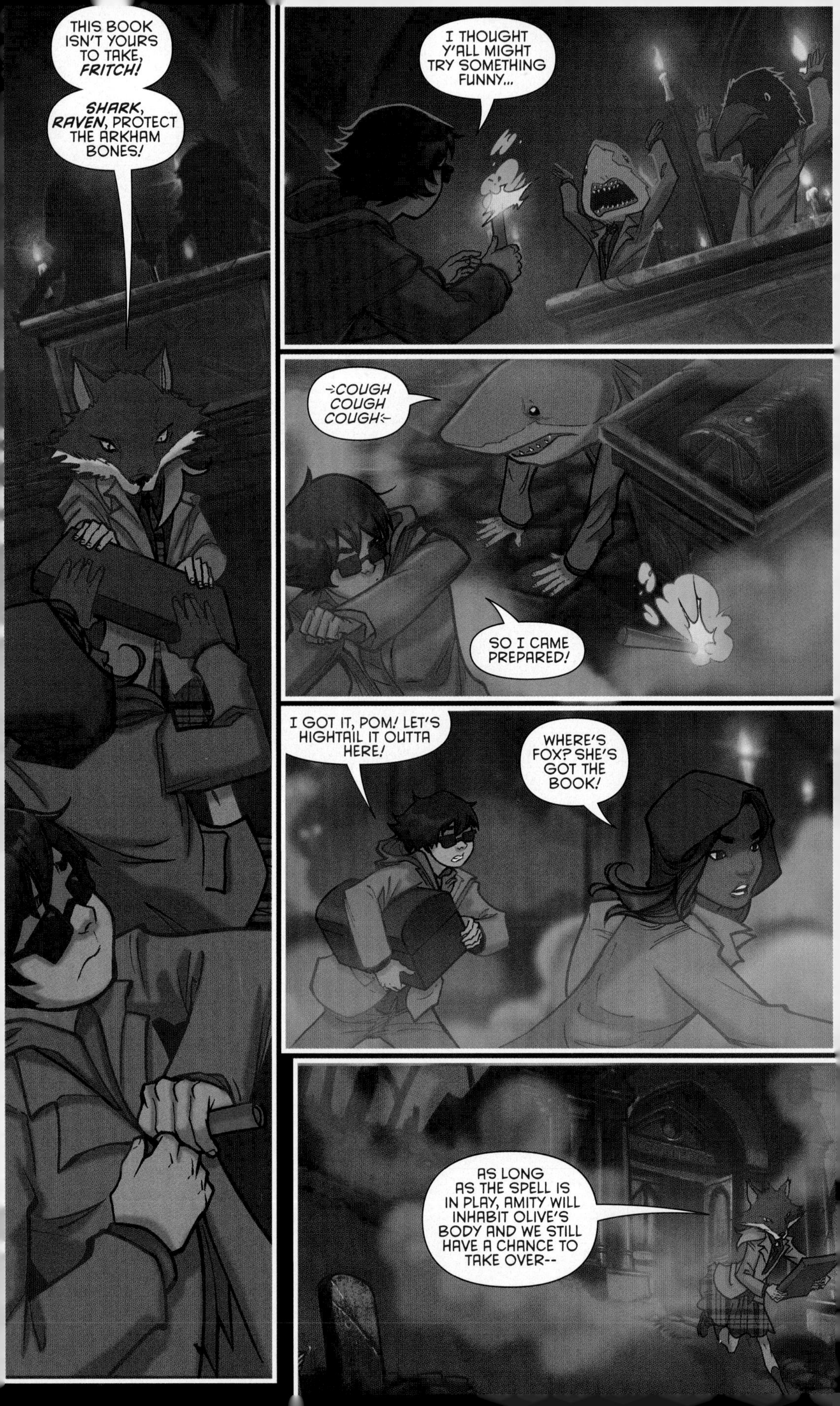

THIS BOOK ISN'T YOURS TO TAKE, *FRITCH!*
SHARK, RAVEN, PROTECT THE ARKHAM BONES!
I THOUGHT Y'ALL MIGHT TRY SOMETHING FUNNY...
-COUGH COUGH COUGH-
SO I CAME PREPARED!
I GOT IT, POM! LET'S HIGHTAIL IT OUTTA HERE!
WHERE'S FOX? SHE'S GOT THE BOOK!
AS LONG AS THE SPELL IS IN PLAY, AMITY WILL INHABIT OLIVE'S BODY AND WE STILL HAVE A CHANCE TO TAKE OVER--

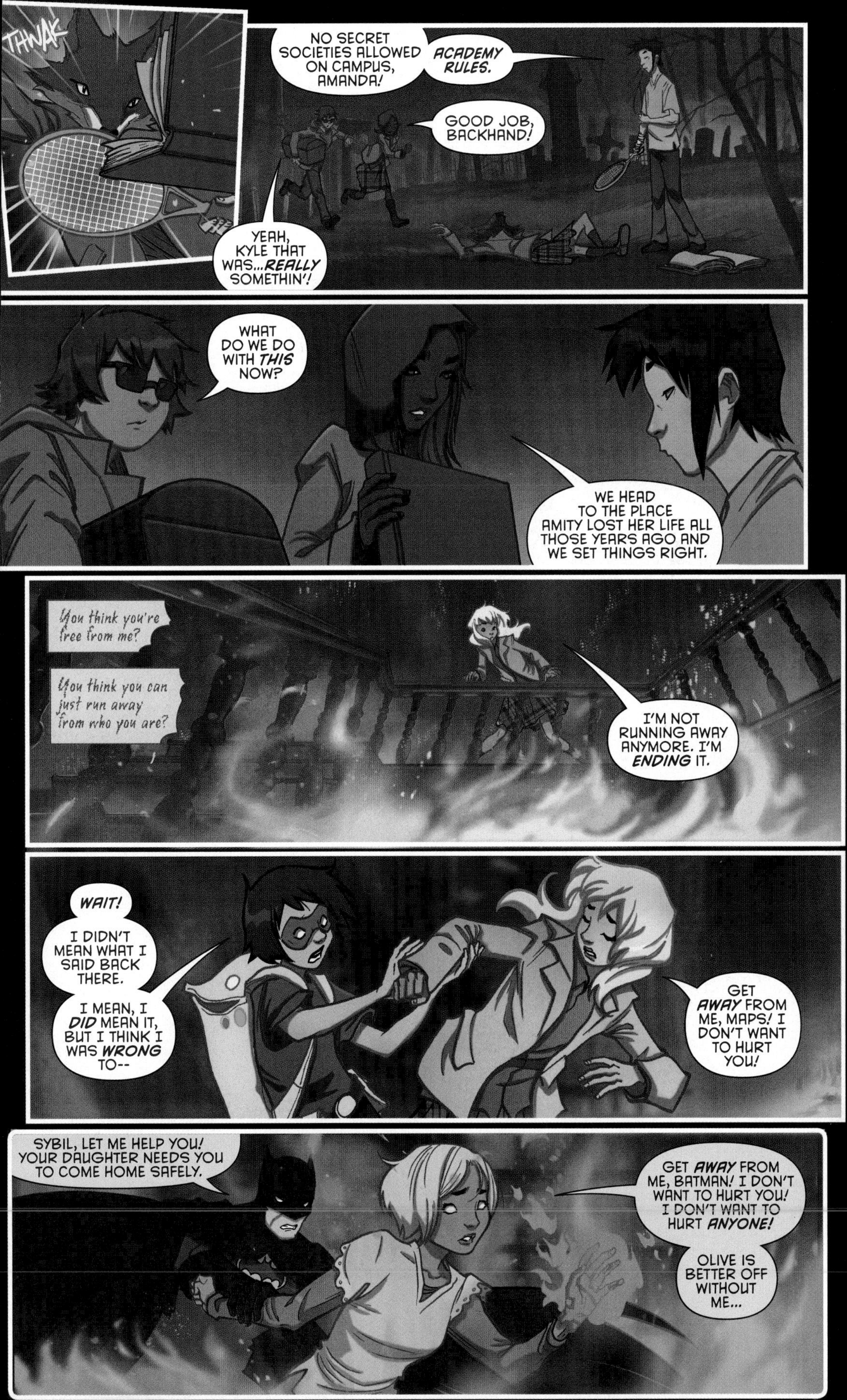
THWAK
NO SECRET SOCIETIES ALLOWED ON CAMPUS, AMANDA!
ACADEMY RULES.
GOOD JOB, BACKHAND!
YEAH, KYLE THAT WAS...REALLY SOMETHIN'!
WHAT DO WE DO WITH THIS NOW?
WE HEAD TO THE PLACE AMITY LOST HER LIFE ALL THOSE YEARS AGO AND WE SET THINGS RIGHT.
You think you're free from me?
You think you can just run away from who you are?
I'M NOT RUNNING AWAY ANYMORE. I'M ENDING IT.
WAIT!
I DIDN'T MEAN WHAT I SAID BACK THERE.
I MEAN, I DID MEAN IT, BUT I THINK I WAS WRONG TO--
GET AWAY FROM ME, MAPS! I DON'T WANT TO HURT YOU!
SYBIL, LET ME HELP YOU! YOUR DAUGHTER NEEDS YOU TO COME HOME SAFELY.
GET AWAY FROM ME, BATMAN! I DON'T WANT TO HURT YOU! I DON'T WANT TO HURT ANYONE!
OLIVE IS BETTER OFF WITHOUT ME...

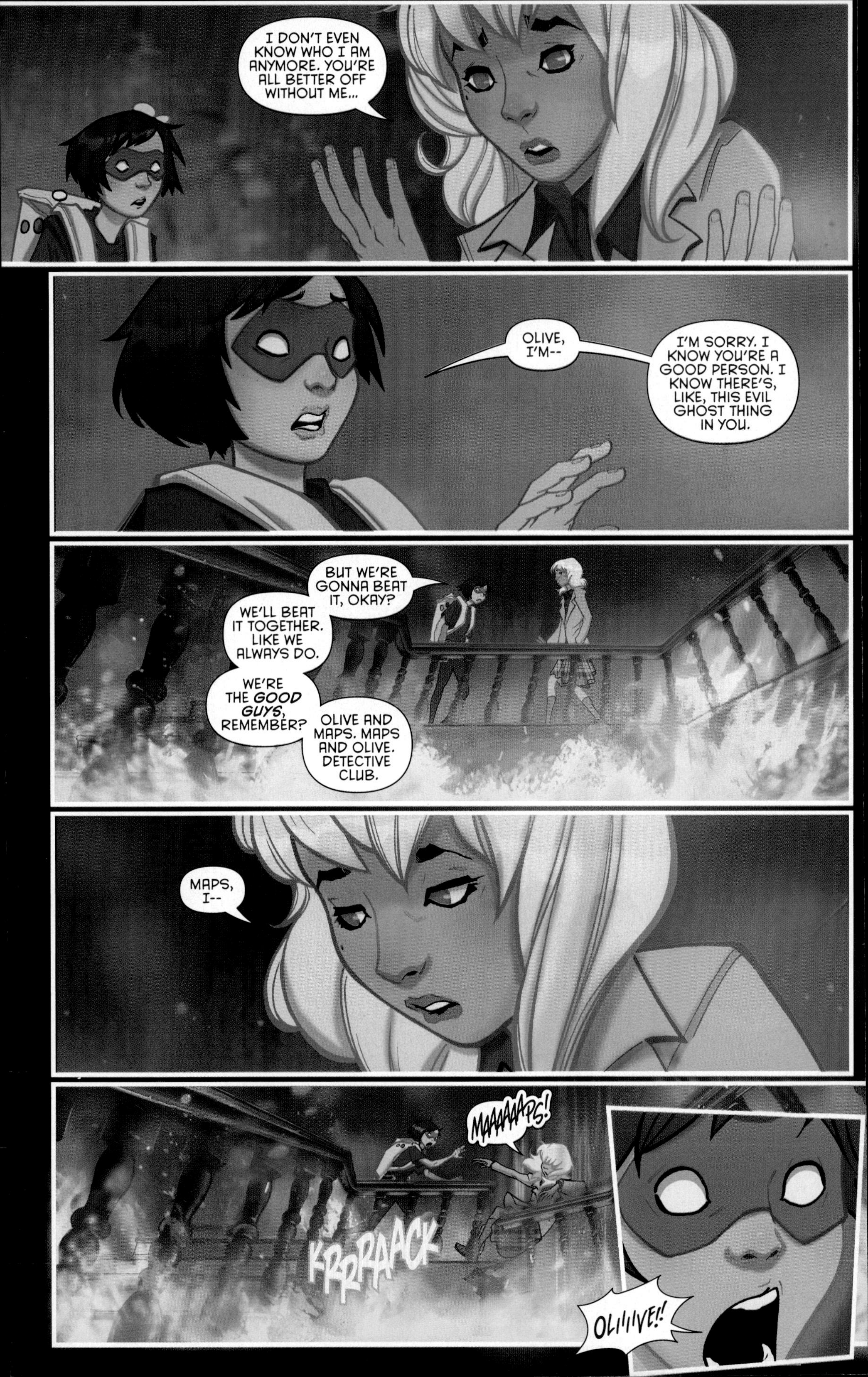
I DON'T EVEN KNOW WHO I AM ANYMORE. YOU'RE ALL BETTER OFF WITHOUT ME...
OLIVE, I'M--
I'M SORRY. I KNOW YOU'RE A GOOD PERSON. I KNOW THERE'S, LIKE, THIS EVIL GHOST THING IN YOU.
BUT WE'RE GONNA BEAT IT, OKAY?
WE'LL BEAT IT TOGETHER. LIKE WE ALWAYS DO.
WE'RE THE GOOD GUYS, REMEMBER?
OLIVE AND MAPS. MAPS AND OLIVE. DETECTIVE CLUB.
MAPS, I--
MAAAAAAPS!
KRRRAACK
OLIIIIVE!!

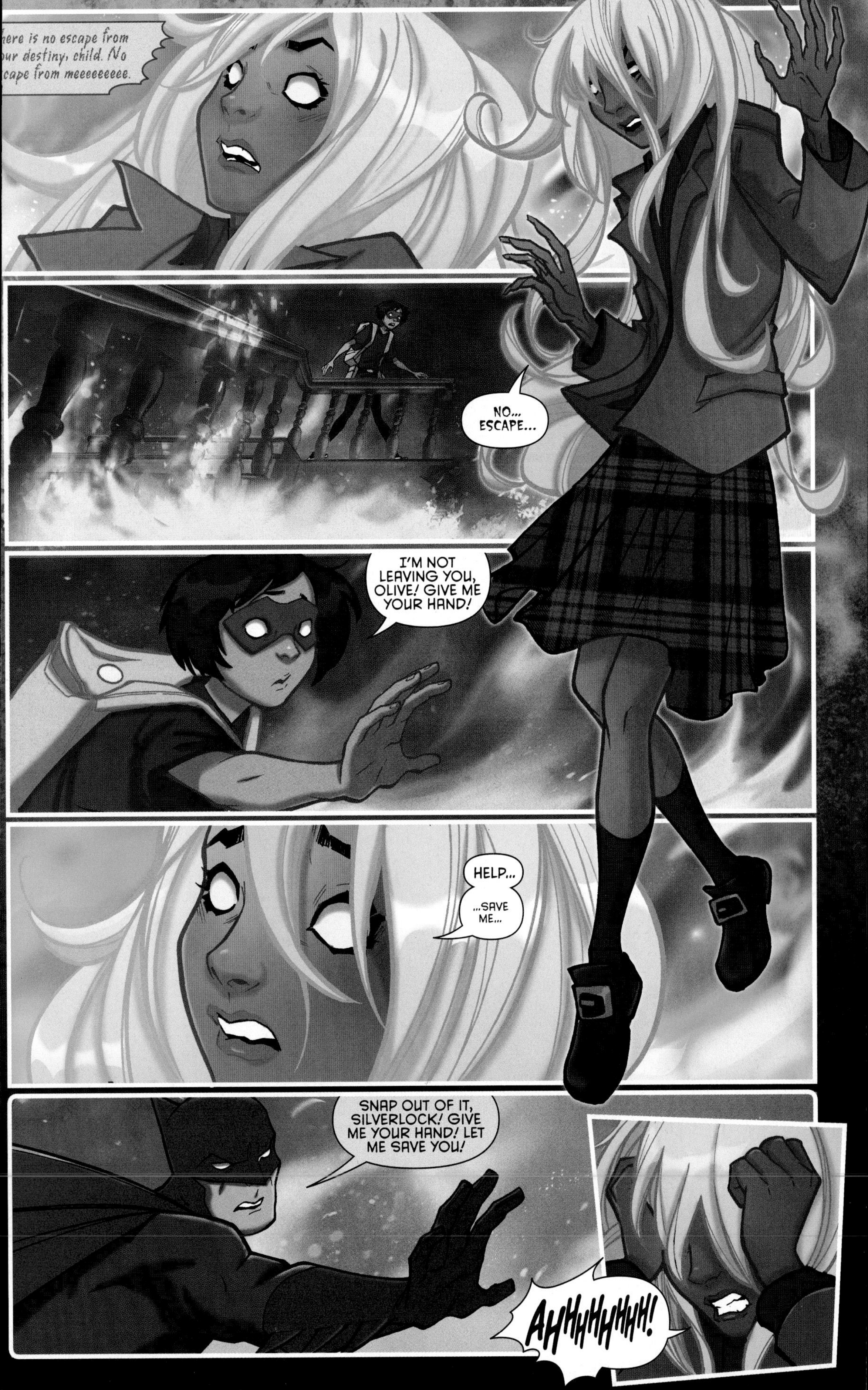
here is no escape from
our destiny, child. No
cape from meeeeeeeee.
NO... ESCAPE...
I'M NOT LEAVING YOU, OLIVE! GIVE ME YOUR HAND!
HELP...
...SAVE ME...
SNAP OUT OF IT, SILVERLOCK! GIVE ME YOUR HAND! LET ME SAVE YOU!
AHHHHHHHH!

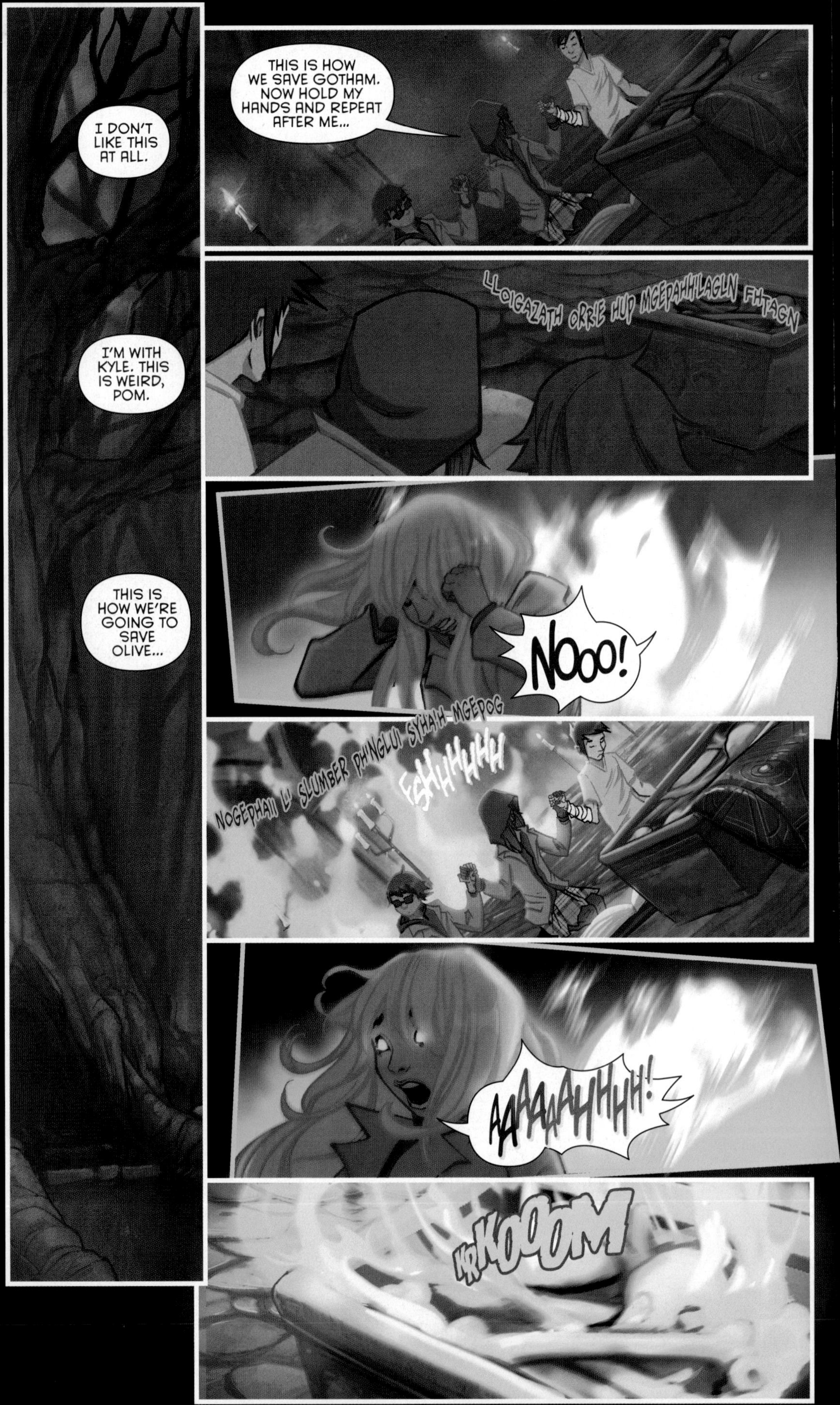
THIS IS HOW WE SAVE GOTHAM. NOW HOLD MY HANDS AND REPEAT AFTER ME...
I DON'T LIKE THIS AT ALL.
LLOIGAZATH ORR'E HUP MGEPAHH'LAGLN FHTAGN
I'M WITH KYLE. THIS IS WEIRD, POM.
NOOO!
THIS IS HOW WE'RE GOING TO SAVE OLIVE...
NOGEPHAII L'I SLUMBER PH'NGLUI SYHA'H MGEPOG
FSHHHHHH
AAAAAAHHHHH!
KRKOOOM

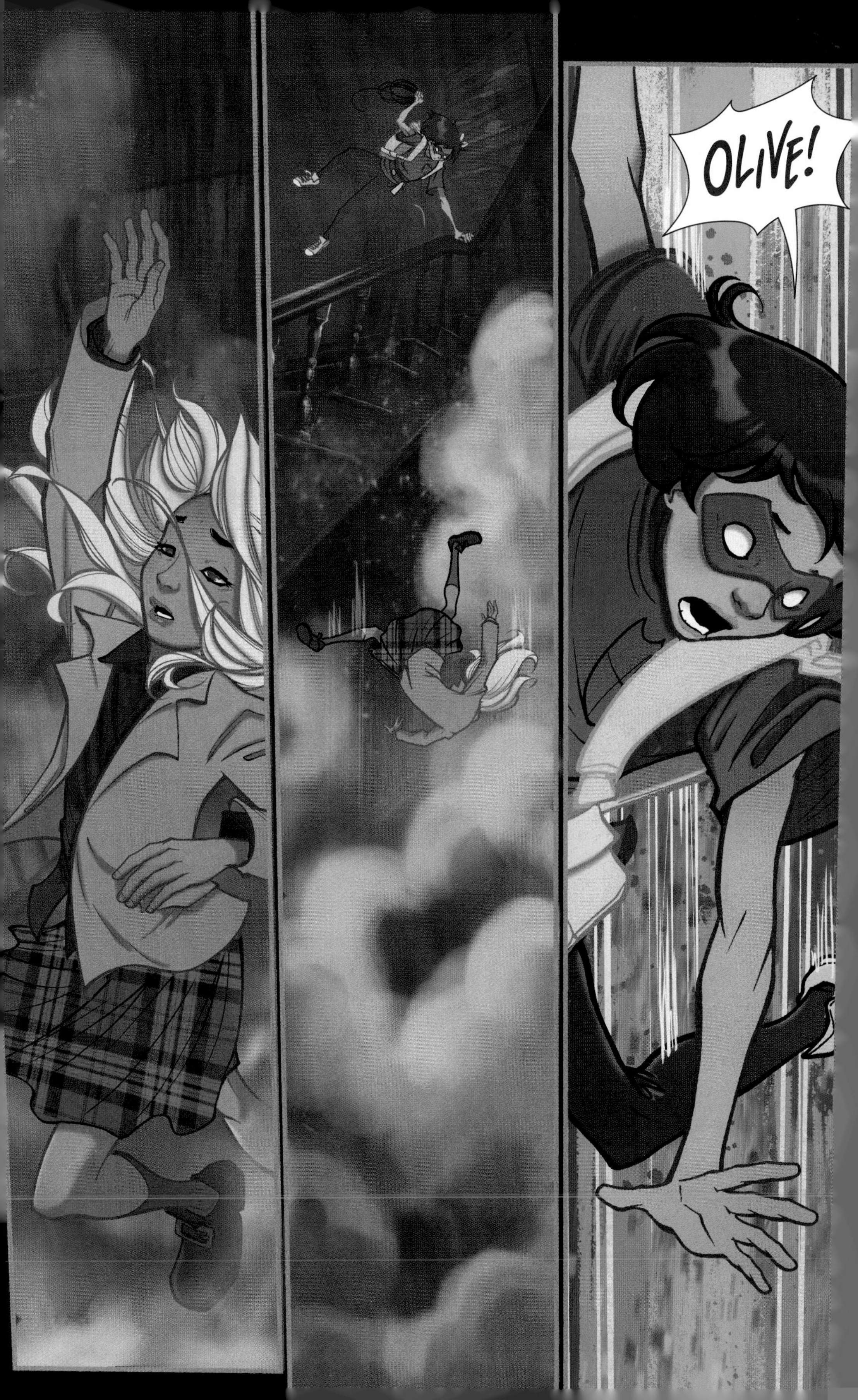
OLIVE!

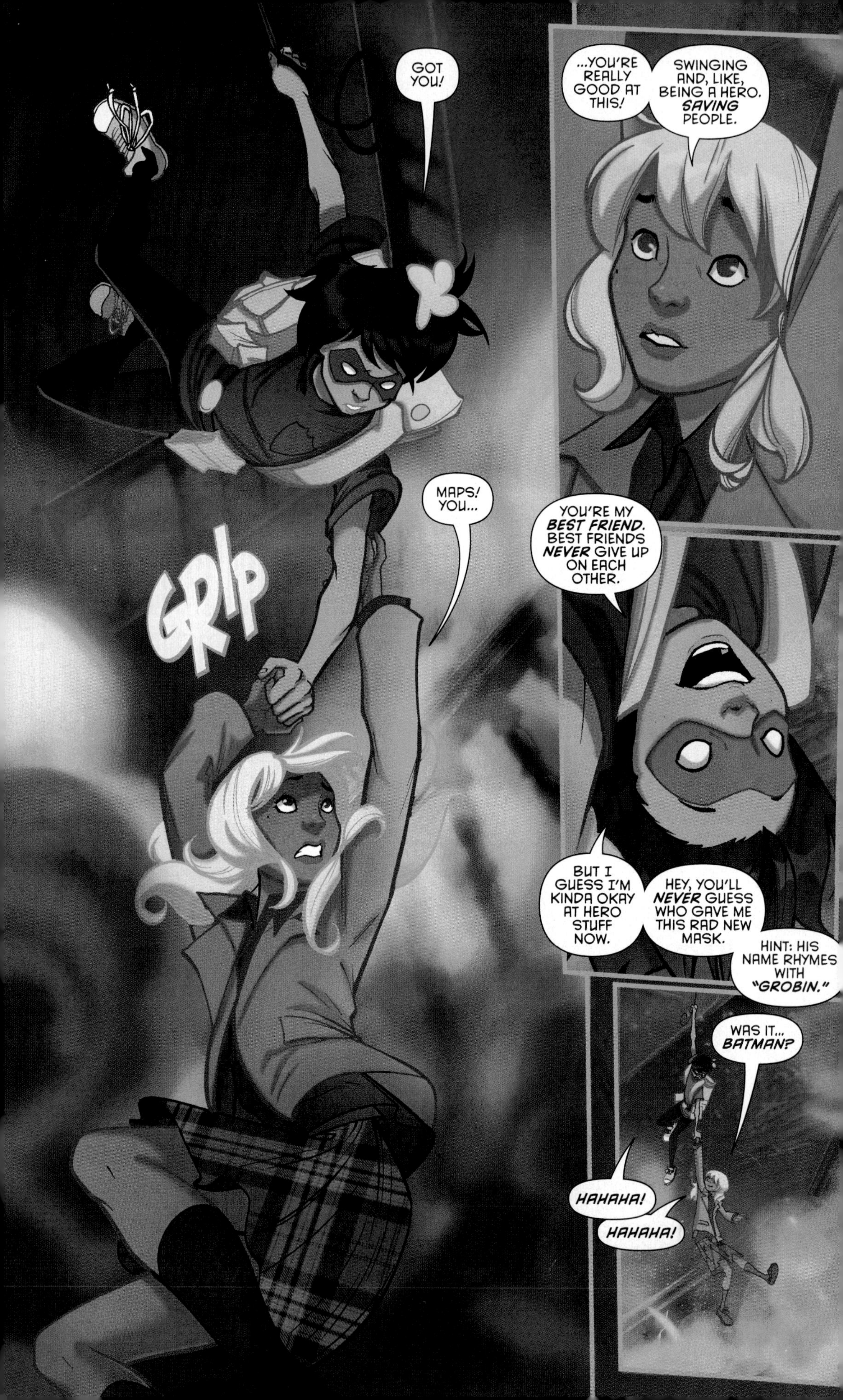
GOT YOU!
MAPS! YOU...
GRIP
...YOU'RE REALLY GOOD AT THIS!
SWINGING AND, LIKE, BEING A HERO. SAVING PEOPLE.
YOU'RE MY BEST FRIEND. BEST FRIENDS NEVER GIVE UP ON EACH OTHER.
BUT I GUESS I'M KINDA OKAY AT HERO STUFF NOW.
HEY, YOU'LL NEVER GUESS WHO GAVE ME THIS RAD NEW MASK.
HINT: HIS NAME RHYMES WITH "GROBIN."
WAS IT... BATMAN?
HAHAHA!
HAHAHA!

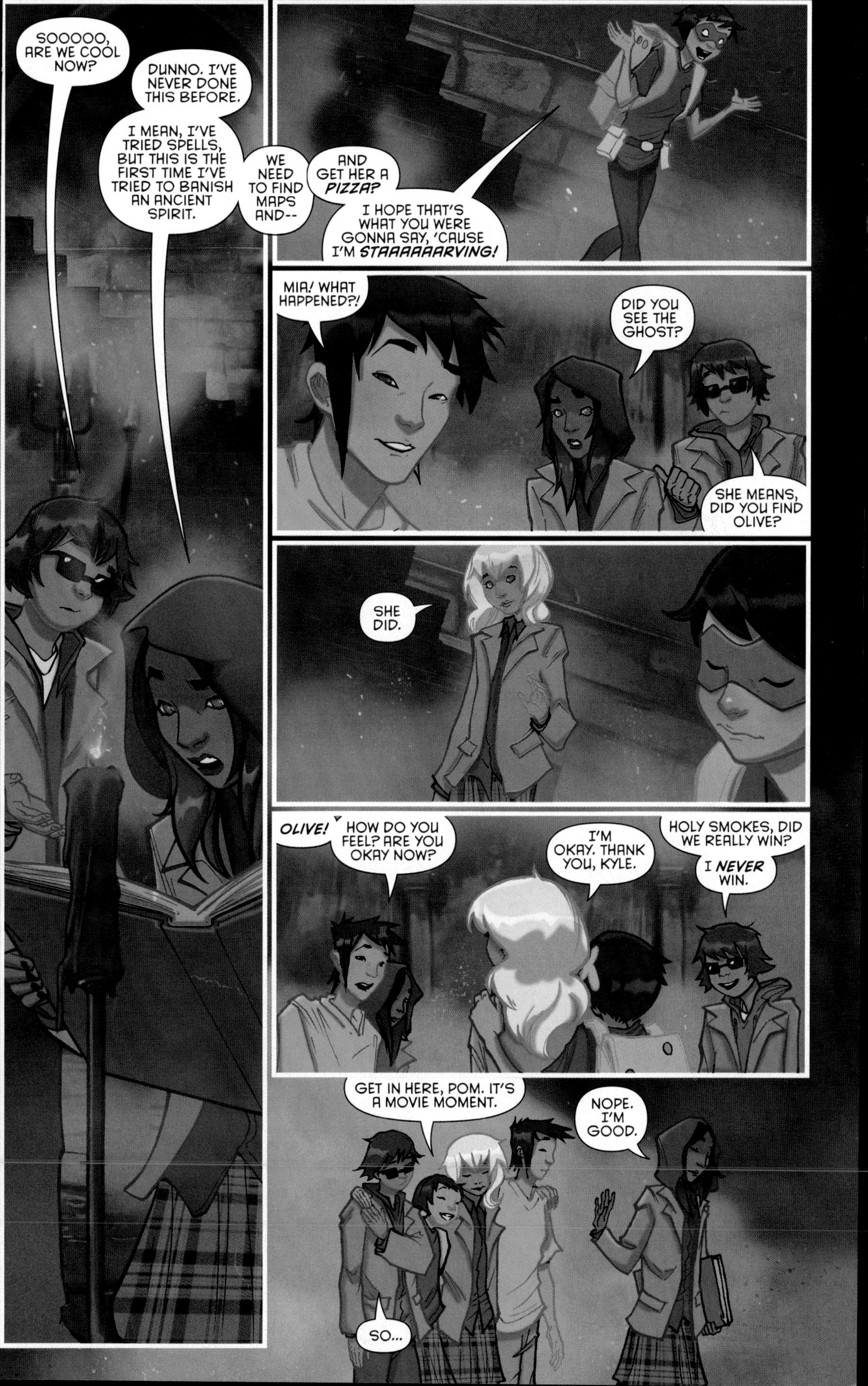
SOOOOO, ARE WE COOL NOW?
DUNNO. I'VE NEVER DONE THIS BEFORE.
I MEAN, I'VE TRIED SPELLS, BUT THIS IS THE FIRST TIME I'VE TRIED TO BANISH AN ANCIENT SPIRIT.
WE NEED TO FIND MAPS AND--
AND GET HER A *PIZZA?*
I HOPE THAT'S WHAT YOU WERE GONNA SAY, 'CAUSE I'M *STAAAAAARVING!*
MIA! WHAT HAPPENED?!
DID YOU SEE THE GHOST?
SHE MEANS, DID YOU FIND OLIVE?
SHE DID.
OLIVE!
HOW DO YOU FEEL? ARE YOU OKAY NOW?
I'M OKAY. THANK YOU, KYLE.
HOLY SMOKES, DID WE REALLY WIN?
I *NEVER* WIN.
GET IN HERE, POM. IT'S A MOVIE MOMENT.
NOPE. I'M GOOD.
SO...

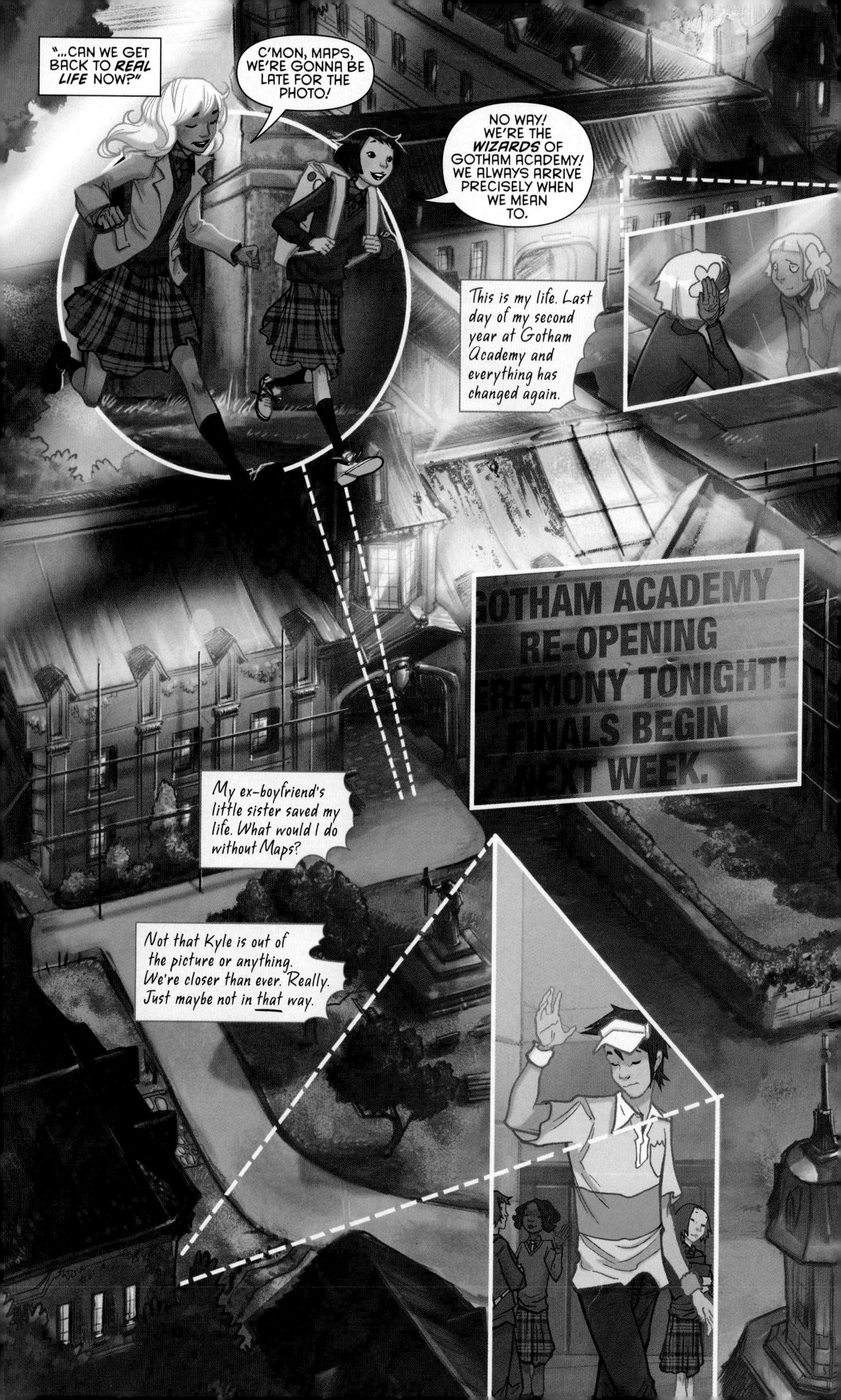
"...CAN WE GET BACK TO *REAL LIFE* NOW?"
C'MON, MAPS, WE'RE GONNA BE LATE FOR THE PHOTO!
NO WAY! WE'RE THE *WIZARDS* OF GOTHAM ACADEMY! WE ALWAYS ARRIVE PRECISELY WHEN WE MEAN TO.
This is my life. Last day of my second year at Gotham Academy and everything has changed again.
GOTHAM ACADEMY RE-OPENING CEREMONY TONIGHT! FINALS BEGIN NEXT WEEK.
My ex-boyfriend's little sister saved my life. What would I do without Maps?
Not that Kyle is out of the picture or anything. We're closer than ever. Really. Just maybe not in that way.

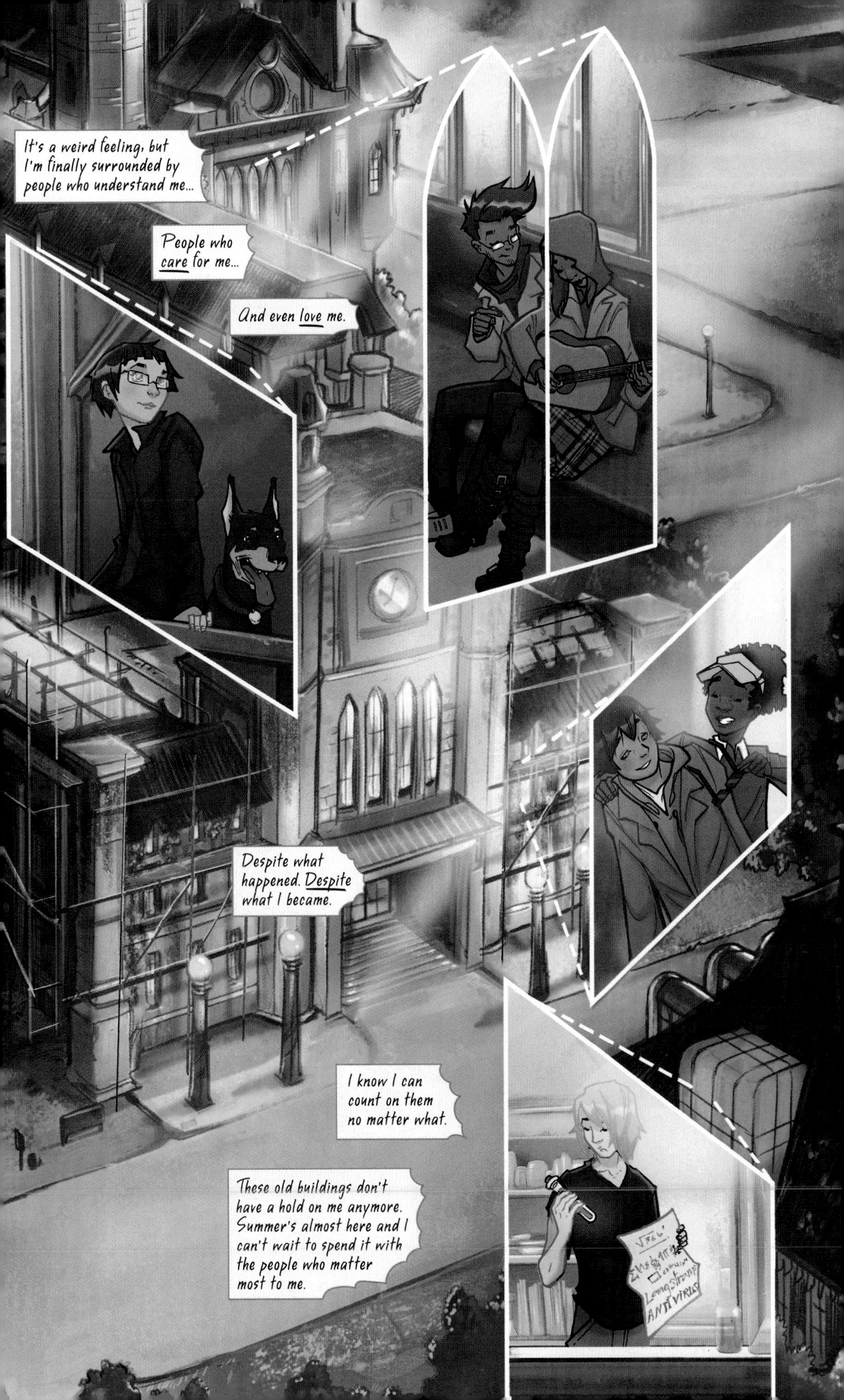
It's a weird feeling, but I'm finally surrounded by people who understand me...
People who care for me...
And even love me.
Despite what happened. Despite what I became.
I know I can count on them no matter what.
These old buildings don't have a hold on me anymore. Summer's almost here and I can't wait to spend it with the people who matter most to me.
Langstrom
ANTI VIRUS

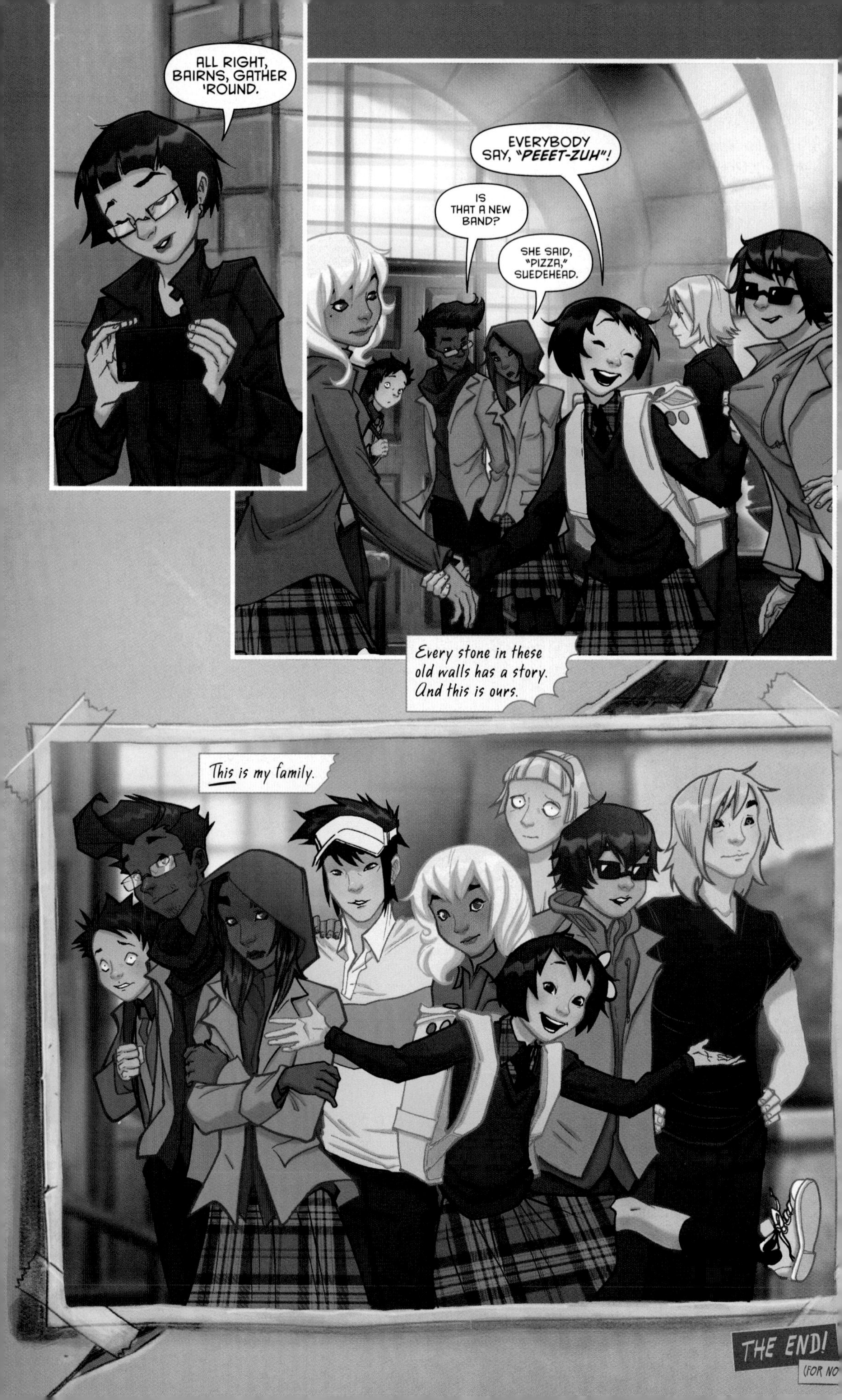
ALL RIGHT, BAIRNS, GATHER 'ROUND.
EVERYBODY SAY, "PEEET-ZUH"!
IS THAT A NEW BAND?
SHE SAID, "PIZZA," SUEDEHEAD.
Every stone in these old walls has a story. And this is ours.
This is my family.
THE END!
(FOR NO

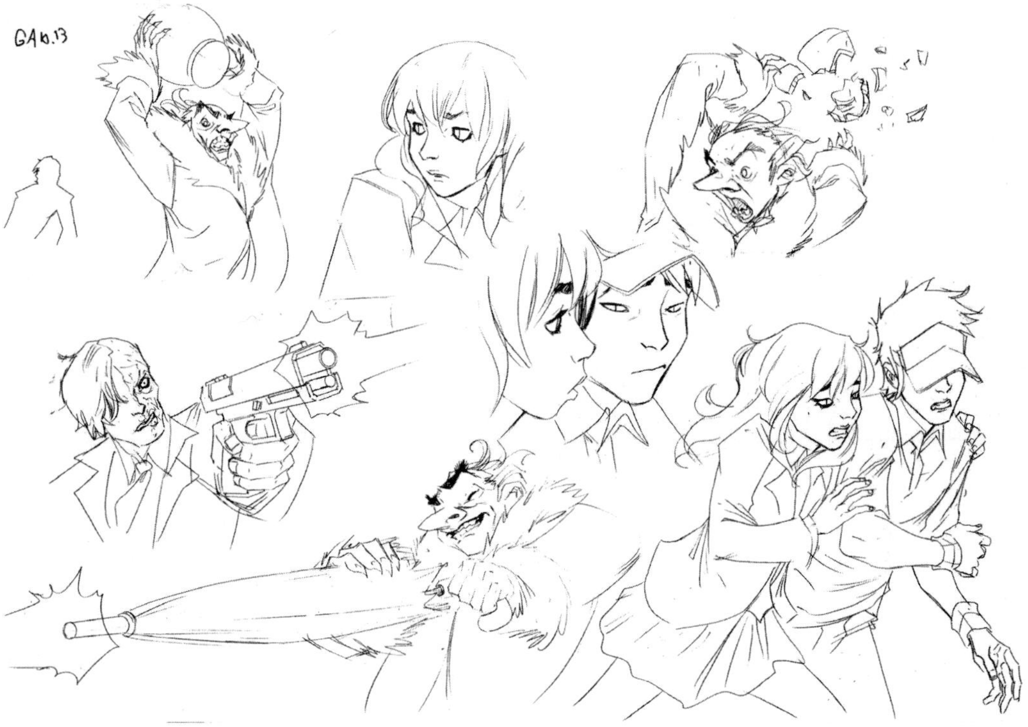
GA6.13

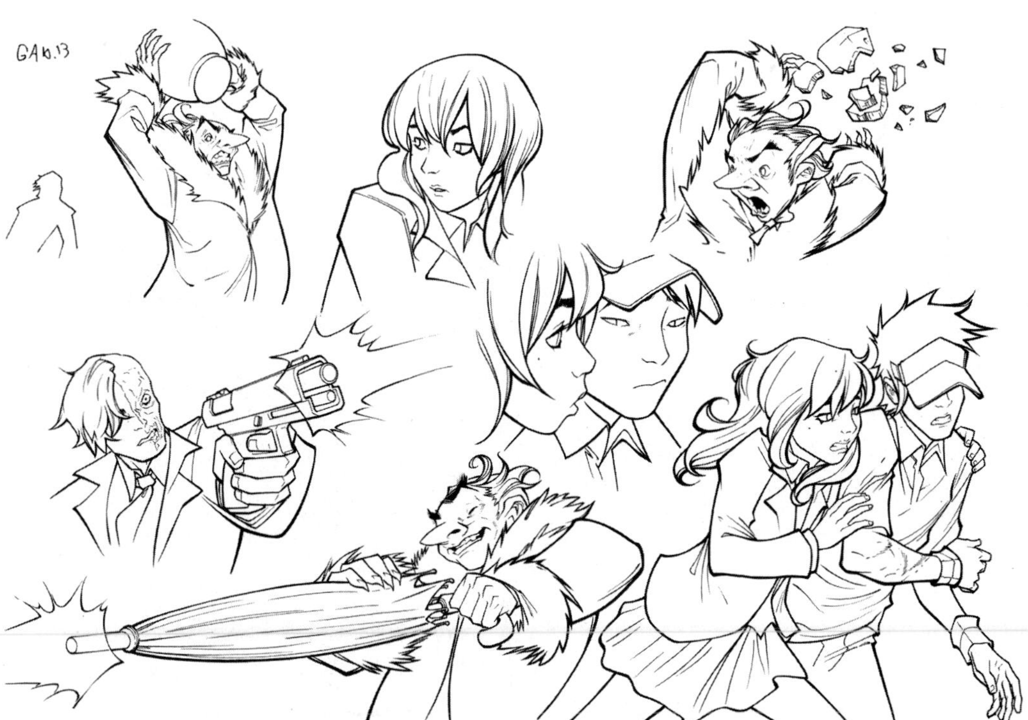
GA6.13

Pencils by **Adam Archer**, Inks by **Sandra Hope**

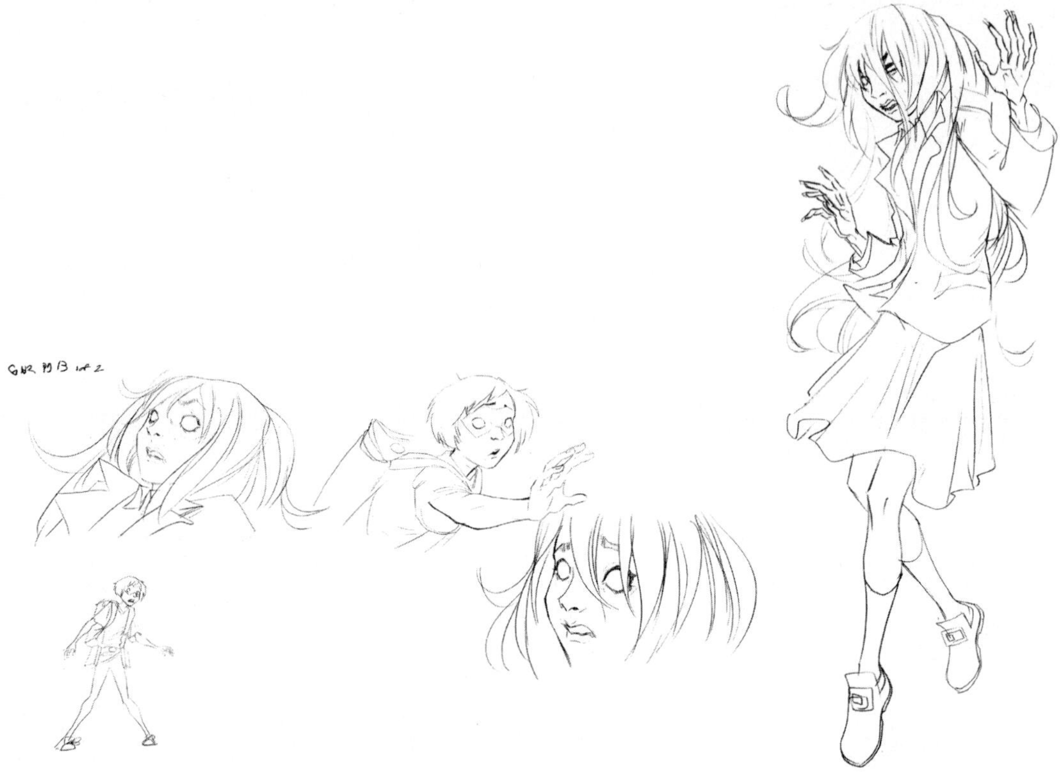

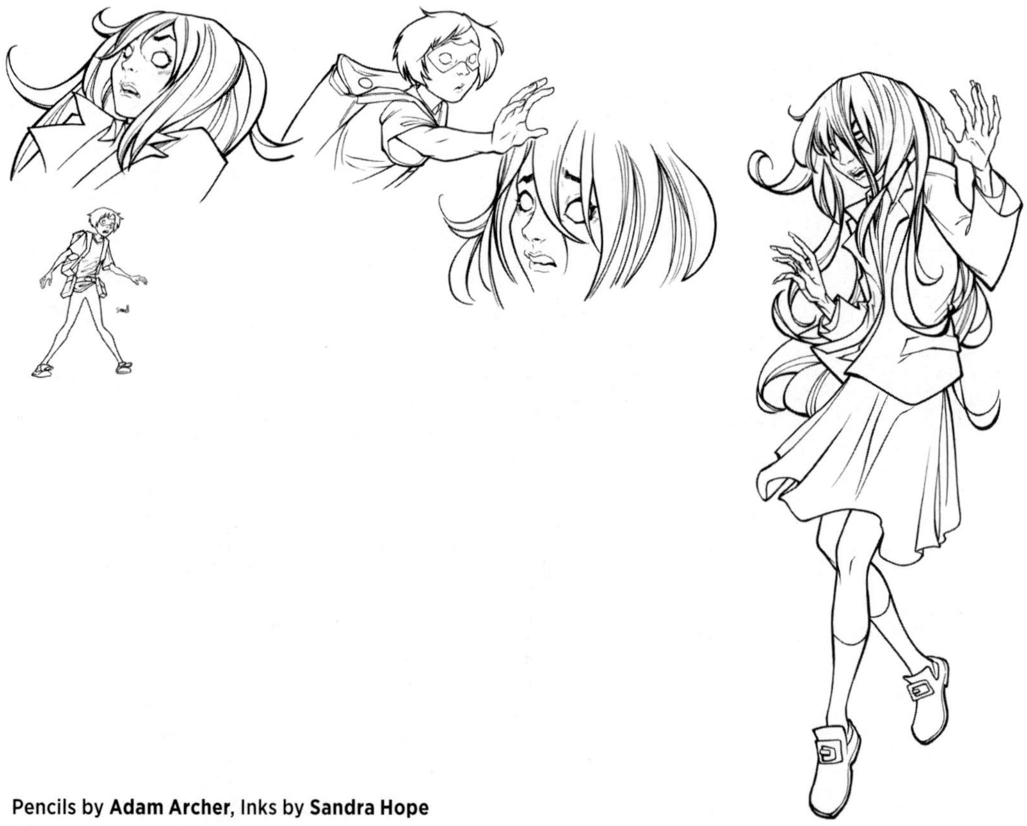

Pencils by **Adam Archer**, Inks by **Sandra Hope**

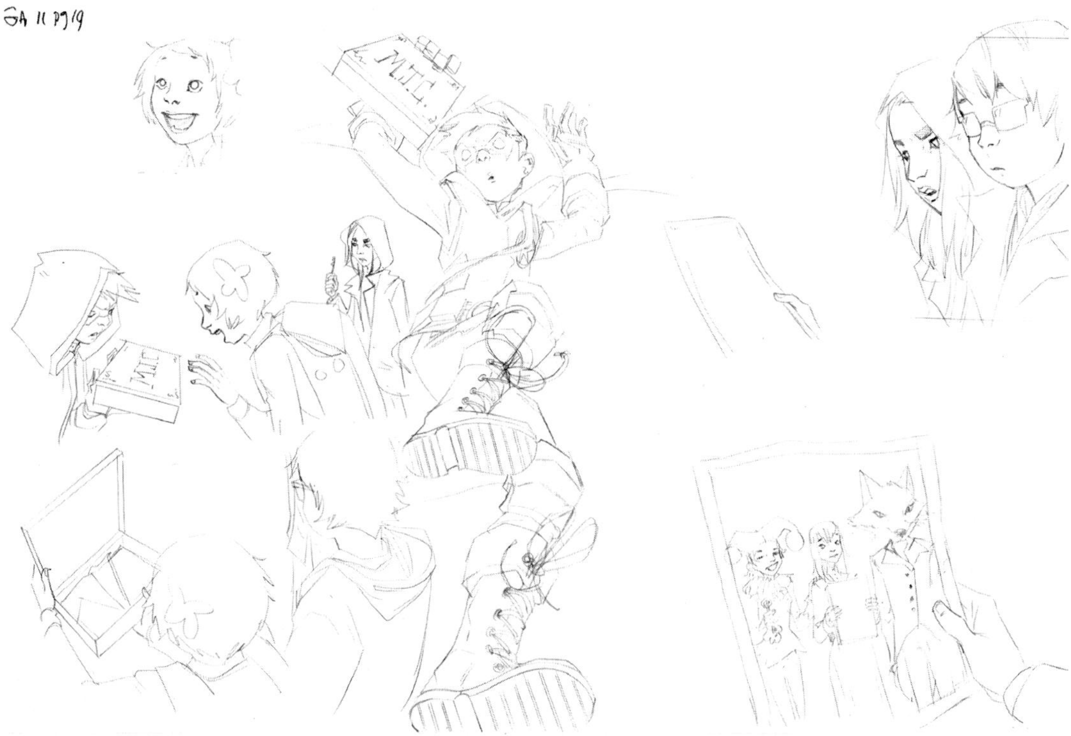
GA 11 pg 19
M.I.T.
M.I.T.

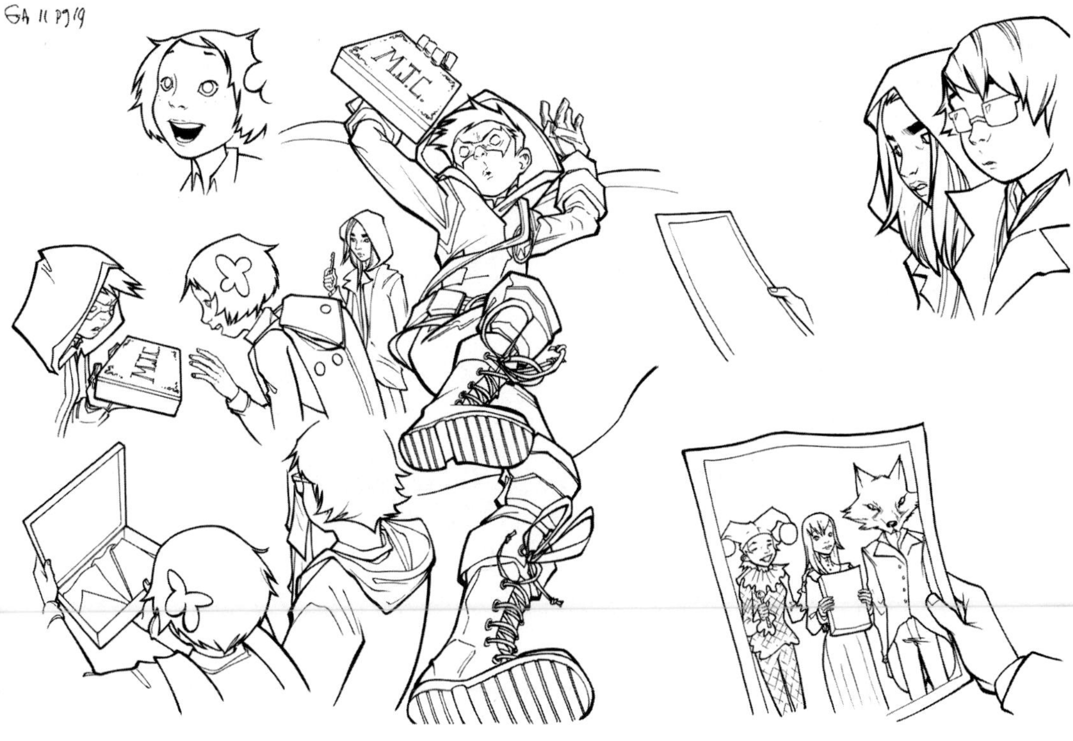
GA 11 pg 19
M.I.T.
M.I.T.

Pencils by **Adam Archer**, Inks by **Sandra Hope**

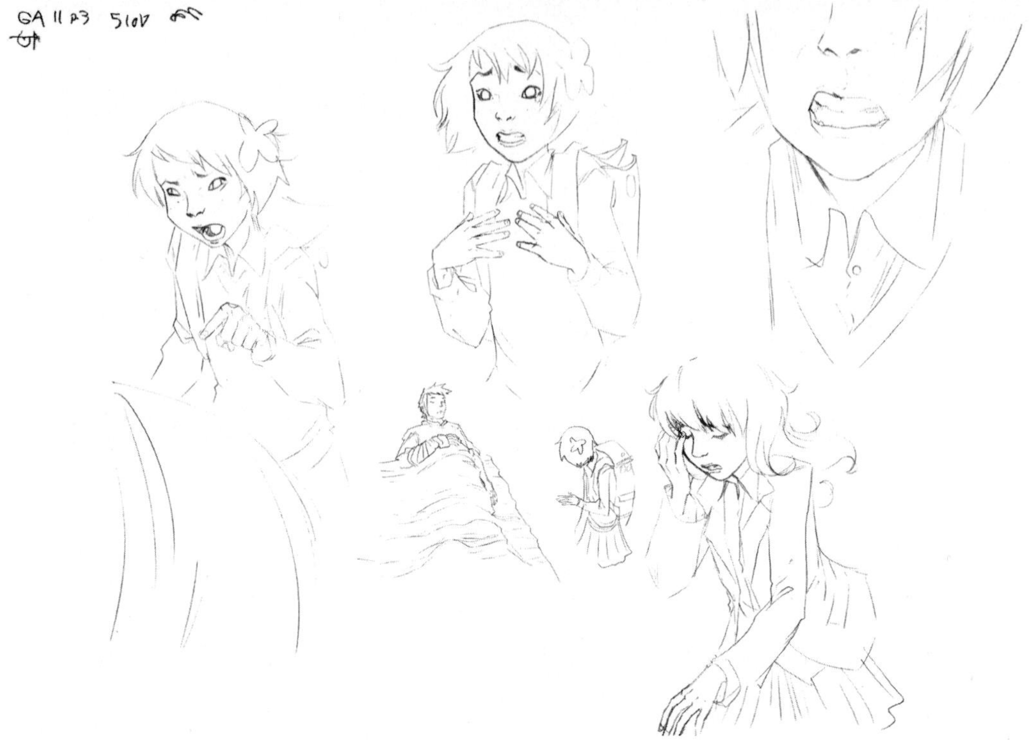

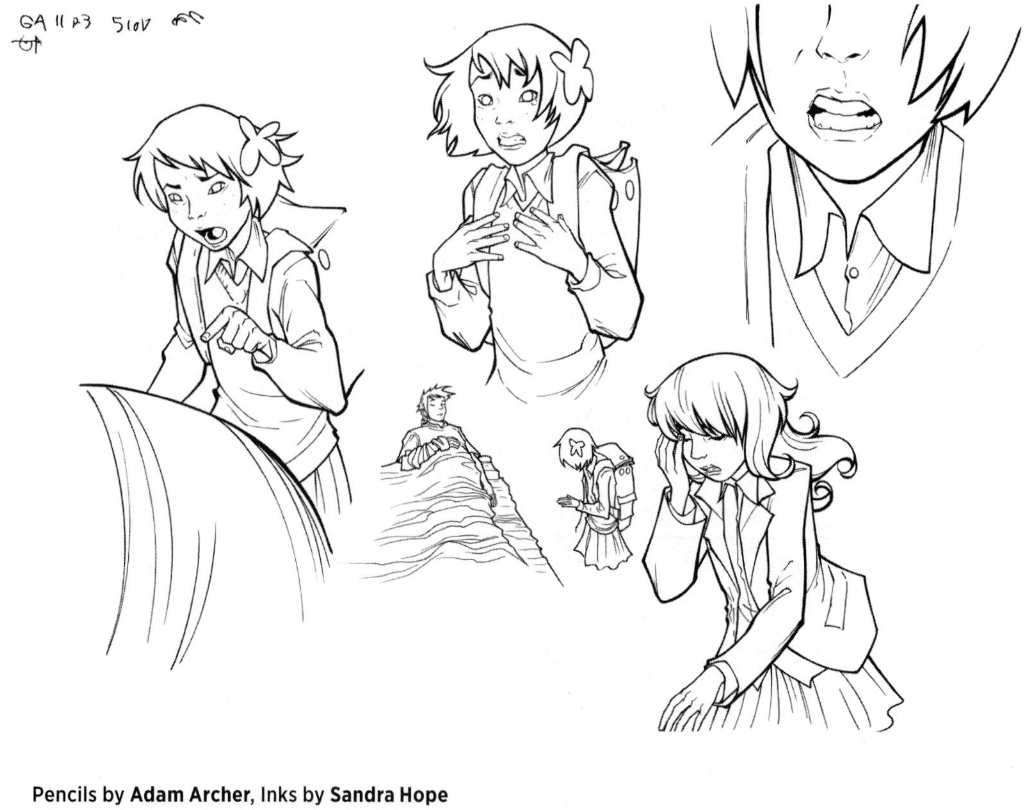

Pencils by **Adam Archer**, Inks by **Sandra Hope**

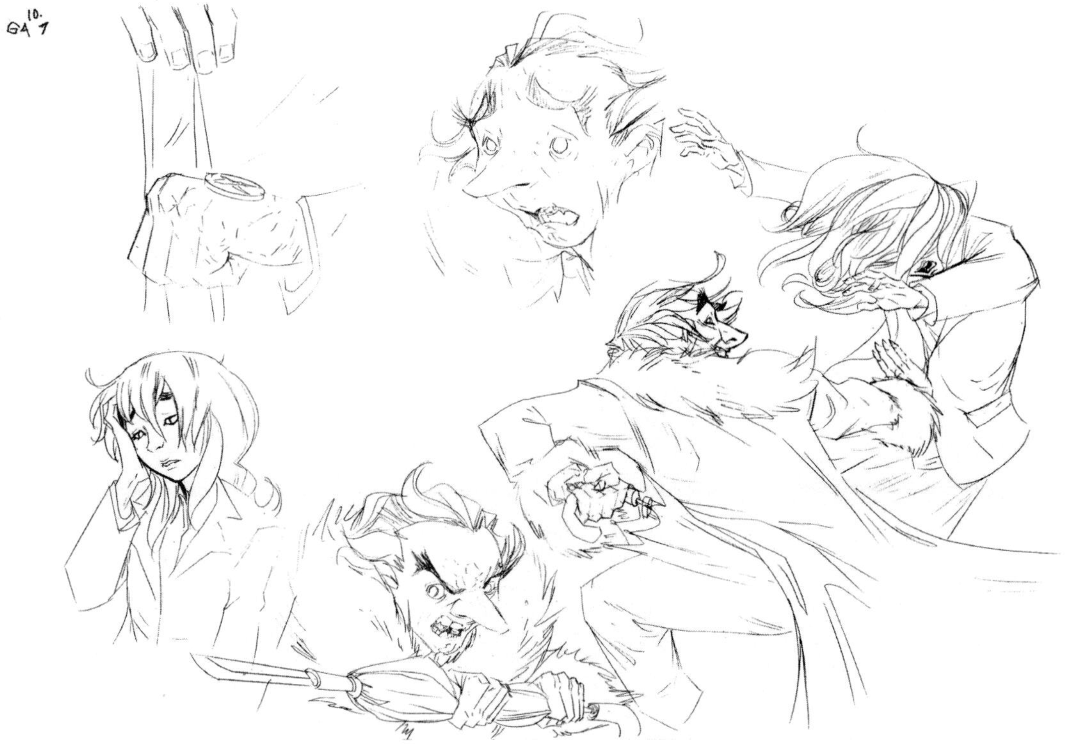

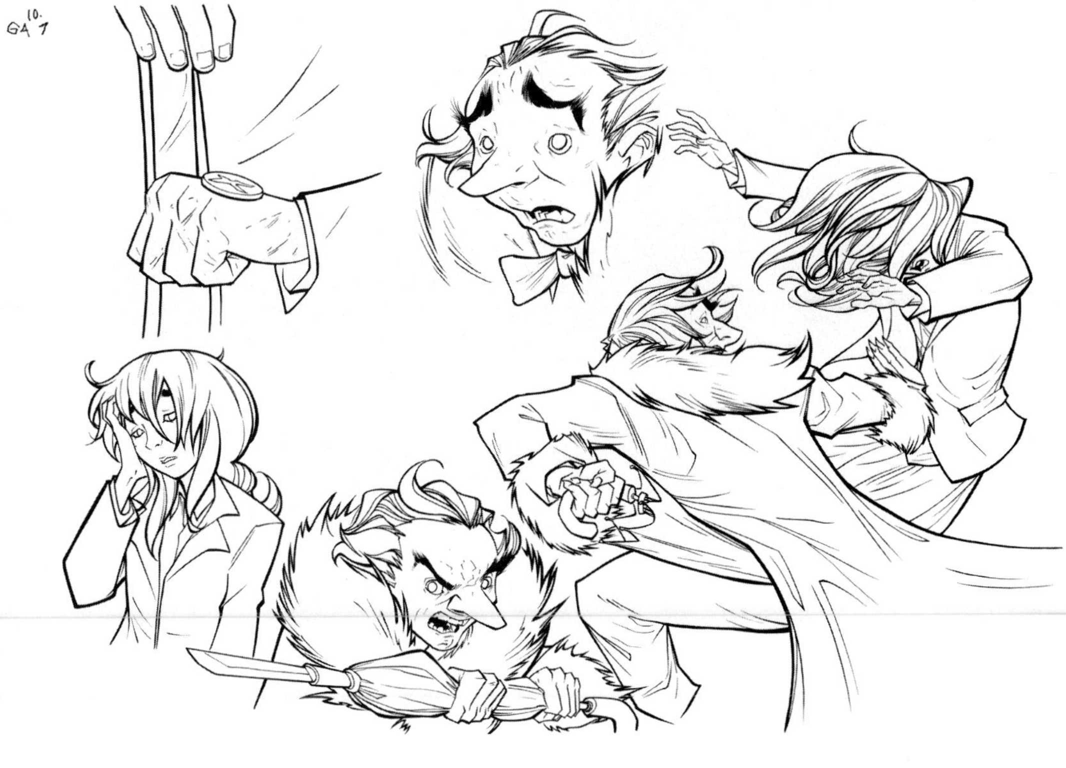

Pencils by **Adam Archer**, Inks by **Sandra Hope**

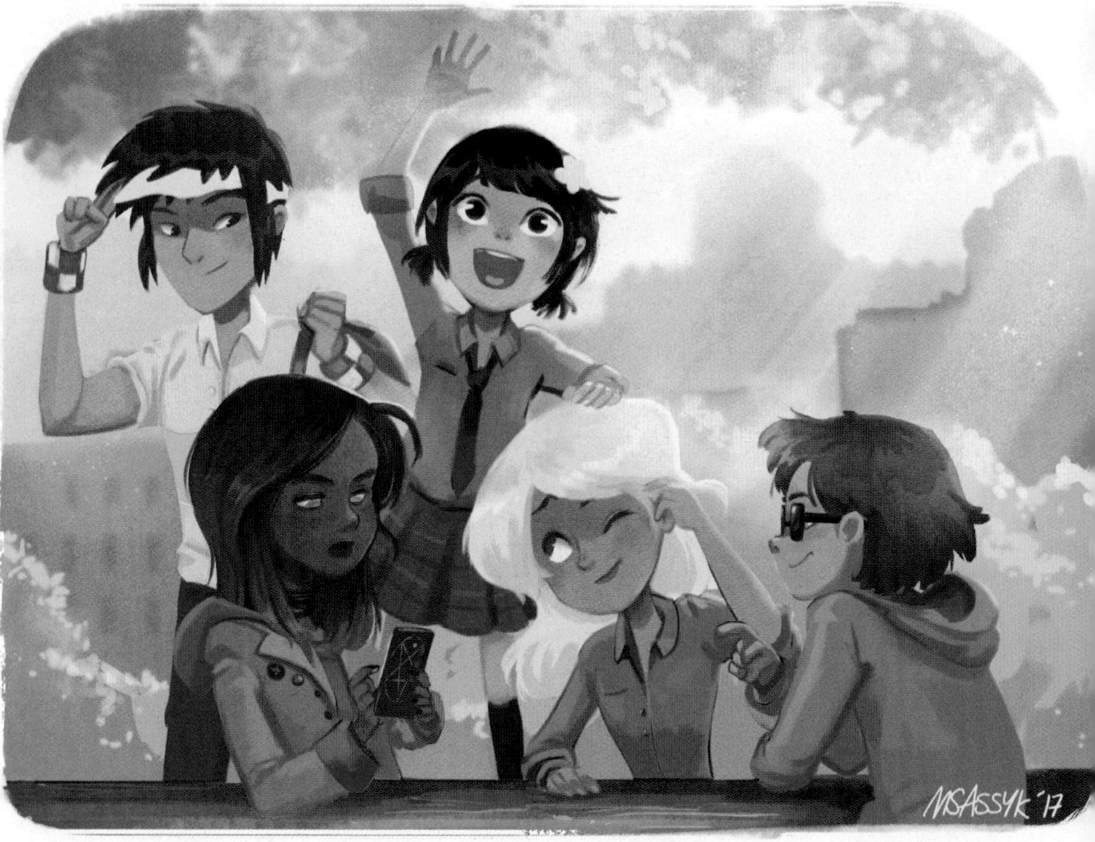
MSASSYK '17

Art by MSASSYK

A look at how the different elements of each Gotham Academy page come together, with figures by Adam Archer and Sandra Hope, layered on top of background by MSSASYK, with a final layer of color by MSASSYK finishing the page

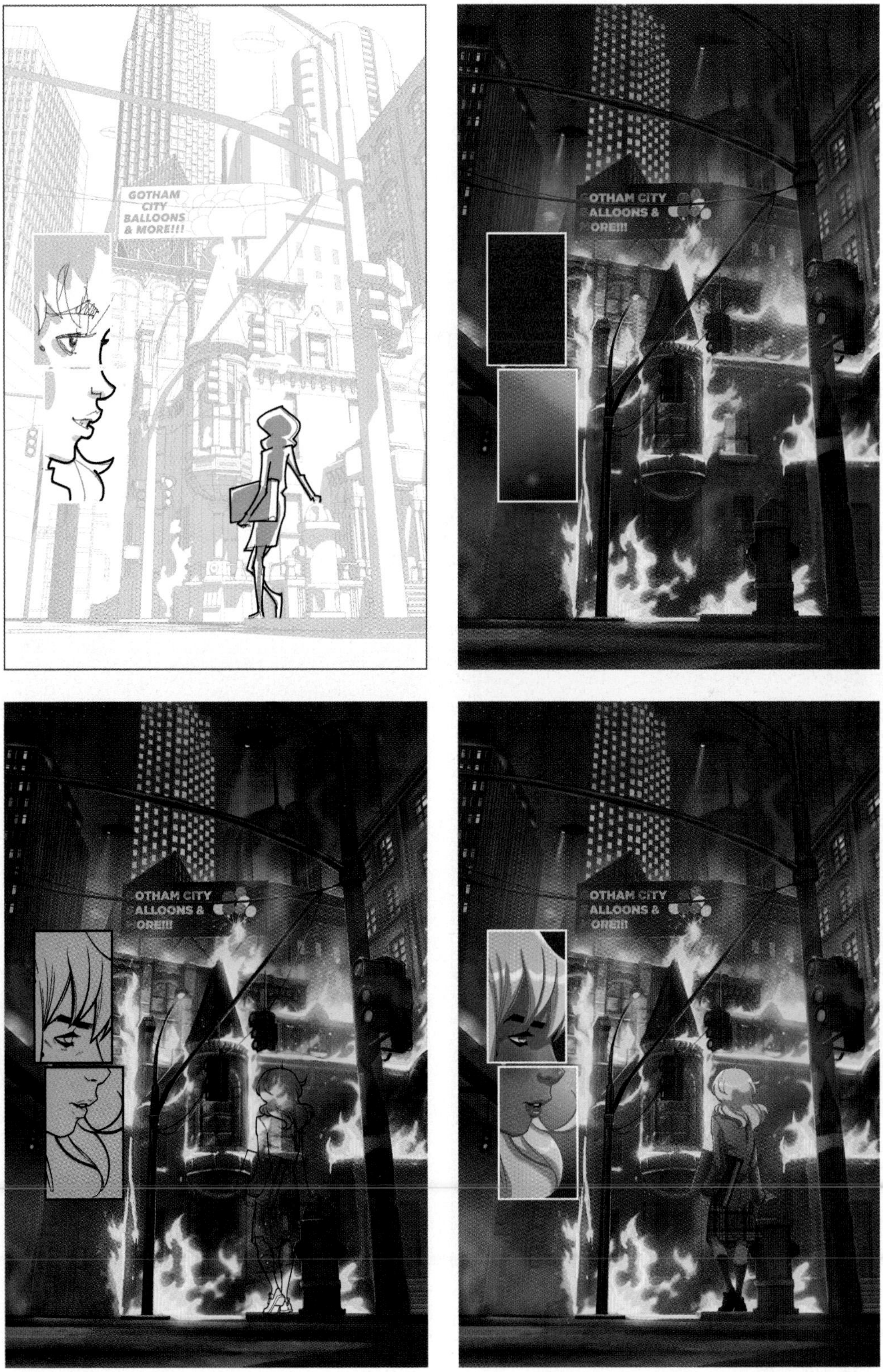
GOTHAM CITY BALLOONS & MORE!!!

Issue #9, page 1

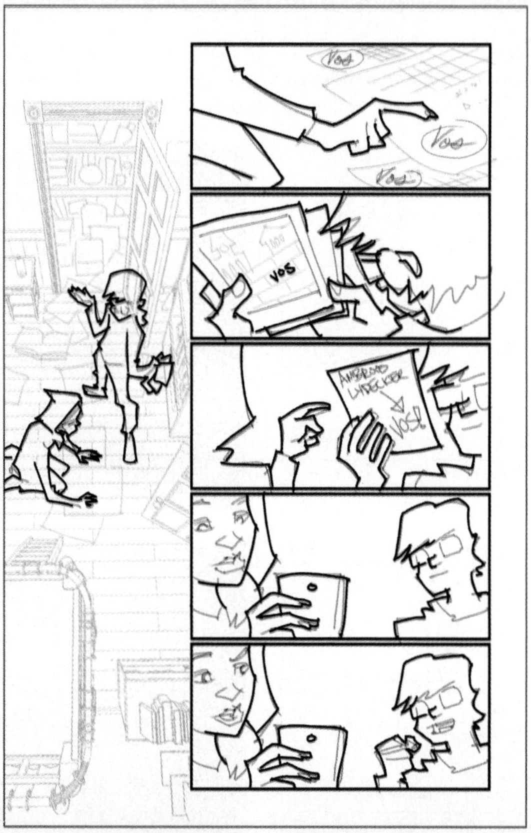
VOS
Ambroos Lydecker
VOS!

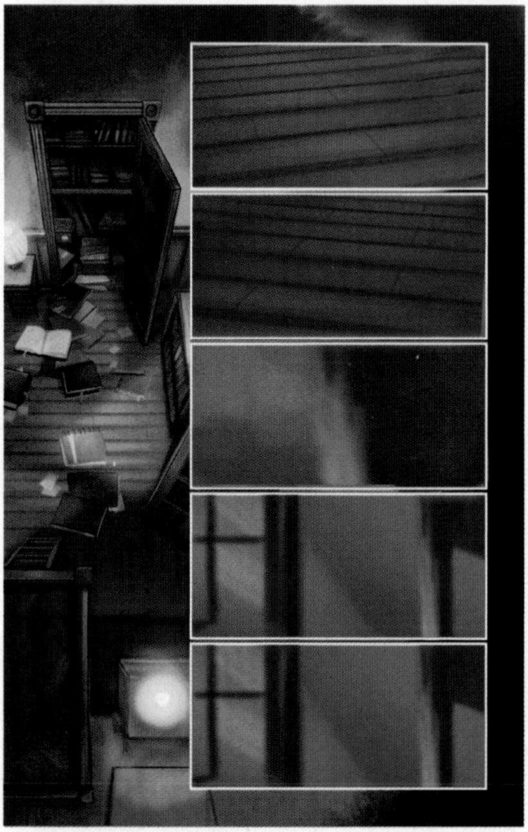

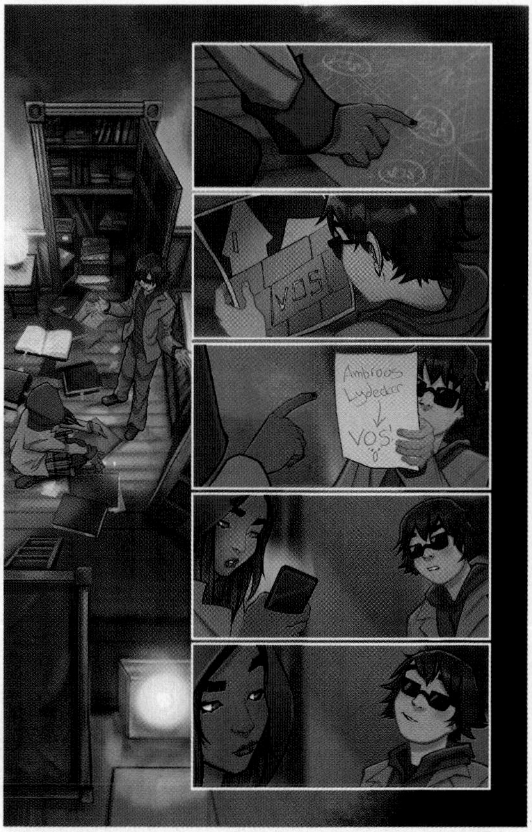
VOS
Ambroos Lydecker
VOS!

Issue #10, page 10

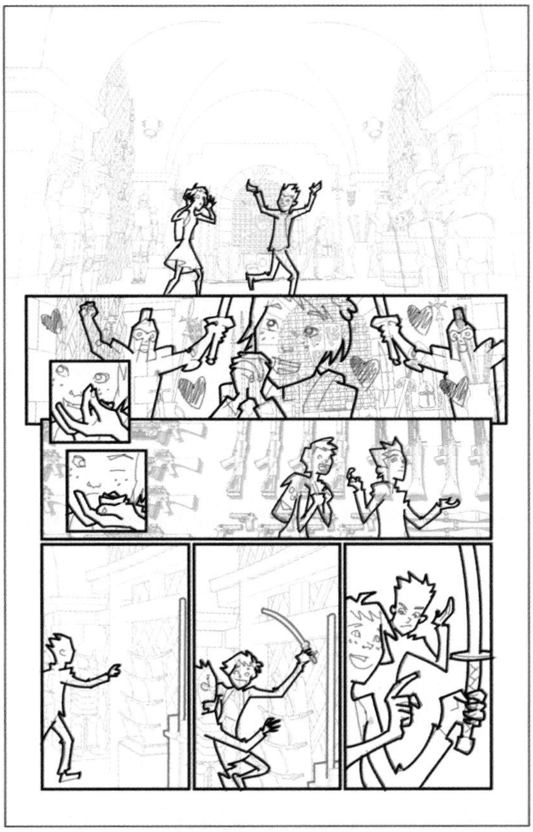

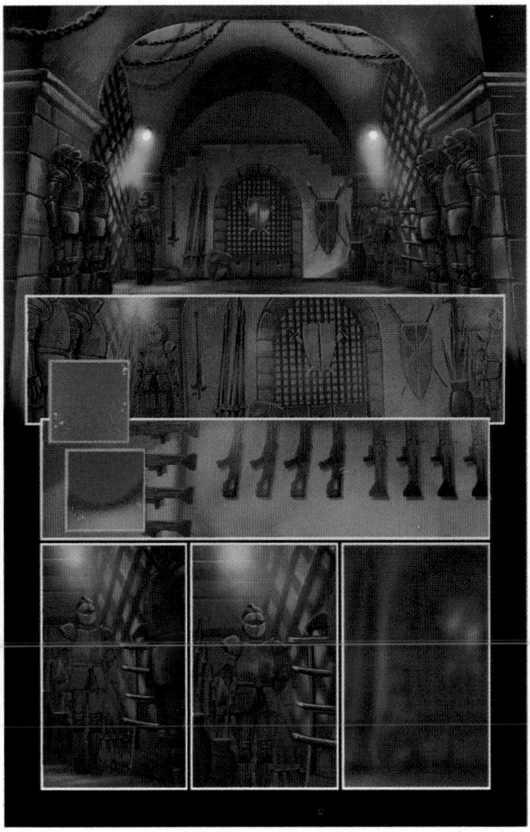

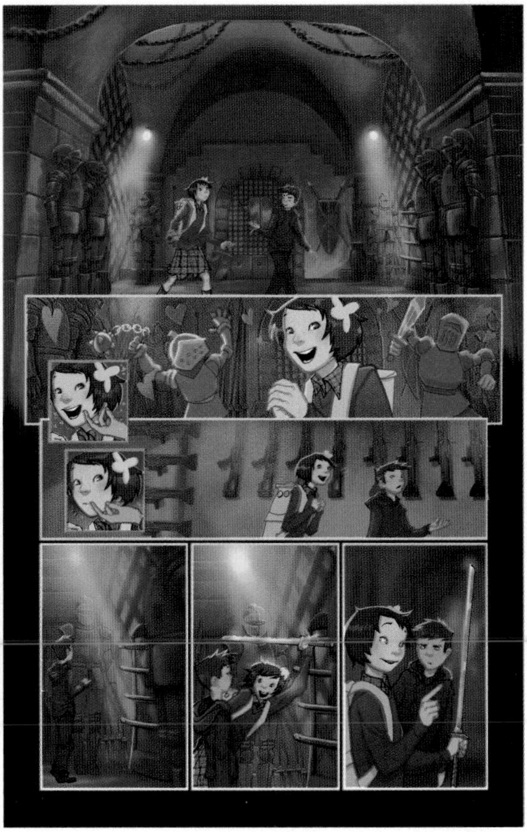

Issue #11, page 11

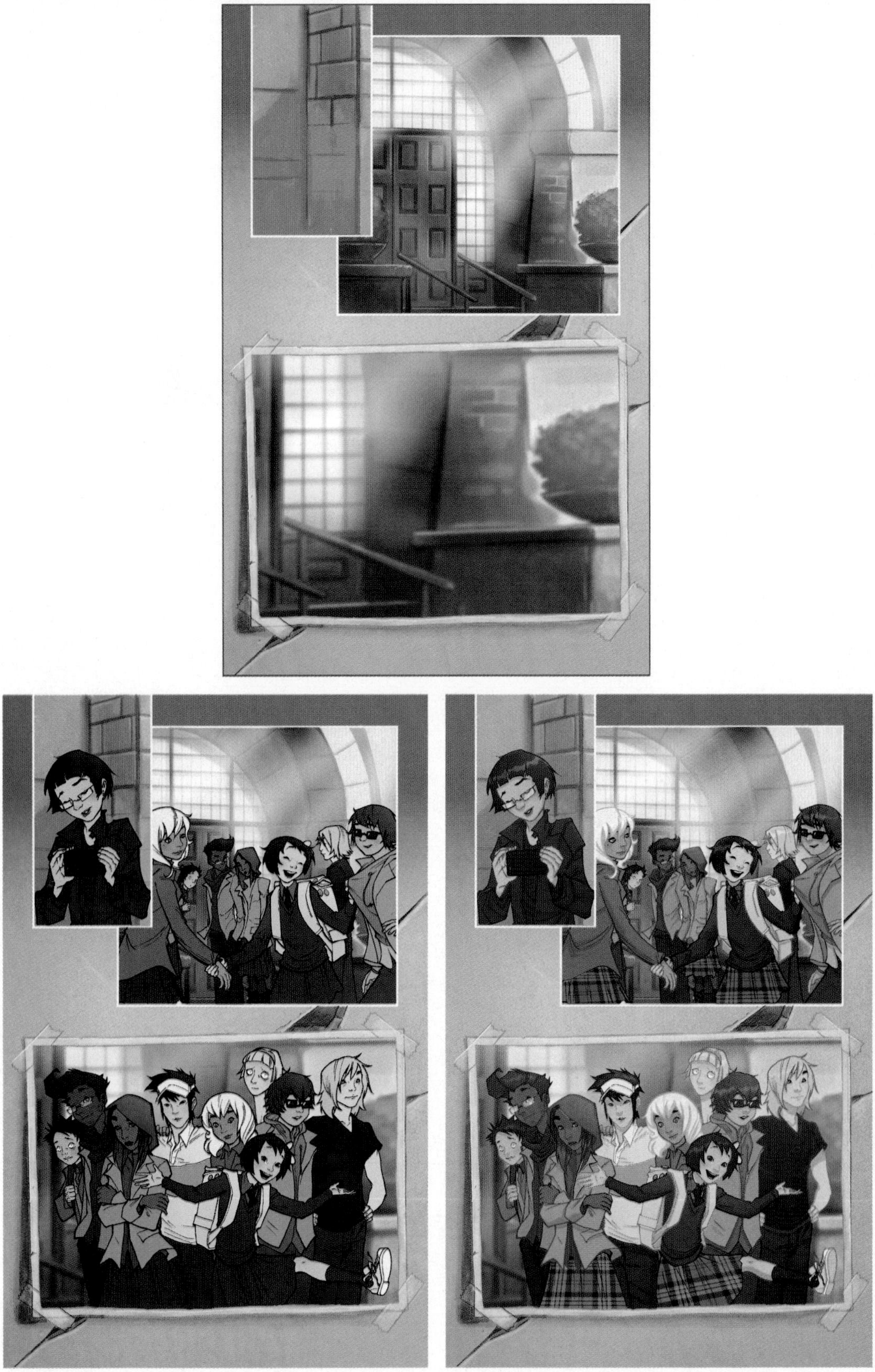

Issue #12, page 20

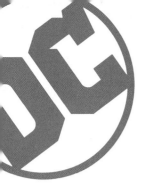

A brand-new take on a classic, and it looks
bsolutely, jaw-droppingly fantastic."
- **NEWSARAMA**

A whole lot of excitement and killer art."
- **COMIC BOOK RESOURCES**

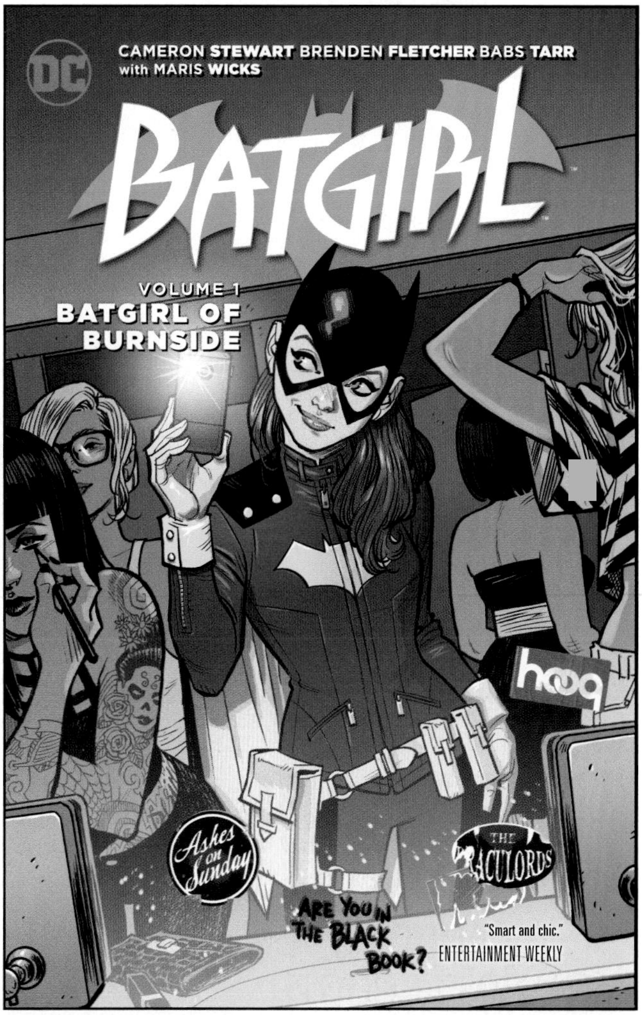
CAMERON STEWART BRENDEN FLETCHER BABS TARR
with MARIS WICKS
BATGIRL
VOLUME 1
BATGIRL OF BURNSIDE
hooq
Ashes on Sunday
ARE YOU IN THE BLACK BOOK?
"Smart and chic."
ENTERTAINMENT WEEKLY

ATGIRL

L. 1: BATGIRL OF BURNSIDE

AMERON STEWART &
RENDEN FLETCHER
ith BABS TARR

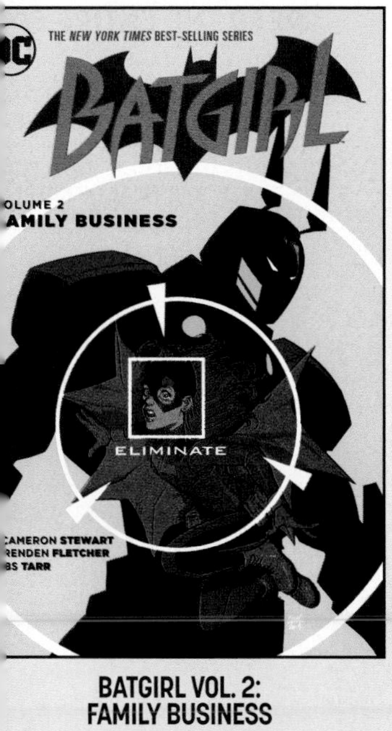
THE NEW YORK TIMES BEST-SELLING SERIES
BATGIRL
OLUME 2
AMILY BUSINESS
ELIMINATE
AMERON STEWART
RENDEN FLETCHER
BS TARR

BATGIRL VOL. 2: FAMILY BUSINESS

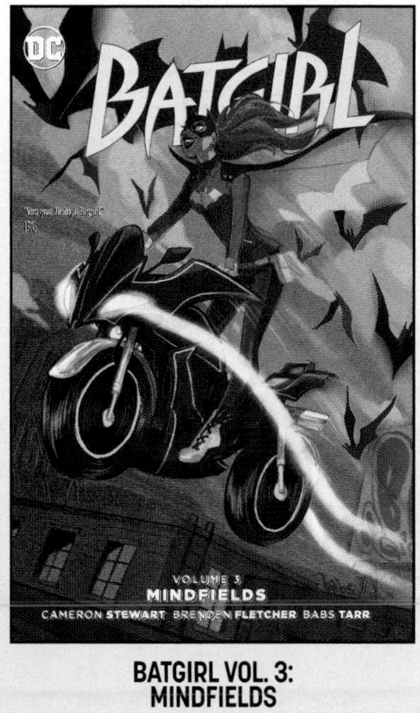
BATGIRL
VOLUME 3
MINDFIELDS
CAMERON STEWART BRENDEN FLETCHER BABS TARR

BATGIRL VOL. 3: MINDFIELDS

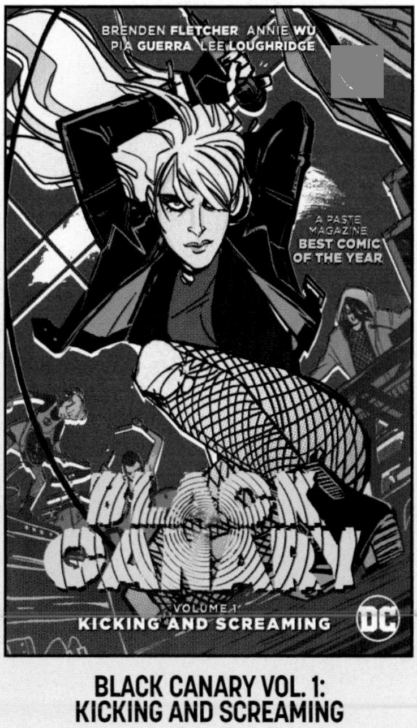
BRENDEN FLETCHER ANNIE WU
PIA GUERRA LEE LOUGHRIDGE
A PASTE MAGAZINE BEST COMIC OF THE YEAR
VOLUME 1
KICKING AND SCREAMING

BLACK CANARY VOL. 1: KICKING AND SCREAMING

Get more DC graphic novels wherever comics and books are sold!

"GRADE: A. [BOOTH'S ART] WORKS FOR THE BOOK'S YOUTHFUL, KINETIC HEROES AND WORKS FOR POTENTIAL TEEN READERS."
– USA TODAY

TEEN TITANS
VOL. 1: IT'S OUR RIGHT TO FIGHT
SCOTT LOBDELL
with BRETT BOOTH

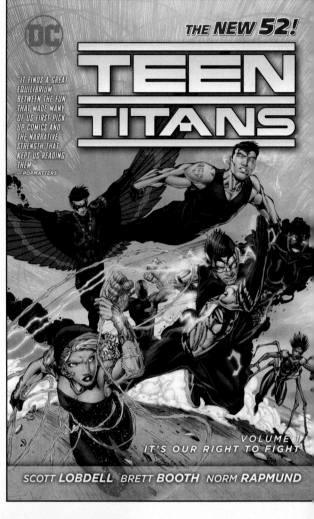

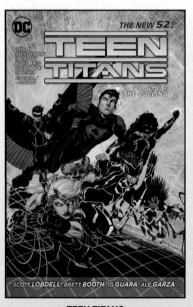

TEEN TITANS
VOL. 2: THE CULLING

TEEN TITANS
VOL. 3: DEATH OF THE FAMILY

READ THE ENTIRE EP▶

TEEN TITA▶
VOL. 4: LIGHT AND DA▶

TEEN TITA▶
VOL. 5: THE TRIAL OF KID FLA▶

"There's just something about the idea of Dick Grayson returning to the role of Nightwing that feels right."– **IGN**

"Equally weighted between pulse-pounding and heartfelt drama."
– **NEWSARAMA**

DC UNIVERSE REBIRTH

NIGHTWING

VOL. 1: BETTER THAN BATMAN

TIM SEELEY
with JAVIER FERNANDEZ

TITANS VOL. 1:
THE RETURN OF WALLY WEST

BATGIRL VOL. 1:
BEYOND BURNDSIDE

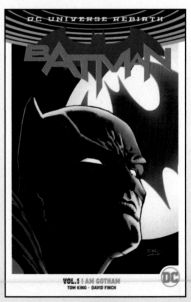

BATMAN VOL. 1:
I AM GOTHAM

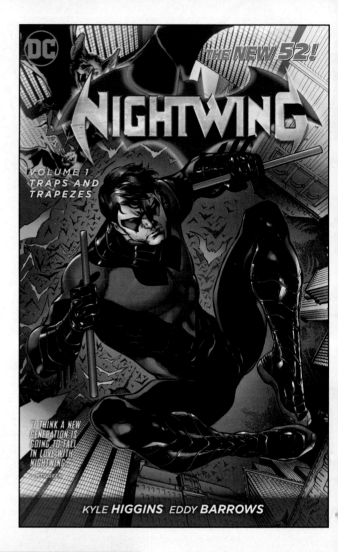